[illegible signature]

Cheltenham Cricket

19/7/96

SOUTH AFRICA

SOUTH AFRICA

THE YEARS OF ISOLATION AND THE RETURN TO INTERNATIONAL CRICKET

MIKE PROCTER

with Patrick Murphy

Queen Anne Press

QUEEN ANNE PRESS
a division of Lennard Associates Limited
Mackerye End
Harpenden
Herts AL5 5DR

First published in Great Britain 1994

British Library Cataloguing in Publication
is available

ISBN 1 85291 540 4

Typeset in Palatino and Helvetica
Editor Caroline North
Editorial Assistant Jacky Cleaver
Index by William Hodge
Cover design and styling by Cooper Wilson

Reproduced, printed and bound by
Butler and Tanner Limited,
Frome and London

CONTENTS

FOREWORD

South Africa is once again competing in international cricket and the standard of our cricket has obviously been well maintained, due to the coaching of enthusiasts, such as Mike Procter.

Great pleasure has been derived by cricket lovers from the excellent performances of our Test players, wherever they have played.

Our development programme is bringing thousands of youngsters from the townships into the game. Very soon now our national team will reflect the new South Africa.

These developments have brought enormous personal satisfaction to me but we cannot rest on our laurels.

The United Cricket Board of South Africa is committed to ensuring that cricket is played and supported by all people of South Africa. It takes moral, cricket and business sense.

I am very pleased to write a foreword to this book because it affords me the opportunity to pay tribute to Mike Procter, surely one of the greatest cricketers produced by South Africa.

It would be true to say that since Procter was unleashed against the Australians in South Africa in the 1966-67 series, he has established an international reputation as a player and a person that will be difficult for any South African cricketer to surpass.

It was not for nothing that the cricket supporters of Gloucestershire re-named their county 'Proctershire' after experiencing his considerable influence.

There is no doubt that had he been allowed to play enough

international cricket, Mike would have been right up there with the records set by modern all-rounders such as Imran Khan, Sir Richard Hadlee, Kapil Dev and Ian Botham.

I always believed that Keith Miller was unique in his absolute feel for all aspects of cricket until Mike Procter emerged.

It would be a grave injustice on my part if I failed to say that I have lent heavily on Procter's advice throughout my administrative career. Whenever I have needed expert opinion on proposed innovations and their effect on the game, he has been my first contact.

I am certain that this book will enhance the vast international cricket library, simply because it will portray that very special Procter quality.

Dr Ali Bacher
Managing Director
United Cricket Board of South Africa.
April 1994

BACK WITH A VENGEANCE

Some days never fade from the memory if you're lucky enough to be a successful sportsman. For me, March 10, 1970 was one. January 6, 1994 was another. A gap of over 20 years which brought heartache, frustration, false hopes and finally a glorious return to international cricket for South Africa. On that March day in 1970, I led the South African side off the field at Port Elizabeth after taking 9 wickets in the match to hammer the Australians. That victory wrapped up the series 4-0 and hardly anyone doubted we were the best side in world cricket. Yet we were not to play Test cricket again for another 22 years. Press the fast-forward button to an emotional South African dressing-room at the Sydney Cricket Ground on the sixth day of 1994. We had just beaten Australia by 5 runs in one of the most amazing Tests of all time, a game in which we had shown all the guts and resilience associated with South African sportsmen. The team kept coming back from the dead, refusing to lie down, and we had triumphed in a breathless finish. In 1994 I was 46 but felt 96 until Fanie de Villiers caught and bowled Glenn McGrath to unleash a great celebration party in Sydney and many more back home in South Africa. As the team's cricket manager, I was naturally overwhelmed with joy and pride in my players but as relief mingled with the adrenaline of victory. I had a reflective moment or two. Through the tears, I looked across the swaying, singing bunch of cricketers and raised my glass to a friend who'd come a long way with me since that day in Port Elizabeth 24 years ago. Ali Bacher.

It was Bacher the cricketer who had ended that Australian innings in March, 1970, catching Alan Connolly to bring us a crushing win by 323 runs. He was 28, our captain, and I was the 23-year-old all-rounder who had taken 26 wickets in four Tests that series and couldn't wait to add to the tally a few months later when we were due to tour England. Bill Lawry's Aussies couldn't live with us in that series: we had several all-rounders, two great batsmen in Graeme Pollock and Barry Richards, a wicket-keeper-batsman in Denis Lindsay who was good enough to go in at number 6 and an excellent captain. Ali was an ideal player at number 3, after Richards and Eddie Barlow, and he had made 73 at Port Elizabeth. It turned out to be his last innings in Test cricket as world opinion turned against South Africa and our sportsmen suffered from the shortcomings of our politicians. The tour to England was cancelled, so was the one to Australia a year later and we faded into isolation: an isolation that lasted until 1991, when we were allowed back into international cricket; an isolation that might have been even longer without the brave, unselfish work of Ali Bacher the administrator.

Ali has always been an emotional man. Tears and over-the-top reactions come naturally to his warm nature. More than once he has got into trouble with South African politicians and sports administrators for his impulsive comments and actions, and it was no surprise when he hailed our Sydney victory as 'the greatest performance by any South African team ever'. This time, it was hard to disagree. A telegram he was clutching supported the view: it was from Sir Donald Bradman, telling Ali that this had been one of the most exciting Tests in history and one of the great comebacks. That was some compliment from such a cricketing legend and it only added to the magic of the occasion. So did the presence in our joyous dressing-room of Joe Pamensky and Krish Mackerdhuj.

Joe had been a fantastic administrator for South African cricket throughout our years of isolation, travelling to London time and again to allow the International Cricket Conference to judge the amount of progress towards multi-racial cricket in South Africa, only to swallow his disappointment as they refused even to give him an official hearing. He never seemed to despair; he always kept the lines of communication open while trying to strengthen our own domestic cricket. He was also brave enough to criticise our government in public when he felt it was right; a more cautious administrator would have kept his head down, but Joe felt the world ought to know the strides we had made towards multi-racial cricket, even if our government was lagging behind in human rights.

Krish Mackerdhuj had been wonderfully supportive of South African cricket in the run-in to our return to the international family of the sport. He had been against the recruitment of English players under Mike Gatting and campaigned against the tour in 1990, but once President de Klerk had dismantled the apartheid legislation and released Nelson Mandela – both historic events which occurred at around the same time as the Gatting tour – Krish threw his weight behind our cause. He had delivered the crucial support of the African National Congress, with the vital public backing of Nelson Mandela, and in no time at all, the bandwagon for our return from isolation had become irresistible. Rival cricket boards had merged into one – the United Cricket Board of South Africa – and with Bacher as its managing director and Mackerdhuj as its president, there was little danger of the petty disputes that had hampered our earlier efforts at rehabilitation.

I am certain that the presence of the non-whites on the new board has been the best thing that's ever happened to South African cricket. They are very genuine guys, they really want all South Africans of whatever colour to be the best. They're also more realistic than some of our traditional white supporters, who were a bit gung-ho when we came back into the international cricket family. A lot believed that we'd go straight back to the top of the ladder, but the non-white officials on our merged board took a more sensible, long-term view that our rehabilitation would take time.

So when Krish Mackerdhuj told the press at Sydney that our victory was by a team playing for all races in South Africa, we all nodded in agreement. It didn't matter that white men had pulled it off because we were all convinced that one day our country would be represented on the cricket field by a side containing perhaps a couple of fast bowlers of African descent, some Asian batsmen, an Afrikaner or two and a few whites descended from British stock. In other words, a side of truly representative South Africans. With the ANC behind us, our administrators united and our cricketers genuinely wanting multi-racialism, that will happen – but not overnight. For the moment, Sydney had been a glorious triumph for a South African team which was at last representing its entire population, not just the white minority. That was clear to us from the hundreds of messages that were faxed to our team hotel after we won, and the feedback we had from phone calls to home. Apparently the phone never stopped ringing all day at the United Cricket Board offices – and the calls came from all races. At home, the Test was broadcast live on television, starting at two o'clock in the morning, and the final two hours were repeated at seven o'clock, as people were getting ready for work and school. We were the front-page story in most of the papers – taking up pages more inside – and we were the lead item on the radio and television bulletins that night.

South Africans are like Australians when it comes to sport: we love winners. Our top sportsmen learn to acquire that ultra-competitive streak very early, and we had been desperate for more than two decades to prove our quality in international cricket. It had frustrated us that we couldn't build on our success in 1970 and two generations of players had grown up listening to our hard-luck story. We understood why we had been isolated and any fair-minded person would agree that South Africa deserved sanctions in the short term, but we cricketers had felt for a long time that we were being made to pay for the attitudes of our politicians. We had shown them the way towards a multi-racial society from the mid-1970s onwards and we knew that if the day came when we got back into the international arena, no South African player would be found lacking in effort and guts. That was the major pleasure for me in that dramatic Sydney Test. When it came to the crunch, we faced up to a collection of great competitors – and we didn't buckle. Unspectacular qualities like that shine through when you're playing for each other and with pride for your country.

Above all, the Sydney win was a team effort. Since our return into international cricket, I had been conscious as team coach that we needed to fight all the way to compensate for our lack of big-match experience. As a player I had been lucky enough to play in seven Tests, learning all the time. My Test career ended at the age of 23 years and six months, but then I had the compensations of a fulfilling career in English county cricket with Gloucestershire and two years with World Series Cricket in Australia, the hardest, most demanding standard I have ever played. All that experience made me realise that the top international players aren't always the ones with the best technique and styles. You must be mentally strong to handle the unique pressure at the top level. Pretty 20s with the bat or an impressive spell of six overs are no use if you then waste your chance by throwing it away because you're just not tough enough. I had been hammering those points into my players ever since our first tour, late in 1991, to India, and I was proud of the way they kept bouncing back. We had learned a harsh lesson in Barbados, in April, 1992, when we really should have beaten the West Indies in our first Test back in the fold. We were chasing a small victory target of 201 and at 123 for 2, we were clear favourites. But Courtney Walsh and Curtly Ambrose summoned up the extra effort and we buckled, all out for 148 – a cruel introduction to the particular mental demands at the highest level. I'm sure that setback in Barbados helped toughen us up and we were able to draw on that experience when things became unbelievably tense in the Sydney Test.

Just consider what we were up against in Sydney. The Aussies were full of themselves after hammering England a few months earlier. They had a settled side of top batsmen boasting an impressive tally of runs in recent Test cricket; Craig McDermott was back after serious illness, roaring towards 200 Test wickets and making up for lost time as their fast-bowling spearhead. And their young leg-spinner Shane Warne had recently dominated a succession of batsmen in Test cricket. He was full of confidence that he would do the same to us. The modern South African batsman isn't at home against spin bowling – there's not a great deal of it in our domestic game – and he's even less happy against a leg-spinner of Warne's class. We knew that the Sydney pitch would turn and help Warne and the off-spinner, Tim May, and when we were bowled out for 169 on the first day (7 wickets to Warne), the Aussies were strutting. Injuries had also cut us down. Our best all-rounder, Brian McMillan, was out with knee trouble, then our captain, Kepler Wessels, broke a finger. Yet he decided he would bat at number 4 in the second innings and his personal example inspired the others. Kepler is no stylist but he is one of the gutsiest batsmen around, someone who has to be prised out, even when the ball is turning as much as it did in Sydney. The way he hung on in that second innings said it all: 'You'll win over my dead body.' No player in his side could fail to dig deeper when he saw Kepler battling away at the crease. Yet on the fourth morning, Kepler and four other front-line batsmen were all out, and we led by only 13 runs. Warne was on the way to another 5 wickets and there could be only one winner in the eyes of everyone but those in the South African dressing-room.

Enter Jonty Rhodes. Now Jonty has made a worldwide reputation for himself with his remarkable fielding, especially in the 1992 World Cup, but in Sydney he showed the importance of a big-match temperament. He just refused to believe we were out of the match, and even though he was struggling against Shane Warne, he played him off the back foot, keeping him out, shovelling away, getting runs here and there. Jonty was certain the game was still there for the taking and he communicated that to our tail-enders. If we had something to bowl at, we could still get among the Aussies. Our wicket-keeper, Dave Richardson, helped him add 70-odd, then Allan Donald came in and they added a precious 36 for the last wicket. That partnership was to prove decisive, because the Aussies were becoming frustrated with Jonty's running between the wickets, his unorthodox style of batting and Allan's blocking. Jonty's 76 not out was more valuable than many a double century in a Test match; he had given us a chance and in the dressing-room I could sense our hope turning into conviction.

We still weren't fancied for two reasons. A target of 117 is almost impossible to defend in Test cricket against class batsmen, and we lacked the cutting edge of a Warne to take advantage of the wearing pitch. So we had to rely on our fast bowlers to win the match on a pitch totally unsuited to them. It was hard to argue with the logic that pointed towards an Australian win, and Wessels' injury meant we would be captained in the field by a 24-year-old. But Hansie Cronje had impressed me as a mature cricketer with a cool brain and I was sure he'd get the boys fired up. Fanie de Villiers and Allan Donald were certainly ready when we took the field. Donald was well known to world cricket through his excellence in English county cricket for Warwickshire and a strike record of 4.5 wickets per Test, which is mighty impressive, but de Villiers was the big surprise to those who hadn't closely followed his career. Fanie is a big Afrikaner with a fantastic attitude to fast bowling. He hadn't done very well in one season of county cricket with Kent, but I knew he wasn't the type to coast when the contest was red-hot. He fired out four Aussie batsmen on the fourth evening, and even though one was the nightwatchman, Tim May, it gave them food for thought. But surely they'd still get home with only 54 needed and 6 wickets in hand? One of those was Allan Border, a man whose fighting qualities are admired all over the world. If we could get him early, I was sure the knock-on effect would seriously bother the other Aussies. Before the boys went out on that final morning, I had a quiet word about the need to contest every run and make things difficult. I didn't need to say much – I could see the determination in the guys' faces. When Donald bowled Border in the first over, you could see our boys grow even more in confidence while the pressure got to the Aussies.

Our fielding was sensational and that just tightened the screw even more. Our stand-in captain ran out Shane Warne with a throw on the turn from mid-off that hit the one stump he could see, and the effect on both dressing-rooms of that wonderful piece of fielding was decisive. The Australians simply buckled under the pressure; only Craig McDermott played a shot in anger when he came in at 75 for 8. He took the game to Donald, realising that with a bit of luck a thick edge from such a fast bowler would travel to the boundary. He added 35 with Damien Martyn, who seemed totally overwhelmed by the tense situation. Martyn had scored a stack of runs in recent seasons at home and abroad but his experience in Sydney illustrated the importance of temperament. While McDermott chanced his arm and I got worried, Martyn lost the battle, spooning up a catch to cover off a shot he would never have played in normal situations. That left the last man, Glenn McGrath, and he had to be the one to get out, because McDermott was still blazing away at the other end, his eye now in. But they only added another single, then big Fanie caught and bowled McGrath and we were home by just 5 runs. Two more blows from McDermott and we would have lost.

Cronje had captained the side magnificently, setting a wonderful example in the field, denying runs with some shrewd field placings and always looking in control. He brought back Donald at the right time to finish off Martyn and he got the best out of de Villiers. The heat was intense that morning – fires were spreading around the outskirts of Sydney – but Fanie just refused to give up. He bowled unchanged for two hours that morning before he finished off the innings and I'm sure he would have demanded to come bustling in after lunch if the game had still been alive. He was named Man of the Match but they were all heroes to me. They refused to lie down thoughout the five days and that bravery was something I have always associated with South African cricket. I was under no illusions when we returned to the international game; I knew we would be rusty and mentally weak until we had been tested. We weren't a team of individual brilliance like the 1970 side, so we had to concentrate on moulding the players into a team in every sense of the word. In Australia, I don't believe we were favoured by certain umpiring decisions, we were troubled by injuries and yet we somehow managed to win a desperately close finish through fast bowling on a pitch that brought Shane Warne 12 wickets in the match. If that isn't a victory for character, what is?

A triumph, then, for South Africa but also for Test cricket. To me that was always the pinnacle of the game and I treasure my seven Tests against Australia. We all enjoy one-day cricket, but the five-day Test is the best you can get. We were second-best for the best part of four days, but still hung on in there to turn it around. Nearly 20,000 people watched that final morning in Sydney and even though the bulk of them were disappointed Australians, they must have gone away thinking that they had watched something special. The change of fortunes would have fascinated any cricket-lover, and I'm sure that back home it opened a few eyes previously only interested in the instant brand of cricket. I was absolutely delighted to reach the semi-finals of the World Cup in 1992, but in strictly cricketing terms, for me Sydney 1994 was the highlight so far of our comeback.

OUT IN THE COLD

By March, 1970 South Africa could fairly claim to be the best international side in the world after thrashing Australia at home. That 4-0 series defeat meant we had won seven of our last nine Tests against the Aussies and although some tried to make excuses for Bill Lawry's side – they were tired after a long tour of India – we were mentally tougher as well as more talented. Men like Eddie Barlow, 'Tiger' Lance and Peter Pollock relished the mental pressures, gloried in the dogfight, while Barry Richards, an undeniably great player already, was still hungry for runs. That was never a problem with Graeme Pollock: he just loved to bat and didn't believe in giving his wicket away through boredom. In the second Test at Durban he gave an unbelievable display, hitting 274 in seven hours. At the age of 26, he was being hailed as one of the greatest batsmen of the past 20 years. Younger players like myself and Lee Irvine were able to come into a confident, tough side that had the measure of the opposition early on, and so we could do ourselves justice, knowing that individual failure would not be a disaster. Our catching close to the wicket was miraculous at times, a fact greatly appreciated by this particular young fast bowler, and in eight separate innings not one Australian century was posted.

Many thought that all Ali Bacher had to do was turn up, win the toss and just let his side get on with it, but that's unfair. Ali was a fine batsman for a start – good enough to score 235 for Transvaal against the 1966 Aussies – and the ideal man to go in at number 3, to blunt the attack in the rare event of a failure by either Richards or Barlow. As our captain, he was a marvellous motivator who had the total respect of the other players. He was also lucky, a vital quality in the best captains. Almost every hunch he played seemed to come off, especially when he brought on the great partnership-breaker, Eddie Barlow. Eddie always thought he should be bowling – he was never one for self-doubt, Eddie – and the trick was knowing when to let loose all that aggression. Time and again, he would be brought on and do the necessary. Barlow would get the credit, but Bacher was the shrewd puller of strings. At just 28, Ali was the ideal captain of an excellent, strong-willed side. Intelligent enough to encourage lively discussions in the dressing-room, he had the knack of understanding each player's own character. Ali was the nearest to England's Mike Brearley in that respect.

With all that going for us, we were desperate to get to England in May, 1970, to show that the Australian hammering was no fluke. It was not to be. A great team simply disappeared and was never seen again on the field of play. Politics had caught up with us. The tour to England was cancelled on the instructions of the British government because it was felt the safety of players and spectators couldn't be guaranteed. The disruption by well-organised demonstrators of the Springbok rugby tour to Britain a few months earlier had rattled the British government and the Anti-Apartheid Movement had claimed a notable scalp. It was clear that cricket was a bigger security problem than a rugby match. Policing a rugby stadium for about three hours is far easier to organise than the kind of massive security operation needed at a Test match ground for five days in a row. Anyone could clamber over the boundary fence and cause trouble. Cricket remains one of the easiest sports to disrupt and it was hard to argue with the logic of the British government, frustrated though we were.

Trouble had been brewing for some time over our government's stance on apartheid, the policy of separate development that had been the official policy of successive National governments since 1948. Even earlier than that – when the Union of South Africa was formed in 1910 – blacks had been excluded from political decisions and policy-making. That's why we had never played cricket against India, West Indies and, later, Pakistan. When Prime Minister Vorster refused to allow the MCC to select Basil D'Oliveira for the tour to South Africa in 1968, our cricket isolation started to gather speed. Basil was a Cape coloured who had emigrated to England to try to further his cricket career, something that was denied him in his own country due to the colour of his skin. He had performed brilliantly to make himself into a Test player at an advanced age and all fair-minded sportsmen in South Africa were delighted for him. Not so our government: the Prime Minister said the MCC touring party was 'the team of the Anti-Apartheid Movement' and refused Basil a permit.

I felt very sorry for Basil and it was hard to disagree with the English cricket authorities when they said they must pick who they wanted. In 1968, it was the South African government which brought politics into sport, not the protesters. In later years, defenders of South Africa's right to play international sport would usually bemoan the blurring of the boundaries between sport and politics, but we have to accept that initially the fault was on South Africa's side. We sportsmen were happy to chug along, playing Test cricket intermittently, hoping that there would be changes for the better eventually, but largely indifferent to the need for radical change.

Meanwhile our government suspected conspiracies everywhere involving people with strong convictions and they failed to understand that a man of Basil D'Oliveira's dignity and achievements would have been a role model to the black community. The government just battened down the hatches and hoped the problem would go away.

The Anti-Apartheid Movement was never going to fade away and the accelerating force of international opinion at the end of the 1960s meant sporting, economic and political isolation was inevitable. For South African cricket, it came in 1971, when we were thrown out of international contention. In practice, that only meant Tests against England, New Zealand and Australia, but as we had played each other since 1889, it was still a massive blow to our pride. When you are closely involved in the actual playing aspect, you see things in a narrow perspective and at first, in common with the other South African cricketers, I was hurt, disappointed and angry at our own government and at world cricket's ruling authority for making the decision. An international sportsman can't wait to have a go at opposition of equal stature, to test his mettle at the highest level. Now we South Africans were out in the cold. On top of the loss of the 1970 tour to England, we would miss out on the 1971-72 trip to Australia, something I had really fancied, because I knew the Aussies would be desperate for revenge.

At the time I felt it would be a short ban, that soon we would be welcomed back into the fold. Then it dawned on me that we were in for a long period of isolation. Like most white South Africans of that period, I had been brainwashed as a boy. Coming from a comfortable background, I went to Hilton College, one of the best schools in the country, and the wonderful sports facilities there brought me great happiness and a drive to succeed in sport. It didn't really occur to me that I came up against only whites on the sporting field, that blacks were mostly involved in the menial aspects of South African society. Everything in my garden was rosy as a teenager, and I took for granted the wonderful climate, the marvellous practice facilities and the fact that the South Africa I wanted to represent was in fact white South Africa. If India, Pakistan and West Indies didn't want to play us at cricket, that was their problem: every two years, we would be up against England and Australia, and when it came to rugby, the New Zealanders and British Lions were also available for some titanic battles. We didn't need anybody else.

It took county cricket in England to help break down my naive attitude towards racial matters. When I joined Gloucestershire in 1968, I was 22 and not exactly well travelled. I didn't question the laws of my homeland and assumed apartheid was the right thing, simply because it was in place and we whites seemed happy. When I started living in England, I remember my surprise at seeing white men cleaning the streets, emptying dustbins and taking train tickets. To my eyes, that was the black man's job. Playing against men of the stature of Clive Lloyd, Basil D'Oliveira and Gary Sobers brought home to me the fact that colour should not be the deciding factor: what's inside the body is more important. I was the typical white young South African sportsman until travel and county cricket broadened my mind. For the first time I had some inkling of the frustrations these great guys had experienced purely because of the colour of their skin. Thank God all that has changed over the years. Now I do not know one South African sportsman who disagrees with the fact that ability is the only criterion for success, that equality of opportunity is the major aim.

It took isolation to make us realise how we South Africans were viewed in the free world. It wasn't until we were in sporting exile that we understood that there was more to our society than just playing sport. Sanctions were justified in the early 1970s, because they helped break down the sporting segregation which had existed. In turn we led the way towards a fairer, multi-racial society in South Africa. Sportsmen started to say publicly that it was wrong that we whites could play with blacks on the cricket field, have a drink with them in the bar (due to some loophole in the law), but then had to watch them travel home on a train that had a whites-only section. Pressure from the sporting community helped change racial attitudes that had been entrenched for generations in South Africa and the politicians should be forever grateful. If it had been left to the demonstrators and the dogmatic politicians, South Africa would still be in the wilderness.

It was frustration with the South African government that led to the first public statement by white South African cricketers in support of mixed cricket, and I am proud to have played some part in that unforgettable day in April, 1971. The year before I had been lucky enough to play for the Rest of the World against England, a series organised at the last minute in place of the cancelled South African tour. My fellow South Africans Eddie Barlow, Barry Richards and the Pollock brothers jumped at the chance to play alongside great cricketers such as Rohan Kanhai, Gary Sobers, Clive Lloyd, the Pakistanis Mushtaq and Intikhab and the Indian wicket-keeper Farokh Engineer. The team spirit was fantastic: we South Africans would pull Gary Sobers' leg about his horse-racing tips and we'd go out and socialise with all the guys. That summer in England was another educational experience for the South Africans and we came home convinced that things had to change in our country, otherwise we would be in the cold for a long, long time.

By the following April, we were still clinging to the fond hope that we still might be able to tour Australia later that year. The South African Cricket Association had asked our government if two non-whites could be included in the tour party to pacify international opinion. Now I know that sounds like tokenism, a patronising suggestion that amounted to window-dressing, but we South Africans weren't exactly sophisticated in those early days of isolation. In any event, the government turned down the idea flat and it was all we talked about on the eve of the match at Newlands which was, in effect, a Test trial with the Australian tour in mind. Over dinner that night, the players discussed what we could do to publicly register our dismay at the government. Denis Lindsay, the Pollock brothers and I wondered if we should refuse to play in the match that was due to start the following day. We were talked out of that – too extreme, and likely to alienate those whose support we needed. We decided to walk off at a certain stage, hand a statement to the press, then go back on the field. Both sets of players agreed to the plan and after I had bowled one ball at Barry Richards, we all trooped off. We knew what we were doing: it was the first time we would come out and say publicly what many of us had been feeling for some time. This is the full text of the statement:

'We cricketers feel that the time has come for an expression of our views. We fully support the South African Cricket Association's application to include non-whites on the tour to Australia if good enough, and furthermore, subscribe to merit being the only criterion on the cricket field.'

Now that may sound fairly unexceptional in these more enlightened times, but it caused a major furore in 1971. We had all agreed that no one would add anything to that statement, but many others had their say. There was one interesting postscript to the walk-off. The players in that match were due to attend a barbecue at the invitation of Frank Waring, the Minister of Sport, but the invitation was withdrawn after our statement was released. The Afrikaner press had a field day, accusing us of unpatriotic behaviour, thereby missing the point. We wanted the politicians to realise that it was about time we had equality of opportunity on the sporting field. We had shown that we were prepared to play with and against anybody and if that led to an improvement in our country's racial policy in future, all the better. For the moment it was a sporting demonstration, but the politicians couldn't see it that way.

For a long time in the early 1970s, it was a case of one step forward and one back as we inched towards multi-racial cricket. There were so many disappointments, so many examples of manipulation by politicians, either blatantly or behind the scenes. And not just South African politicians. When I was Rhodesia's national coach I invited Gary Sobers over for a double wicket competition and the amount of flak he took back in the Caribbean was unbelievable. After that my invitations to West Indian, Pakistani and Indian players were always enthusiastically welcomed by the guys – but each time their governments refused permission. Making new friends and breaking down racial barriers didn't seem to be on the agenda. In 1974, Barry Richards and I were delighted to accept an invitation to play in India for a charity match in aid of flood victims. The Indian government wouldn't let us in, even though we had played county cricket with some of the Indians and we weren't getting money out of the trip. On another occasion I captained a Rest of the World side against the Australians at Arundel, and among those playing for me were three Pakistanis, Zaheer Abbas and the Mohammad brothers, Mushtaq and Sadiq. I couldn't understand why all three were being called to the phone all day and finally I asked Zaheer what was going on. He told me that high-ranking officials back in Pakistan were rollicking them for playing under a South African. I wondered whether those officials were aware that Zaheer and Sadiq also played under my captaincy in county cricket with Gloucestershire!

Two great Indian players also bore the brunt of unnecessary pressure after they agreed to come to South Africa to play in a double wicket competition. Bishen Bedi and Farokh Engineer had to withdraw after death threats and warnings that their homes would be burned down. It was desperately sad to see how much dogmatic, wasteful thinking was still hampering our efforts to open up cricket in those early years of isolation. I had first-hand experience of that in September, 1971, when an exciting plan for a mixed tour by an England XI which included Basil D'Oliveira was scuppered. Two young South African newspapermen organised a sponsor, worked out an itinerary and somehow managed to get the government's permission for Dolly to come on the tour. Barry Richards and I were instantly keen on the plan and we persuaded Dolly it was a good idea. Players of the calibre of Tony Greig, Alan Knott, Fred Titmus, John Snow and Dennis Amiss were ready to come and Dolly had done a great job setting up the players in conditions of strict secrecy. We were well aware that the tour would have sparked off a lot of angry demonstrations and it was imperative that the news was kept quiet for as long as possible.

Everything was in place until, astonishingly, the South African Cricket Association vetoed the tour. The Association's president, Jack Cheetham, refused to give any concrete reasons, and to this day I don't know if he was acting on a government instruction or whether SACA thought our country wasn't ready for such a breakthrough tour, with D'Oliveira returning to his homeland so soon after the Prime Minister had said he was not welcome. Cheetham can't have thought we were undermining SACA's authority; we thought permission would be a formality because the tour would obviously benefit South African cricket, both financially and in terms of international prestige. It would have told the world that things were on the move in South Africa towards a better society, that we had the self-confidence to invite Dolly here and to withstand the efforts of the less tolerant demonstrators. It had been agreed that any tour profits would be handed over to SACA for the development of black cricket. With four unofficial 'Tests' scheduled for the major Test match grounds, the profits would have been considerable. A golden opportunity to salvage some credibility for South Africa was lost due to bloody-mindedness and I still get annoyed when I think about it. We never got to the bottom of the real reasons why that tour was aborted, and it served only to set us back a few more years.

I was just as disappointed with SACA a couple of years later when they knocked back my plan to bring a Rest of the World team to South Africa. I was due a benefit with Gloucestershire and as part of the operation I would be asking many world-class players to turn out in games for me in England. I thought it would be a great idea to bring such a side over to South Africa, a side of mixed race, but a team of world class. There would be no window-dressing: the sole criterion would be the ability to play cricket at the highest level. The colour of skin would be irrelevant. Although it would be part of my overall benefit year, I did not expect to make much money out of it because the costs would be huge, flying the guys from all parts of the world, making sure they had reasonable expenses and then bearing the cost of staging the game itself. If the trip made a loss, then I was prepared to make that up out of my own pocket. My main motivation was to bring some excitement to South African domestic cricket, because we were being starved of glamour players as isolation began to take effect.

My plan was favourably received by the Transvaal Cricket Union's chairman, Joe Pamensky, and he suggested I wrote to SACA, who also reacted positively at the outset. Later I was told that SACA had gone cold on the idea and the reasons given to me by the secretary, Charles Fortune, were baffling. He said that SACA were worried that South Africa would be beaten out of sight inside a couple of days because the opposition would be strong and our players would be out of season and not geared up for such a big match. The morale of South African cricket would be badly damaged as a result. I couldn't believe it: the very idea that the top players in South Africa wouldn't be good enough or competitive enough! I was certain that the guys selected would have got themselves fit and ready, because such a prestigious game would have galvanised them after a slow decline in interest and motivation during the early years of isolation. Later SACA tried to blur the issue by saying there was a problem with the dates, but that was nothing that couldn't have been sorted out with goodwill. Once again South Africa had missed a great public relations opportunity to show that we were more progressive and open-minded than our detractors. The presence of great cricketers with dark skins would have provided role models for some of the black community while offering a different viewpoint to some bigots among the whites. At times, I wondered if certain influential South Africans in cricket and politics really *wanted* an end to sporting isolation. Didn't they care about bringing top-class cricket to a sports-mad nation recently starved of such attractions? Wouldn't the sight of non-whites competing with and against whites on the cricket field send out signals of hope and a desire for change to the outside world?

If I criticise SACA for being obstructive on those two occasions, it is only fair that I redress the balance and admit that its leading officials eventually came round to the necessity for a more progressive attitude towards mixed cricket. It was SACA which encouraged the millionaire Derrick Robins to bring over sides which contained a number of prominent non-white players like John Shepherd and Younis Ahmed at a time when hardly anybody was interested in a tour of South Africa, and in 1973 SACA sanctioned a significant event, the Datsun Double Wicket Competition. This was the first time the South African public were allowed to see blacks and whites compete together. The Indian, Pakistan and West Indian Boards of Control vetoed their top players from taking part, but some – Younis and Saeed Ahmed, Bill Ibadulla, John Shepherd, Mohammad Ilyas and Geoff Greenidge – broke ranks and played. These developments were straws in the wind, but they were nevertheless encouraging. They would have made an even more significant contribution to the cause of multi-racial cricket if the support of the South African Cricket Board of Control, which represented the interests of coloureds and Indians, had been given to such well-intentioned initiatives. Now, as a sportsman first and foremost, I have a natural suspicion of rival sporting bodies who purport to speak on behalf of those who only want to get out there and compete to the best of their abilities, and a close examination of the actions of SACBOC in the early 1970s justifies my scepticism.

Throughout that bleak period, Hassan Howa was SACBOC's spokesman and a powerful advocate he was, too. When he was president of SACBOC in the early 1970s, it seemed that in the eyes of the international media he was the spokesman for South African sport. A former teacher with a glib turn of phrase and the kind of self-confidence that appealed to the media, Hassan Howa it was who coined the memorable phrase, 'no normal sport in an abnormal society'. It's hard for any fair-minded person to object to such sentiments but there were times when Howa seemed to exceed his brief of improving the lot of the non-white cricketer. He could be abrasive, persuasive and maddening to those who tried to work with him. He always seemed available to the media for a quote and there is no doubt that he did immense work, and you have to admire his tenacity and sincerity. But he could be as dogmatic as the proudest Afrikaner at times and too often he was obstructive. There was a crying need at that time for the rival cricket boards to amalgamate and present a unified front to the government so that they could press on with the desired reforms. But too often Howa would put SACBOC in the opposite corner to SACA. He thought our walk-off at Newlands in 1971 was just a public relations gesture; he said SACA was hypocritical in telling the government that two blacks would be included on merit in the proposed Australian tour party – even if the government agreed, he said, SACBOC wouldn't allow any of its players to go on tour.

Hassan Howa always said that white cricketers in South Africa didn't give a damn about the interests of black players before isolation and he's probably right, but he was wrong to keep questioning our sincerity once we had admitted our faults and tried to make good decades of neglect. He was too hard-line at times. What was the point in turning down a grant from SACA of 50,000 rand, which had been earmarked for the development of non-white cricketers? That was looking a gift horse in the mouth, and not looking after those he was elected to represent. Then he banned a coloured player, Dickie Conrad, for going along to Newlands to watch the Derrick Robins XI play Western Province! So if you go along to watch some coloured players, you are banned by the organisation that represents coloured cricketers. Howa also leaned rather too firmly on Basil D'Oliveira at times. He persuaded Dolly not to take part in the first Datsun Double Wicket

Competition in 1973. Basil was due to partner Tony Greig, the white South African who had become one of England's best players, and that would have sent out the most positive of vibes to those who were happy to be stuck in their isolationist mud. But Basil pulled out and another great chance for multi-racial cricket was lost because of Howa's obstructiveness. I can understand how difficult it must have been for Dolly during those years after he had been banned from coming back to South Africa, especially with Hassan Howa giving him hawkish advice while others preached the gospel of conciliation. The problem was that Howa was a very persuasive character, a courageous guy who wouldn't admit defeat.

Yet far too often he seemed more of a politician than an administrator. In 1973, the Minister of Sport met him in private to try to find some way that SACBOC and SACA could agree to a plan for normalisation of cricket. Howa would not budge and the three-year plan was shelved. It was understandable that SACBOC would be sceptical of white motives, believing that we would use their approval to get us back into Test cricket, then cast their interests aside, but that was unfair to those of us who genuinely wanted radical change. Many had spoken up on behalf of multi-racial cricket and for concessions outside sport too, but Howa rarely seemed to acknowledge that shift in white attitudes. He tarred us all with the same brush and didn't seem interested in reconciling any differences. The only realistic way to accelerate change was to have one unified cricket body speaking for all South Africans. It was hard enough trying to persuade the government to give a little as the years went by without all the destructive infighting among the various cricket administrators.

By the mid-1970s, it was clear to me that as far as the international cricket family was concerned, it was a case of out of sight, out of mind. In London, the Cricket Council had ruled that there would be no England tour of South Africa in 1976-77, and for once, Hassan Howa echoed the views of most of us when he said that the decision was premature, that progress towards multi-racial cricket was being made. Yet no official from Lord's had come over to South Africa to assess the speed of change and we had the feeling their minds were closed. The New Zealand Cricket Board of Control had scotched a proposed tour by Kiwi Test cricketers, the excuse being that the board was simply following the views of other members of the International Cricket Conference. In 1976 the Australian government made it clear there was no chance of our tour – scheduled for later that year – going ahead; the door was closed because the ICC said so. The Australian government would not even allow SACA's president, Boon Wallace, to travel there after he had requested a hearing on our behalf. Mr Wallace wanted the Australian cricket chiefs to be aware that genuine efforts were being made towards multi-racial cricket, but he never got the chance to state his case. Twice he applied for a visa to get into Australia and each time the government refused his application. The world was turning its back on us just when we needed encouragement.

When South African officials lobbied the ICC meeting in 1976, I was not optimistic about our chances. The official view was that there had 'not yet been significant progress towards multi-racial cricket'. We were to get used to the cold shoulder from the ICC at most of their annual meetings in London; it would be another 15 years before the barrier came tumbling down.

I can't remember exactly when I gave up hope of playing Test cricket again, but I know I felt very pessimistic when I watched the 1975 World Cup in England, wondering what it would have been like to play against the other countries during that marvellously hot month of June. A year later, I watched Viv Richards thrash the English bowlers all over the place and I wondered how I would have bowled at the young genius, and how Graeme Pollock would have countered the brilliance of Michael Holding. I wasn't bitter; I became philosophical and did my best for Gloucestershire in county cricket and in the Currie Cup, for Rhodesia and then Natal. At least I had played Test cricket, unlike fine young players such as Peter Kirsten, Clive Rice and Ken McEwan. Without that incentive, South African cricket was marking time at first-class level. There was nothing higher to aim at and for a time there was an excessive amount of needle in Currie Cup games because they had acquired an importance that was out of proportion to their status. There was talk of getting the captains around the table to sort out major disciplinary problems and I'm sure some of that extra aggression stemmed from the frustration of our top players.

Interest in the schools was declining as well, and I saw how different it all was from my schoolboy days, when all I ever wanted to do was bat or bowl all day and check how my own particular heroes were doing for South Africa. In the mid-1970s, the keen schoolboy had only the scores in the Currie Cup, and there wasn't much to fire his imagination there. There was none of the excitement and incentive we'd given when hammering the Australians a few years earlier. The number of specialist cricket coaches at schoolboy level was dropping off and the quality was inferior at first-class level. Cricket was crying out for a revival in South Africa, but where would it come from? The administrators, black and white, seemed to spend too much time bickering in petty disputes, and I felt they were too defeatist in the face of a cautious government that seemed obsessively worried about change. It was obvious that any return to international cricket would have to come about through the proper channels (cricket is like that, very conformist and conventional), so we had no chance unless we organised a unified body with a powerful voice that wasn't frightened of the politicians.

It seemed to me that first-class cricket in South Africa was a poor relation to rugby in those days. We were trying to put our house in order after being expelled from the international community, but rugby went on its own sweet way, oblivious to the need for reform. The National government was traditionally associated with the Dutch Reformed Church and the game of rugby; cricket was perceived to be the game of whites descended from British stock. When the British Lions toured South Africa in 1974 – and again in 1980 – it was seen as a great triumph for the traditionalists against the forces of anti-apartheid darkness. If you could get through to the rugby folk about the need for a multi-racial society, then you would make progress in South Africa, but that was a tough one to crack, especially as they didn't have to cope with isolation like the cricketers. Some liberal-minded South Africans were pleased for Willie John McBride's magnificent Lions side in 1974 which beat the Springboks in their own backyard. That heavy series defeat was a choker for the die-hard Afrikaners and the theory of white supremacy in South Africa took a blow. We had been punished for the political sins of our country, so why were the rugby guys still playing internationals?

I felt our cricket image was poor in the 1970s. There didn't seem to be much effort to raise money through sponsorship, to galvanise the country's cricket community. Having played for several years in county cricket in England, I had gained some appreciation of the need to generate cash, to drum up publicity and freshen up the game's image. Not enough was being done in South Africa to get the major companies involved – and this in a country of great wealth where sport is normally a huge passion. There was no television coverage of cricket worthy of the name and the feeling was that we were just marking time, waiting for something to turn up. That something was a return to Test cricket, but with political considerations merging more and more into those of sport, and the increase in sophisticated forms of political demonstration, I didn't feel at all optimistic about a hasty return. Things had to change internally – and politically. Meanwhile those South African cricketers who weren't lucky enough to play in English county cricket were getting stale, and there was an enormous amount of natural talent going to waste. We had deserved our ban initially, but I now felt we had served our time. The carrot was now needed rather than the stick, and I felt that the exposure to other views which would have been provided by tours was vital. The cancellation of tours had made us question our values but now was the time for contact. Yet the prospects looked bleak.

THE LOST GENERATION

For a decade after isolation started, many cricket fans in South Africa played the 'if only' game. If we hadn't been forced out of Test cricket, how would we have done against England and Australia over the next couple of years? We felt we were top of the heap on the eve of the 1970 tour to England, and that heap included India, Pakistan and the West Indies, even though we hadn't played international cricket against them. The scheduled Australian tour would probably have marked the swansong of players such as 'Tiger' Lance, Denis Lindsay and Peter Pollock through age and Ali Bacher for business reasons, but we had enough talent coming through to convince me that we'd have given anyone a good game for a few years to come, as long as we were able to keep our competitive edge sharp by regular tilts at the opposition in Tests. That was the Catch 22 situation; once we were out in the cold, we were bound to be a bit of an unknown quantity when the unofficial world rankings were being compiled. Success at the top level is cyclical – people talk about our isolation in the 1970s, but we played only one four-match Test series in three years after Australia, and that was against the same opposition. The England tour to South Africa in 1968-69 was called off after the fuss over Basil D'Oliveira, so we hadn't played them since winning a three-match series in 1965 in England by 1-0. As the decade progressed, the Indians developed a brilliant spin attack, the Pakistanis found two great fast bowlers in Imran Khan and Sarfraz Nawaz as well as some class batsmen, while the West Indies started a production line of wonderful quick bowlers that has lasted to this day. England became a fine side under Mike Brearley, with the aid of a great young all-rounder in Ian Botham. So the balance of power was being moved at various times during the period and it would be foolish to state with any degree of certainty that South Africa would have been top dog. What I can say is that the following players would have played significant parts in South Africa's Test fortunes over the following decade – if things had worked out differently.

GRAEME POLLOCK

Now I've never been a great one for statistics, but when you get a player like this guy who was so good to watch, such a high-class murderer of bowling, and with such a great career record as well, then you've got a truly great batsman. Only Bradman has a higher Test batting average than Graeme's of almost 61 (and he was not out just four times in 41 innings, so there was nothing artificial about that average). He scored 64 first-class hundreds in a career that centred around just a few innings per season in the Currie Cup and six years of Test cricket. It's terribly sad to think that his last big innings in England came in 1970 when he played for the Rest of the World. We had been looking forward all summer to seeing Graeme bat with that other great left-hander, Gary Sobers, but Graeme struggled for a time on the slow wickets and he seemed a little rusty in his timing. In that final match at the Oval, they finally shared a stand of 150-odd that was simply magical. He even overshadowed Sobers, and the great man was generous enough to acknowledge that afterwards.

I can still see that innings of Graeme's in the Durban Test of 1970 when he slaughtered the Aussie bowlers, making 274. In one hour after lunch on the first day, he and Barry Richards made 103 and their contrasting styles were fascinating, Barry easing the ball into the gaps with so much calmness, Graeme standing tall and smashing it through the offside. He just went on and on, playing with amazing ferocity. That was the difference between Richards and Pollock – where Barry would get bored with his mastery, Graeme always wanted more. He had a hunger for runs and just loved to bat. He didn't particularly like fielding, he never bothered much with his bowling, but tell him he could bat all day and he was delighted. He was certainly not one to relish the obsession with physical fitness you see in professional cricket nowadays. Graeme was not of the tracksuit brigade, preferring to conserve his energies for batting.

He had a very uncomplicated batting method. He would stand at the crease with his legs wide apart and hit through the line of the ball with an easy, graceful swing. A tall man with strong arms, he was one of the first to use a heavy bat (around three and a half pounds) and he would batter the ball with immense power. His offside play was glorious, either along the ground or the one-bounce four over extra cover's head, but he was just as good with the square cut and the pull shot over mid-wicket. Whenever I bowled at Graeme, I used to think I had a chance against him, because he played so many shots. I thought my natural in-swing would make the ball leave the left-hander in the off-stump area. Now and then I'd get him caught behind or in the slips, but not until he'd made a pile. I remember one game when he kept smashing me out of sight from just after lunch until close of play and the madder I got, the further he hit me. Graeme just loved to bat! In one Gillette Cup final, Western Province scored 355 and if ever victory seemed certain, it was surely that day. But Graeme smashed us for 169 and it was no fault of his that Eastern Province lost by just 13 runs. We just couldn't bowl at him that day.

I believe he kept his hunger for batting because he didn't give himself full-time to first-class cricket. Graeme never fancied county cricket in England because the thought of playing every day simply didn't appeal to him. He concentrated on building up his business career, working in sales and marketing, keeping fresh for the amount of cricket he wanted to play. He was almost 43 when he last played first-class cricket and he went out in style, making a magnificent hundred against Kim Hughes' Australian XI. It was such an emotional farewell that the South African Broadcasting Corporation had told radio and television producers that the innings was to be covered in full, in English and Afrikaans. There were to be no interruptions. When Graeme first came in, he scratched around a bit as Rodney Hogg and Terry Alderman tried everything to get him out. He saw little of Hogg's first three deliveries, but after his first cover drive to the boundary off Hogg, he was on his way. After he reached his hundred he conserved his energies – he went from 103 to 144 with ten boundaries and a single! In the end it was tiredness that got him out. He hadn't picked up a bat in the previous month and he had been so worried about a finger injury that he only agreed to play as long as he didn't field in his normal slip position. But Graeme's sense of occasion didn't let him down, even if he wasn't fully fit. You wouldn't have known that by watching him bat that day.

I'm sure that some of the modern judges would say that Graeme wouldn't have made so many runs in Test cricket nowadays because the bowling is more attuned to short-pitched attrition, to wear the batsman down. It's true that Graeme was more comfortable off the front foot, but he could handle the short stuff. For years he wasn't bothered with a helmet but he started to use one towards the end of his career and the way he coped with the aggression of the West Indies bowlers on their two tours when he was nudging 40 left me in no doubt of his capabilities in that direction. His desire to dominate the bowling and bat all day would have been ideal for the longer game, because six hours of Pollock at his best usually meant a double hundred for him, whatever the type of bowling. I never saw Graeme try to get away from the bowler, unlike other big-name batters I could mention. He hated giving up the strike, he had such a quiet confidence about him. In short, he was a genius. One thing I particularly remember about that 274 against the Aussies in 1970 is that he never picked John Gleeson's googly. Gleeson impressed us all in that series and hardly any of us could fathom him out. In that Durban knock, Graeme occasionally changed his mind, checking his stroke, nodding in acknowledgement to the bowler. If he'd been totally sure about Gleeson that day, he would have scored 400. What I wouldn't give to see Graeme Pollock take on Shane Warne!

BARRY RICHARDS

Barry was the best player I ever saw, the batsman I would choose to play for my life. If Barry felt like it, he could bat all day and there was little the bowler could do, unless it was hope for an unplayable delivery. His technical mastery was complete – there was no weakness I could ever see. I hardly ever got him out, no matter how hard I tried. We were born in Durban within a year of each other and first toured together in 1963 – to England with South African Schools – and I never tired of watching him bat. Unfortunately Barry himself began to tire of batting rather too early because it was simply too easy for him.

His wonderful technique wasn't God-given, though. Barry worked very hard as a boy in Durban and again in the summer of 1965 when he and I played for Gloucestershire Seconds. We spent hours in the nets, getting the feel of English conditions, and in those days he was desperate for success. At school, he would throw a golf ball against a wall then hit it back with a cricket bat to sharpen up his reflexes. He may have looked the finished product when he came into Test cricket, but Barry deserved that success for his talent and earlier dedication. He played in only four Tests, those against the 1970 Australians, but he looked a master. When he scored 94 before lunch on the first day in the Durban Test, it was hard to imagine how another mortal could approach such perfection. He got into position so quickly and with such easy grace. Barry was the only player who could handle Gleeson's leg-spin with comfort during that series because he reacted so swiftly and was so balanced.

Although he was a superb technician, he also learned to improvise. County cricket helped. When he joined Hampshire in 1968, he was predominantly an offside player and the one-day game there was essentially legside. So he started to come down the wicket to the medium-pace bowlers, backing away to leg and hitting them over extra cover's head. That was a major breakthrough in style for many batsmen and Barry was the originator of that type of daring unorthodoxy. But he never lost his core of pure technique. He played so late, waiting for the ball to stop moving, and his square driving was never surpassed in my time. When Barry decided to occupy the crease, he gave such an air of permanence. Ask Dennis Lillee, Graham McKenzie and Tony Lock: they were the main bowlers for Western Australia in the match at Perth when he hit 325 in a day for South Australia, with no false stroke. In the 1972-73 season in South Africa, his Natal side finished bottom of the Currie Cup table, but Barry broke the record of runs for a South African season, all gathered at an incredible rate, with an air of complete certainty.

I believe our isolation in the 1970s hit Barry harder than any of the other top South African players. After a time, he became jaded with his dominance in English county cricket and in the Currie Cup; he had proved his worth in the Australian Sheffield Shield, so what else was there for him in cricket if he couldn't play Tests? He didn't handle his departure from Hampshire at all well, packing it in after his county had been understanding enough to let him stand down from the three-day games so that he could concentrate on giving his best in the Sunday League. Within a week or two of agreeing to that, Barry headed off to Australia and never came back. That did nothing for the image of the overseas player in English county cricket at a time when some were being criticised for a lack of effort and cynical acceptance of good money.

Barry was so frustrated at not being able to shine any more in the Test match arena that he allowed himself to get sidetracked by financial considerations. He kept pointing to the vast sums earned by golfers and tennis players. He thought he should be paid more for playing and also get large sums for advertising and giving interviews to the media. He didn't seem to understand that cricket didn't have the worldwide appeal of golf or tennis or the backing of major sponsors through global television coverage. He used to say, 'You can't eat a century and cups don't pay for the rent,' and many sponsors and officials were put off by his lack of diplomacy. Having known Barry since we were schoolboys, I knew that he was at heart a good guy who was a little too dogmatic for his own good. He might have phrased things better at times, but I'm sure that his mercenary attitude stemmed from having just four caps to show for his fantastic talent. He was at his peak in the period when the prospects of a return to Test cricket were at their gloomiest and that must have gnawed away at him as he outclassed current Test players from all the other countries whenever he came up against them in county cricket. I believe that he would have done a Kepler Wessels and qualified to play for Australia if he had known that isolation was to last so long.

Barry didn't feel an enormous amount of loyalty towards those who ran South African cricket. He hadn't forgotten how an incident outside an hotel in East London meant he had to wait another three years for his Test debut. In 1967 he hit a wonderful hundred for a South African Invitation XI against the Australians, and it was such an impressive display from a 21-year-old that he seemed certain to be picked for the Tests. Later that evening, Barry and I tried to get into a cabaret after being invited earlier that day. We were a little the worse for wear and, as young men are, a shade boisterous. The doorman wouldn't let us in and eventually I accepted that and started to leave, but Barry was furious and in his frustration he kicked out at a vase near the hotel swimming-pool. In a moment, we were surrounded by bouncers. I called one of the South African selectors to try to smooth things out. A big mistake, even though Barry would have been in a jail cell that night otherwise. In the second innings, Barry was sent in at number 8 and he was never picked for the series. When you consider that the South African selectors were never slow to pick young players if they were good enough (I was 20 and Graeme Pollock 19 on our debuts), it was certainly not Barry's tender years that told against him.

At his peak Barry was seeking extra enjoyment from his genius by asking for more and more money. Kerry Packer's offer in 1977 was perfect for him and he showed his brilliance with a succession of brave, controlled innings against some of the most hostile fast bowlers in the world. At last he had a stage worthy of his talents once again, but it was only two seasons before Australian World Series Cricket was wound up. Then he took off to Australia and Holland to play some lucrative club cricket. It was only the prospect of playing against international touring sides that brought him back to South Africa, and typically he showed he could still do it. The masterful way he coped with the West Indian fast bowlers – especially the hostile Sylvester Clarke – only confirmed his enormous talent. With his technique, it seemed that the passage of time was less of a problem for him than for the rest of us nearing retirement age. The eyes may dim a little, the reflexes get a touch slower, but when a master of the art of batsmanship like Barry Richards comes along, you never want him to pack it in.

He knows he was headstrong when younger, that he might have given more to his teams on occasions, that he allowed the frustrations of isolation to get to him. All he wanted to do was prove himself against all the other great players of his time, year after year. Those of us who saw him at close quarters had no doubts of his superiority, and it would have been a thrill for me to have watched him demonstrate that in more than four Tests spread over two months early in 1970.

EDDIE BARLOW

If ever a cricketer made everything count it was Eddie Barlow. He had the ideal Test match temperament and it would have been fascinating to see him up against other great all-rounders like Ian Botham, Richard Hadlee, Imran Khan and Kapil Dev. He lacked their natural talent, but I suppose he was nearest to Botham in terms of self-belief. Eddie had such faith in his own ability and to this day I don't know how much of that was bravado and how much complete conviction. His mental toughness was a vital ingredient in our success against Australia before isolation. At the time he was 30, a very experienced Test player and due to be Ali Bacher's vice-captain on the 1970 tour. His confidence just seeped through to the rest of us, so that we always believed we could turn a game round. As a bowler he was a bit of a 'golden arm', a great partnership-breaker. He'd bustle in, bowl what seemed to be innocuous medium pace and go through the whole routine of staring at the batsman, making him think he was lucky to survive. Now and then he'd come up with an unplayable delivery, good enough for the best batsman, and Eddie would just accept the wicket as a natural reward for his skills. He never seemed surprised when he did well. Yet his batting technique was a little shaky; he would play across the line and sometimes lose his timing. That's when he showed his character, because he would graft away, refusing to buckle to the bowlers, playing his way out of his bad form.

When we played together for the Rest of the World in England in 1970, he scored a remarkable hundred in the Lord's game. It was at the start of the tour, and like many of us, Eddie was out of season and rather rusty. He never looked in any sort of nick in that innings and, a day later, I couldn't recall one decent shot he played. But he got his hundred, and did it through sheer guts and self-belief. He scored another hundred later that series, topped the bowling averages (ahead of people like Sobers, McKenzie, Gibbs, Intikhab and Peter Pollock), did the hat-trick at Leeds and took more catches than any other fielder.

Eddie never batted an eyelid – it was almost as if he accepted that he would outshine a collection of world-class players.

If his batting was at times a purist's nightmare, if his bowling appeared unimpressive, his fielding was world class. I'm struggling to remember Eddie dropping a catch at slip for South Africa. In the 1970 series against Australia, he took eight beauties and the boost he gave to bowlers like Peter Pollock and myself was immense. In contrast the Aussies dropped a bucketful of catches and time and again we wriggled out of trouble. If Eddie had been standing at slip for them, we might have struggled at times. Given Eddie's enthusiasm for the game, it was inevitable that he would try his hand at county cricket and equally certain that he'd inspire his side . Derbyshire were the lucky county. He introduced new standards of fitness, drove himself harder than anyone, and transformed a modest outfit into one that bristled with confidence. He took them to a Cup final at Lord's, saw three of his players (Bob Taylor, Mike Hendrick and Geoff Miller) make the England side, and when he left them, Derbyshire were at last a force in the English game. I seem to recall that they were the first team to start lapping the ground early each morning before the start of play: that was Eddie's idea and those from other counties who stood around scoffing were all doing the same within a year. Eddie had the knack of proving people wrong.

A restless character, Eddie. He always seemed to be on the move. He was still playing first-class cricket at the age of 42 in South Africa, transforming Boland in the Currie Cup 'B' section with his unique brand of optimism. In the mid-1980s he came over to London for a couple of years as director of the South African Sports Office, promoting the cause of South African sport at a time when international opinion was still very critical. Eddie's intelligence and persistence in stating his case did our country a great deal of good in that period – it was the kind of task ideally suited to someone like him. After running a pig farm, then a vineyard, thena stint as Gloucestershire's coach followed by a spell as Orange Free State's cricket manager, he has now settled in Transvaal as their cricket manager. I've no idea how long he can stay in one place, but it's certainly a lively spot when he's there.

When you look at his Test record – six hundreds, a batting average of almost 47, a ratio of one catch per 30 Tests – you realise the importance of the right temperament. Players with far greater natural talent have struggled but this stocky, short-sighted guy just wouldn't accept his own limitations. You couldn't possibly bracket him alongside Pollock or Richards when it came to brilliance, but he was crucial to our success. I'm certain that, had we stayed in Test cricket, when the inevitable transitional period came Eddie Barlow would have helped paper over the cracks by the sheer force of his personality and his own never-say-die example.

CLIVE RICE

Clive was South Africa's first captain after we returned to the international fold in India late in 1991. Unfortunately it all came a little too late for him – he was 42 and creaking a little in the field, so he wasn't picked for the World Cup in Australia. It was a huge disappointment for him and I could understand his frustration. He had been selected for the tour to Australia in 1971-72, only to see that cancelled. For the next two decades he was a terrific all-rounder in English and South African cricket, leading Nottinghamshire to the County Championship twice and guiding Transvaal to consistent dominance of the Currie Cup. As someone who had captained a county in England, I could appreciate how much was involved in addition to having to perform up to scratch as the side's leading all-rounder. I thought he did superbly well to transform Nottinghamshire from also-rans to a team that played positively and expected to win trophies. He was helped greatly by the contributions of Richard Hadlee, but it was Clive who had to nurse Hadlee through the times when he didn't fancy bowling or coming back for another season. I thought Clive did a great deal for the image of the overseas cricketer during his time at Nottinghamshire.

He was a great success in the second year of World Series Cricket out in Australia. A typical South African, he was no respecter of big reputations out on the field and he made an immediate impression. You could see him grow in stature the longer the series went on; he was now 30, desperate to make up for lost time on the international scene, and he bowled with pace and aggression as well as batting confidently. Clive was one of the real casualties when WSC was disbanded after its second year. Like the other South Africans, he needed the stimulus of competition against other top performers and now, without WSC, it was back to whistling in the dark for a return to the official brand of international cricket.

Clive has always been a big-occasion player and he could be impatient with those who didn't meet his standards. He certainly whipped a few Nottinghamshire players into shape when he took over as captain and he has consistently ruffled a few feathers in South Africa with his frank comments on administrators, politicians and fellow players. But the fact that he was still playing in the Currie Cup in his 40s says a lot for his enthusiasm and self-motivation. In his prime, he was quick and hostile as a bowler and a fine batsman with a sound technique, with the temperament to raise his game. I have no doubt that Clive Rice would have been a major player for South Africa.

VINCE VAN DER BIJL

Many good judges think this guy was the best bowler never to play Test cricket and it's hard to think of anyone better qualified. At six foot seven and a half inches, he was the Joel Garner or Curtly Ambrose of South African cricket, getting lift and bounce from the slowest of pitches. He swung the ball too, and never gave you a moment's peace with his accuracy. In a 15-year career, he took more Currie Cup wickets than anyone else in history, almost 5 per game. That is high-class bowling. Apart from one season in county cricket and some productive bowling against Graham Gooch's England XI in 1982, Vince just toiled away in the comparative obscurity of South African domestic cricket. At the age of 23, he had been picked for the aborted Australian tour and that was the nearest he ever got to Test cricket. He took 10 wickets on his debut for a South African side against the Gooch team, but Vince would never accept that as the real thing. So his frustration at continued isolation was huge, possibly even bigger than Clive Rice's, because he never played in World Series Cricket.

In his only season in England, for Middlesex, he showed his class, taking 85 wickets, topping the first-class averages and helping Middlesex win the County Championship. Having played alongside him for Natal for several seasons, I didn't need any reminders of his quality but I was delighted for him that so many English players were unanimous that he was a world-class performer. A massive man, Vince's stamina was remarkable: another record he holds is the 93 consecutive games he played in Currie Cup cricket. He would have had no problems at all with the need to keep fit and strong on a gruelling international tour. Vince just loved to bowl!

He was 20 when he started out for Natal, in the season before we thrashed the Australians, just before we went into the wilderness. He had learned his trade with the Western Province Schools side on the slow, low pitches at Newlands and his move to the University of Natal helped his development as a fast-medium bowler, because the pitches there were quicker and helped his steep bounce. From then on he won more matches than any other South African in first-class cricket for the next 15 years. When you consider that most Test matches are played on slow pitches that favour the batsmen, a bowler like Vince would have been a godsend because of his bounce and his ability to hit the seam consistently and to get late swing. He was a lovely guy off the field, but he was a real handful with a ball in his hand. He never knew when he was beaten, and resented the batsman scoring even one run. A typical South African bowler, I suppose!

PETER KIRSTEN

I first saw this fellow bat when he was 18 and I was immediately impressed. He was batting for Western Province against Rhodesia and he came in at a very delicate stage in the match. I immediately crowded him with close fielders, trying to bother him with hints that the ball was doing all sorts of things, but he didn't turn a hair. He looked so composed, playing elegant shots as if he had been in first-class cricket for years. It was hard to imagine any English player of that age playing with so much maturity: possibly only David Gower could compare favourably.

So his temperament wasn't a problem and he showed that in another sport the following year when he played for his state against the British Lions rugby side. He could have been outstanding at both sports but one had to fall by the wayside, and he decided to try his hand in English county cricket. Eddie Barlow, who had been a big influence on him at Western Province, brought him over to Derbyshire and he was a brilliant success there for five seasons. Peter's all-round game developed, but after a time he was hungry for greater fulfilment. He didn't quite go down the Barry Richards road but by his late 20s, a stream of centuries in county cricket weren't giving him enormous satisfaction. He needed the stimulus of a higher grade of the game and he never returned to Derbyshire after the age of 27. The succession of rebel tours to South Africa in the mid-1980s gave him fresh incentives and he kept form and fitness for a long time as South Africa's cricket isolation drew to a close. He played in the 1992 World Cup and he was still playing Test cricket as he approached his 40s.

We will never know just how good he might have been in Test cricket if he had played at his peak. There were times when the faster bowlers troubled him and that was usually the staple diet against the top teams. But he looked a high-class player: a crisp driver, very nimble on his feet, a skilful manipulator of the ball through the vacant areas and a brilliant runner between the wickets. At least he had the satisfaction of playing Test cricket late in his career, but he would have been far happier if the call had come a decade earlier.

KEN McEWAN

Another player whose career fell precisely within the years of isolation was Ken McEwan. He was still playing for Western Province until 1989, at the age of 37, so he just missed out on the chance of Test cricket. It would have been interesting to watch him combat the short-pitched stuff that would surely have come his way: that was an occasional weakness of Kenny's, although he had such a good career record that you felt class would get him through any short-term crisis. Only Barry Richards among South African batsmen scored more first-class centuries than Kenny and the hallmark of his batting was a lovely sense of timing. He seemed just to ease into the stroke, never smashing the ball like a Pollock, more like a Richards. It seems amazing that he never played at all until he was 12, and yet within a few years he was the captain of the South African Schools team. He owed a lot to Tony Greig, who coached him at Queen's College, Queenstown and it was Greigy again who recommended him to Sussex. Their loss was Essex's gain and the ten years he spent in English county cricket helped toughen him up mentally without compromising his attacking style. He was very popular at Essex for his unselfishness and his positive approach to the differing demands you meet in the English game day after day, and he made a stack of runs for them in all competitions.

Although a charming, modest guy, Kenny had an inner strength about him and I wasn't at all surprised that he went off to Western Australia to try his hand in Sheffield Shield cricket. He helped them win the Shield in his second season with WA, only confirming what a lucky omen he was. In three countries, he helped his team win the major honour: the County Championship with Essex, the Shield with Western Australia and the Currie Cup with Western Province.

In the end, the demands of his family farm curtailed his career – that and the lack of the incentive Test cricket would have brought. Among the South African players of my time, only Barry Richards could surpass Kenny's elegance.

GARTH LE ROUX

The ideal fast bowler in the traditional South African mould. Friendly enough off the field, he gave his all when bowling. Nicknamed 'Grumps', Garth always expected to get wickets and had a very low opinion of batsmen, a point he was always happy to emphasise. Big and strong, he could bowl all day at his peak and he was a great success in the second year of World Series Cricket. At the age of 23, he forced his way into the World XI and didn't seem at all overawed playing alongside bowlers such as Derek Underwood, Imran Khan, Clive Rice and myself. During that series, he was up against batsmen of the calibre of Viv Richards, Desmond Haynes, Gordon Greenidge, the Chappell brothers and Lawrence Rowe, but big Garth took it all in his stride. Imran was so impressed by Garth that he recommended him to Sussex, and for a few seasons those two were a devastating opening attack, one of the best in county cricket. It was only the brilliance of Richard Hadlee that stopped Sussex winning the Championship in 1981 and facing a fiery le Roux on a quick wicket at Hove was not high on any batsman's list of priorities for a season or two in the early 1980s.

Big Garth managed to gain some consolation for missing out on Test cricket when he appeared for South Africa in a few matches against those touring sides dubbed as 'rebels'. Some sceptics may have doubted just how competitive those games were, but they didn't understand how important it was for us South Africans to show we could still perform at a higher level than the Currie Cup. When Garth took a hat-trick at Johannesburg against Kim Hughes' side early in 1986, I can confirm he was trying! Having played with Peter Pollock in Test cricket, I am certain that Garth le Roux would have been a worthy successor in the business of unsettling batsmen with pace, hostility and an aggressive personality. 'Whispering Death' he was not: you knew when big Garth was on his way!

DENYS HOBSON

In 1977, when World Series Cricket was launched, this fellow was the best leg-spinner in the world, yet only the real scholars of the game outside South Africa knew of him. So when his name was added to Kerry Packer's list, I looked forward to seeing how Viv Richards and the other great batsmen in WSC would cope with him. Sadly, it was not to be. Denys and Graeme Pollock had to return home after some Boards of Control objected to their presence because they had not played county cricket and therefore certain coloured players had not been on the same first-class pitch as them. Very petty. More politics. What was the difference, for heaven's sake? Did those meddling officials not realise how much Hobson and Pollock had done for the cause of multi-racial cricket?

Denys was a terrific bowler, one of the rare leg-spinners who could bowl accurately with four fielders round the bat. He bowled quick leg-breaks, the top-spinner and the googly. He once took 14 wickets in a day, for Western Province against Natal, and he's one of only two spinners to have taken over 300 Currie Cup wickets. Yet he was unknown outside South Africa. He was too young for Test cricket before we were banned and he retired in 1985, at the age of 34, a few years before we got back. He never tried county cricket, even though he had several offers. On his day he was devastating and even when he was not quite at his best, he never got collared because he was so accurate and comparatively quick. When you consider that at the start and end of our isolation we were not particularly strong in the spin department, I think Denys Hobson would have been a match-winner in Tests during the '70s and '80s. He would have been given an extended run and wouldn't have drifted away from the game so young: 34 is no age for a spinner to retire, unless the incentives are scarce.

JIMMY COOK

I believe Jimmy would have been ideally suited to the demands of Test cricket if it had come a little earlier for him. He had made his first-class debut two years after our last Test appearance, and when he was pitched straight into the Transvaal side from league cricket in Johannesburg he came up against Vince van der Bijl at his most devastating. He made a half-century, pulling his side round from 20-odd for 4. That calmness was the hallmark of Jimmy Cook's batting. His home pitch at the Wanderers ground is traditionally hard and grassy and the ball jags about a lot; an opening batsman needs to see the ball early and play it late. Jimmy was a master at that. A calculating yet stylish player, he was one of those who scored faster than you realised. Not one for the flamboyant stroke, he would tuck the ball away to the square-leg boundary without any fuss or lean into the off-drive. Jimmy thought a great deal about the art of batting; he was excellent off the back foot, a vital asset in a Test batsman, and when some of the West Indian fast bowlers troubled him on their tour in the mid-1980s, he worked hard to overcome the fault. I can barely remember a time when he seemed out of position when playing a shot – he reminded me sometimes of Barry Richards in the way he got into position so quickly.

Jimmy played in every one of those rebel internationals from 1982 (Graham Gooch's side) through to 1990 (Mike Gatting's team), and it was only as he approached his 40s that he came to be appreciated by a wider audience. He went to Somerset to play three years of county cricket – no county had asked him before 1989 – and he was a huge success. He didn't miss a game, made masses of runs in great style and impressed everyone with his approach to the game and its supporters. He was highly rated by the world-class bowlers that you meet day after day in county cricket, and the records that he set up came naturally to him – he was no Boycott in terms of personal goals. He was as relaxed as his batting style, but no pushover. You always had to work for Jimmy Cook's wicket.

It was a pity that our recall to international cricket coincided with a loss of form for Jimmy in the Currie Cup and then on our hurriedly arranged trip to India. He missed out on the World Cup as the selectors went for younger players who would also be more agile in the field. It wasn't Jimmy's fault that time had moved on: he shared the heartache of many top-class South African cricketers who were born at the wrong time.

In addition to the players I have already discussed, four other top-class batsmen came through the South African coaching system to become international players. Allan Lamb qualified for England through British parentage, while Chris and Robin Smith served a number of years before becoming eligible for England. I don't blame them at all, even though it was ironic that Lamb first played for England in place of those players who had just been out to South Africa with Graham Gooch, copping a three-year ban in the process. These three players all felt there was little prospect of a return to the international fold for a number of years and they were perfectly entitled as ambitious professionals to use the qualification rules to better themselves as sportsmen. Kepler Wessels took the same attitude. After playing in World Series Cricket, he moved to Australia, married an Australian girl and eventually represented his adopted country at Test cricket. It was 1982, the politicians were still wrangling over South Africa and the ICC appeared reluctant to hold out any hope of a return. It's hard to argue with Kepler's logic or his decision, even if his subsequent moves back and forth to the country of his birth have been rather bewildering! From a personal point of view I would not have wanted to play Test cricket for any other country, even though technically the option was there in my last year at Gloucestershire. I had been classified English for registration purposes so that we could continue playing two Pakistanis, Sadiq and Zaheer, in the same Gloucestershire side, and although the press drummed up a 'Procter for England' line, I wasn't at all keen. It would have been wrong to deny a place to someone far better qualified for England and besides, I was proud of having played Test cricket for South Africa and didn't want to tarnish that memory. Having said that, the Smith brothers, Lamby and Kepler were quite entitled to look elsewhere. I have no doubt, though, that if we had still been in the Test fold, or close to a return, all four of them would have been delighted to play for the country of their birth. That would have been an interesting selection problem!

One thing has struck me about all these fine South African players. With the exception of Graeme Pollock and Denys Hobson, they all played English county cricket. That made them all better players – they experienced different conditions, came up against world-class opponents, learned to cope with the mental and physical demands of the daily grind and developed their skills. With the exception of a genius like Pollock, I believe county cricket is the common ingredient in assessing those players likely to have made the most important contributions if we hadn't been banned over two decades. It simply hardened us all up and the wide experience gained in such a short time gave us all greater self-confidence and increased professionalism. Without Test cricket, it was also an additional incentive. I was doubly lucky, enjoying a fulfilling county career that lasted 14 years, then two hugely satisfying years with World Series Cricket. Others weren't so fortunate. Signing for Kerry Packer was the easiest decision I ever had to take in my cricket career. For South Africans like me, Pollock, Hobson, le Roux, Rice, Barlow and Richards, it was to be the nearest we would get to the real buzz of Test cricket. It proved to be the hardest cricket I ever played, to the highest standard, and don't let any of the traditionalists who hated Packer tell you any different. It was even more satisfying that most of us did well in WSC, a fact I once remarked on to Ian Chappell after a particularly tense, hard-fought game. I told him there should have been even more South Africans signed up, because the World XI would have beaten the Aussies even more comfortably!

There were many other fine players who missed out on international careers during our period of isolation. Who now remembers Grahame Chevalier, a left-arm spinner who played for South Africa after just 16 first-class games, took 5 wickets in his first Test against the 1970 Aussies and was never picked again? John Traicos, an accurate off-spinner, took his place, but didn't add to his three caps for another 22 years, until Zimbabwe was elected to Test cricket. John kept himself very fit, and his flourishing legal practice meant he was financially secure and could therefore carry on playing at a high level for pleasure, but who knows how good he might have been after breaking into the South African team at the age of 22? Arthur Short was the same age when he was selected for the 1970 tour to England, then he was picked a year later for Australia, but this sound opening bat would never wear his country's colours. Lee Irvine, another success in county cricket, had only four Tests to display his punishing batting, and in the last one, at Port Elizabeth, he scored a hundred. Later in the 1970s, Henry Fotheringham, an aggressive batsman, struck up a tremendous opening partnership for Transvaal with Jimmy Cook. They were the best openers in the Currie Cup, playing for the best team, and they must have been close to selection if we had been a Test nation then. Alan Kourie was an accurate, slow left-arm bowler who used to pick up a lot of wickets on pitches that helped the seamers. He and Denys Hobson are the only spinners to take more than 300 wickets in Currie Cup matches. For a few seasons, Chris Wilkins was an exhilarating opening batsman who scored a lot of runs in both Currie Cup and limited-overs matches. During that period, we were also blessed with two fine wicket-keepers: Ray Jennings and 'Tich' Smith, who was the better batsman of the two. All things considered, there was more than enough talent to go round if the ICC had seen fit to use it.

To mark the tenth anniversary of our absence from Test cricket, I was asked to pick a South African side to take on any opposition, with myself as captain, which was very flattering! It was a harmless enough exercise – in 1980 we were still a long way from feeling optimistic about our return. I fished out that selection the other day:

Jimmy Cook
Peter Kirsten
Allan Lamb
Eddie Barlow
'Tich' Smith
Garth le Roux
Alan Kourie
Barry Richards
Graeme Pollock
Clive Rice
Mike Procter
Vince van der Bijl
Denys Hobson

I've gone for 12 to cover all conditions. I assume one of the spinners would drop out, with Eddie Barlow convincing the captain he could easily shoulder the extra burden – a fair amount of talent in that squad. In purely cricketing terms, that was the tragedy of our prolonged spell in isolation.

THE WIND OF CHANGE

By 1977, seven years into our isolation from the international game, there had been dramatic and welcome changes in the organisation of South Africa's domestic cricket. Yet it would be another 14 years before we were welcomed back. If ever we needed proof that the matter was now a political football, beyond the influence of cricketers and our administrators, here it was.

Consider two separate statements of major importance that would eventually become irrelevant. In 1970, the Cricket Council, acting on behalf of England, spoke from Lord's about its regret in cancelling our proposed tour there on the advice of the British government. The statement held out hope, though. The main requirement for a resumption of Test cricket between England and South Africa was 'that South African cricket should be played and teams chosen on a multi-racial basis'. The statement didn't say how much mixed-race cricket it would deem acceptable, but to us, that message was very clear – put your house in order. Four years later, the ruling body of world cricket, the International Cricket Conference, discussed the South African question at its annual meeting in London. There were two key paragraphs in the subsequent ICC statement:

'The Conference... reaffirms its statement made in 1970 that there is universal concern for, and condemnation of, the effect of South African racial policies on the right of individuals anywhere and of any colour, race or creed, to play cricket together.

'The Conference repeats its hope that there will soon be effective changes in South Africa which will enable a single body truly representative of all cricket in that country to take its place at their conference.'

So South African cricket had to have one ruling body speaking for all cricketers while the progress towards multi-racial cricket must be general and sincere. That sounded fair enough to us in 1974; we realised there was a price to pay for a political philosophy we cricketers didn't believe in and we were willing to do everything possible to make sure cricket at least was squeaky-clean. The international game's rulers seemed genuine in their desire to keep politics out of sport and that was fine by us. Recently there had been a greater awareness in South Africa that we needed to make things happen in our domestic cricket structure and change was definitely in the air. Many of us thought it wouldn't be long before we had cleared the slate and were back in Test cricket.

Within a year or two of our official ban, pockets of resistance to government policy began to spring up. In 1973, my old Test colleague Dennis Gamsy and his provincial team-mate Andre Bruyns set up the Cricket Club of South Africa, drawn along non-racial principles, with members from all over the country. They were to provide black cricketers with facilities and coaching and a tour to India was mooted. The matches would be classified as friendlies and would be played only when games under the affiliation of the other ruling bodies weren't taking place. It was a short-lived scheme, but the seeds of non-racial cricket were planted. In the same year the Aurora club of Pietermaritzburg defied the government by setting up the first non-racial cricket club under the umbrella of the South African Cricket

Association (SACA), the body which looked after white cricket. The Minister of Sport, Dr Piet Koornhof, expressed his disapproval of the plan, saying that the club were using cricket for political purposes. At Aurora's first game, security officials took the names of all the players, but the matter wasn't followed up and the following year Aurora started to play cricket in the provincial league.

At a higher level, there were significant breakthroughs. The Datsun Double Wicket International Competition at the Wanderers ground in Johannesburg brought black cricketers to a wider audience alongside white players for the first time. The two Africans picked for the event, Edward Habane and Edmund Ntikinca, beat the New Zealanders, Bruce Taylor and Bev Congdon – both experienced Test players – before losing gallantly first to Barry Richards and Eddie Barlow, then to the Chappell brothers from Australia. It was marvellous to see the rapport between the two Africans and the other guys and their quality as cricketers meant there was no suggestion of window-dressing. A few weeks after the Datsun tournament, there was another significant development. Derrick Robins brought a strong international side to South Africa, including the West Indian John Shepherd and the Pakistani Younis Ahmed. They were the first black cricketers to tour South Africa with a mixed side. The first match of that tour was against an all-African side at the Maroko Jabavu Stadium in Johannesburg and the Robins players were given a fantastic reception.

Two years later, the Robins team returned to South Africa, playing two games against an African XI, and once again, it was clear that cricket was taking hold in the African community. They had a real folk hero in Edward Habane, who was the best African player in the 1970s. He and Sedick Conrad did so well for the African side that they were picked for a mixed South African Invitation XI to play the Robins team at Newlands. The match was officially sanctioned by the government, with one eye on attempts to salvage the forthcoming tour to Australia. That piece of political compromise failed – the tour never materialised

– but at least there were more and more public displays of a desire for multi-racial cricket. Soon after becoming one of the first two blacks to play in a mixed South African side in a first-class game, Sedick Conrad notched up another notable achievement. When he played for Green Point against Claremont in a First Division match in Western Province, he became the first black cricketer to play in a whites-only league. The teams weren't released to the press and when Sedick turned up to play, he fully expected to be barred by the police, but the game went ahead. His next game for Green Point was even more significant. It was against the students of Stellenbosch University in a town that was a traditional breeding-ground for Nationalist leaders. The university had always reflected the thinking of the government, proud to have educated various cabinet ministers and funded by wealthy white businessmen. Yet Sedick was warmly welcomed by players and spectators and he showed his gratitude by hitting 73 to help Green Point to a surprise victory over Stellenbosch.

Things were on the move. 'Tiny' Abed, who used to play with Basil D'Oliveira in the SACBOC national side, joined Green Point as well. The all-rounder Imraan Hendricks teamed up with Port Elizabeth Cricket Club, the oldest club in South Africa. Kantilal Kanjee, an Asian from Salisbury in Rhodesia, became the first black umpire to stand in a first-class match in South Africa, something that would have been unthinkable just a few years earlier – whites subject to the discipline of a black man! John Shepherd, the West Indian all-rounder, became the first black man to play in the Currie Cup, then the Gillette Cup. He was playing alongside me for Rhodesia and when he was due to play in South Africa for us for the first time, we were understandably keyed up. When he walked out to bat at the Wanderers, he was cheered to the wicket by 25,000 spectators. He made 60-odd and he was cheered all the way back. John had been getting stick from various quarters – back in the Caribbean and in Rhodesia, where the ANC said he was a traitor to the black man – but it was brave guys like him who were helping to push us down the right road. If the Shepherds of the day could show character, then those of us who were luckier had to keep the faith as well.

Some cricket administrators were particularly brave about pushing on towards multi-racial cricket. In Transvaal Joe Pamensky, a prominent Johannesburg businessman, worked very hard in the early 1970s to try to move the government away from its entrenched attitude. It was a new administrative style; previously SACA had been conservative and keen not to rock the boat. Now and then SACA would say that it disapproved of apartheid, but the cause of South African cricket needed something more dynamic, a style of leadership that was pitched somewhere between the passive stance of SACA and the hawkish dogmatism of Hassan Howa, of SACBOC, which looked after the interests of Indians and coloureds. At the time Joe Pamensky was a board member of the Transvaal Cricket Union and he knew Ali Bacher, a former Transvaal captain, very well. Ali was equally determined to foster multi-racial cricket and the two men worked tirelessly to try to get some sort of understanding with the SACBOC officials in their province.

They were lucky that the Transvaal president of SACBOC was more sensible than Hassan Howa. Rashid Varachia, a wealthy Indian businessman, loved cricket and believed that political influences could be kept at bay, given goodwill on all sides. He certainly had that, and he agreed with Bacher and Pamensky that mixed trial matches would be far better than separate trials involving the same racial group. The idea was that everyone should play with each other right from the start. Pamensky hired the best legal brains he could afford to see if there was any way that mixed cricket could be played within the law of the land. He was told that there could be mixed cricket in certain cases: if the grounds were private and the matches weren't advertised to the public then the games would not be harassed by the security forces. Sounds a very limited concession, I agree, but Pamensky,

Varachia and Bacher knew that the reforms couldn't be an overnight sensation. Towards the end of 1974, the Transvaal Cricket Union and the SACBOC provincial branch announced there would be integrated club leagues the following season. Pamensky said: 'Cricket cannot wait for other sports to take the lead.' Although non-white cricket was strong in Johannesburg, this was still a brave thing for a white administrator to say to his white Minister of Sport. And Dr Koornhof was not impressed, warning that mixed club competitions were against government policy, and that violation of that policy would be seriously judged.

At times, it looked as if progress towards multi-racial cricket in the Transvaal was doomed as mixed games were cancelled at the last minute due to the behind-the-scenes activities of militant members of SACBOC, who had been stirred up by Hassan Howa. But Rashid Varachia kept the lines of communication open. He came up with the idea of 'normal cricket' and Pamensky was sold on the idea. Varachia thought that distinctions like 'multi-racial', 'multi-national' and 'non-racial' should be dropped from cricket. Cricket should simply be played without government interference and every club should be allowed to pick any player they wished. The Transvaal Cricket Union put the plan to all its clubs and with just one or two exceptions, it was gladly accepted. Every player in the Transvaal League was asked to fill in a questionnaire asking if he was willing to play against non-whites and with non-whites. They voted unanimously in favour.

Pamensky and Varachia approached the Minister of Sport and Dr Koornhof admitted that the findings of the questionnaire were important. He proved to be more flexible than previously in his dealings with the cricket authorities, but said that the problem would be selling the idea of 'normal cricket' to a government whose philosophy was against breaking down racial barriers. The Minister believed that Transvaal's revolutionary proposal needed national support among the cricket fraternity before he could sell the formula to his cabinet colleagues.

Now the leading cricket officials started to move away from their softly, softly stance. Boon Wallace, the SACA president, said: 'Cricket is not only a game in which a man's colour is neither significant nor important, but cricket is indeed a great catalyst of goodwill in the field of race relations.' He said the government's apartheid policy was not SACA's and that mixed cricket was inevitable. So the pace was quickening. Soon the government would be faced with an overwhelming desire for change among our cricketers.

Four other provinces then announced that they would be looking at integrating their league cricket structure along the lines of the Transvaal model. When Rashid Varachia was elected president of SACBOC in place of Hassan Howa, all of a sudden the prospects of 'normal cricket' throughout South Africa looked much brighter. The hope now was that there would be no more blind opposition just for the sake of it. January 2, 1976 was an historic day for South African cricket. The three national bodies that controlled cricket in South Africa agreed to unite and play the game on a non-racial basis. The non-racial South African African Cricket Board (SAACB) had traditionally been a more moderate organisation than SACBOC and they joined forces with SACA so that cricketers of all races could be united in a country where racial divisions were so painfully clear. Cricket had set a precedent that would be followed by many sections of South African society in the years ahead. It would take another 20 months of hard bargaining and frustration before the merged body – the South African Cricket Union – was officially in place, but the significance of the agreement in principle between the three cricket boards wasn't lost on anyone who had followed our efforts to normalise our game. Peter Hain, a thorn in our flesh since the days of protests in Britain over rugby and cricket tours, promised that South Africa's cricketers wouldn't be hassled by his group if the plans came to fruition. South African soccer officials said they'd be looking soon at a similar scheme, but predictably, rugby dragged its heels. The president of the South African Rugby Board, Dr Danie Craven, said there were no immediate plans for similar change in rugby and he warned that nothing would be done without the government's approval. Cricket was always ahead of other sports in South Africa when it came to a sincere commitment to multi-racialism.

We were all very optimistic when the move towards 'normal cricket' was warmly welcomed in London by the ICC secretary, Jack Bailey. He said it was great news and the plan augured well for South Africa's position in international cricket. For their part, Australia seemed equally happy, their board issuing a statement that this important development would be a major step in getting us back into the Test arena. Remember, this was early in 1976. Within six years of being shown the door, South Africa's cricketers and administrators of all colours had shown a common agreement on the way forward, on most occasions against the express wishes of our government. An enlightened approach had emerged in a country of deep conservatism and entrenched social attitudes. It was a miracle that things had moved so quickly. No wonder we got rather bitter as the years moved on and we got no nearer to winning the ICC's approval.

While many were getting excited about the progress towards 'normal cricket', Basil D'Oliveira sounded an understandable note of caution. Dolly knew all about raising false hopes through bitter experience and he warned that the crux of the matter was the approval of the South African government. The Minister of Sport, Dr Koornhof, gave cautious approval to the idea of a unified cricket body and he put the formula to the government late in 1976. He did an excellent job selling the scheme to his colleagues and just before the 1976-77 domestic season started, we heard the great news: there could now be a policy that allowed multi-racial sport to take place from club level upwards. Cricket had been the driving force in making the government change its mind and adapt to the general feeling in the country. When the government's decision was criticised by the Herstigte Nasionale

Above After taking 6 wickets against the Australians, Mike Procter leads the South African team from the Test arena in March 1970.
Below Looking on the bright side – Barry Richards and Mike Procter share a joke at D.F. Malan Airport, Cape Town in April 1971.

Above Dennis Gamsy playing for Natal against Western Province in 1971.
Above left Morris Garda of Transvaal hooks in a match against Western Province in 1971.
Left Lee Irvine scoring a centruy for Transvaal against Western Province in 1974.
Below Peter Kirsten on the way to his maiden first-class century at Newlands in 1978.
Facing page Graeme Pollock - master batsman.

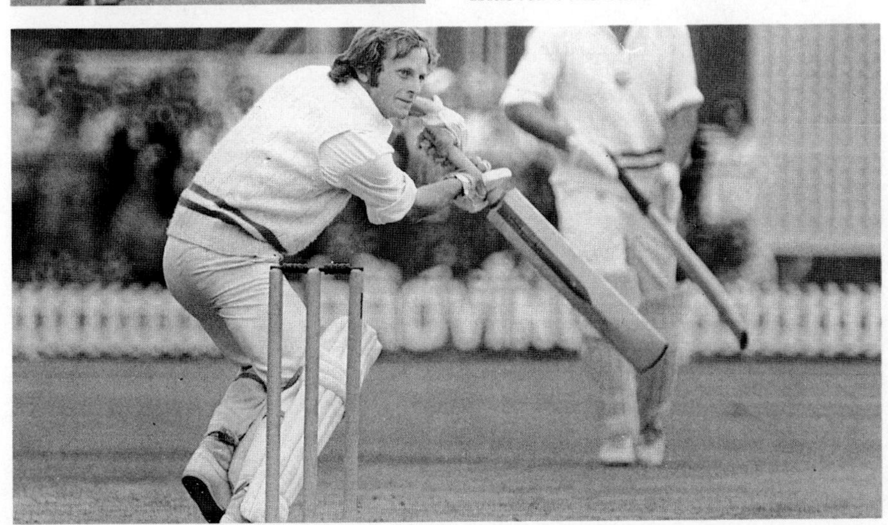

CRUSADERS
SUID
MAR

Facing page Garth le Roux at full tilt against the Australians in 1987.
Above right Another wicket for Denys Hobson, for Western Province against Rhodesia at Newlands in 1977.
Above left The batsman's view of Vince van der Bijl.
Below Eyes on the target – Peter Pollock leaps into action.

Facing page Ali Bacher on his final first-class appearance in January 1974, at Newlands.
Far left Joe Pamensky, a leading member of SACU.
Left Dr Piet Koornhof, former Minister of Sport.
Below left Edward Habane receives a bat as the best batsman of the African Junior Cricket Week at Langa in 1974.
Bottom left John Passmore offers words of encouragement to Langa batsman M. Vazi in 1976.
Bottom right Kantilal Kanjee takes the field (with Ken Craig) at Newlands in January 1975 and makes history as the first non-white umpire to stand in the Currie Cup.

Above right Allan Lamb playing for Western Province at Newlands in 1979.
Above left Lawrence Seeff makes an impressive start to his international career with 188 against the Sri Lankans in 1982.
Below More runs for Jimmy Cook in 1983.

party, the extreme right-wing branch of the Afrikaner philosophy, we knew what a revolution we were witnessing.

So, in October 1976, official mixed club cricket came to South Africa for the first time. The various cricket authorities decided that the new policy meant any club could pick any player, that selection of teams in the Currie Cup would be entirely on merit and that elections to the various cricket associations would take place on a non-racial basis. The door was opening to non-whites in cricket committee rooms as well as on the field of play. In the Transvaal leagues alone, more than 30 non-white teams joined the 60 white clubs. The Minister of Sport attended a match at the Wanderers ground in Johannesburg featuring the home side against the Crescents, a largely Indian team, and he declared that sport should be kept out of politics. Now that was a change of official policy! Crescents had been boosted by the recruitment of two former Test players, Colin Wesley and Dennis Gamsy, and they also fielded an African, Duncan Stamper, a good enough bowler to dismiss Barry Richards, Eddie Barlow and a certain M. J. Procter when we played in the Datsun Double Wicket Competition. I turned out for Chatsworth, a mixed club side, that season and Basil D'Oliveira played in Durban's Inter-City League for Pirates when he paid a short visit towards the end of 1976.

It's true that at the start the all-black teams were weaker than the all-white ones, but there was a lot of talent around. In that first season of 'normal cricket', two SACBOC players – Trevor Roberts and Yacoob Omar – represented Natal 'B'. Eventually Omar, a fine batsman, became the first black cricketer to play for Natal in the Currie Cup. Three SACBOC players – Morris Garda, Solly Chotia and Tiffie Barnes, were picked for a Transvaal Invitation XI against Western Transvaal and then Garda and Chotia went on to play for Transvaal 'B' later that same season. In Eastern Province, the Pioneers club produced Jeff Frans, who, on his debut for Eastern Province, dismissed one of Rhodesia's openers in his first over. Two other SACBOC players – Bravo Jacobs and Devdas Govindjee – were included in Eastern Province's training squad for the Currie Cup season.

There was one other significant change: whenever a game was played at Durban's Kingsmead ground that season, spectators were constantly reminded over the public address system that they could sit wherever they liked. There were no segregation areas based on the colour of your skin: no longer could the whites have exclusive use of the shadiest parts of the ground. The old order was truly changing.

The year 1976 also saw a momentous tour that did a great deal towards healing divisions. Greg Chappell brought an International Wanderers side to play mixed sides. Richie Benaud, who managed the team, insisted on multi-racial opposition and he was good enough to say that the atmosphere in South Africa had changed dramatically – and for the good – since his last visit ten years earlier. He was very optimistic about a return to Test cricket, on the basis of what he had seen. In the Wanderers side were players of the calibre of Dennis Lillee, Greg and Ian Chappell, Max Walker, Bob Taylor, Derek Underwood, Phil Edmonds and Glenn Turner. It was a tremendously popular tour, not least because the Wanderers players took the games seriously and there was never any danger of the non-whites feeling patronised. Initially there were problems with some hard-liners in the SACBOC ranks and Rashid Varachia had to put his personal reputation on the line by insisting that the black cricketers weren't selling out to the white man by agreeing to play mixed games. He won the day after agreeing that mixed trials would be held and that there would be total integration on and off the field. After the first game at Newlands, where black players such as Howie Bergins and Baboo Ebrahim did so well, the SACBOC support for the games increased greatly. Eddie Barlow, who captained the South African Invitation XI, said it was a fantastic experience to be part of the first South African team to represent the three major cricket bodies. He said that the rapport between players of all colours was very moving and that, within a game or two, there was a massive waiting list of non-white cricketers desperate to play. Eddie issued a statement to the press which spoke for everyone involved in the series:

'All the players who represented the South African Invitation XI want to express their feelings of enthusiasm and honour at having been part of a new era of South African cricket. We are unanimous that these games have shown that cricket knows no barriers and that the way is now open for South African cricket to be normalised as soon as possible. We are delighted that the faith invested in us by the South African government and the far-sighted SACBOC administrators has been so completely justified.'

So South Africa's cricketers were becoming louder in their desire for 'normal cricket'. The word was spreading to other cricket centres in the world that we were changing rapidly, and for the better. A year after that International Wanderers tour, the Minister for Sport announced an official change in government policy towards sport. Dr Koornhof finally came out and said publicly what he had hinted at to the cricket family – that mixed sport was permissible, that there was no government law prohibiting it. Any sports club in South Africa could decide who joined. Multi-racial teams were allowed to socialise after a match and to use the same facilities. Before this statement, Dr Koornhof had pursued a stealthy policy of chipping away at the idea of segregated sport, encouraging cricket administrators just to get on with the reforms. Now he had broken ranks and said things that would be bound to upset the right wing of his party. This was a major breakthrough in abolishing sports apartheid. It allowed all sports club officials to accept members of different races and to stop hiding behind the confusion caused by different interpretations of apartheid laws like the Group Areas Act and the Liquor Act. It was a brave decision by the Minister, who was proving himself a friend of sport and its ideals. One month after Dr Koornhof's speech we had confirmation that at last South Africa would have one official body controlling cricket. So

SACU – the South African Cricket Union – was formed, after nearly two years of wrangling, misunderstanding and mischief-making in some quarters. It was thanks to great tenacity by men like Joe Pamensky and Rashid Varachia. Varachia was elected president of SACU, further proof that our cricket was becoming progressive. The very idea of an Indian supervising our domestic cricket would have been unthinkable just a few years earlier, but he had proved to be an outstanding administrator, with the best interests of all our cricketers at heart. He outlined four essentials for the success of 'normal cricket':

Membership of clubs to be open and not governed by race, creed or colour;

Merit selection;

To implement that merit selection, cricket should be played from club level upwards;

Sharing of all common facilities.

At the time of the official formation of SACU I was in the High Court in London, giving evidence on behalf of Kerry Packer when he took the Test and County Cricket Board to court over his plans to play world-class cricket in Australia later that year. I suppose Packer was the better story, with all those big names being bandied about in the witness box and the top brass from Lord's being cross-examined, but I was keen to know what was going on at the meeting in Johannesburg that launched SACU. A few phone calls established the situation and later I was very impressed by one quote from Rashid Varachia: 'There is no way anyone can stop this healthy and exhilarating wind of change that is blowing through the corridors of world cricket.' It was the most important event in South African cricket since the ICC banned us from international competition in 1971. For the first time in the history of South African cricket, one official national body controlled the game. It was also the first time a large cross-section of South African sportsmen of all races had formed an organisation outside the framework of apartheid with clear, non-racial principles. There had been non-racial bodies in South Africa for the previous 20 years or so, but they had been almost exclusively full of black sportsmen. Now the whites had come together with all other colours.

The formation of SACU also fulfilled the requirements of the ICC for allowing us back into international cricket. There was now a single body truly representative of our domestic cricket. So why couldn't we now look forward to inviting touring parties to our country? We were certain there'd be no need for barbed wire around the boundary edge, for security officials to patrol the ground at night-time, for the police to be ready to march away demonstrators. The rest of the world had an out-of-date opinion of South African society in 1977 and those English folk who worried about the safety of touring players needed only to remember the Headingley Test in 1975. When supporters of a guy in prison dig up the Test pitch just to make a crude point, you have to look at your own backyard before you start criticising other countries' security and those who just use sport for their own ends. I was more optimistic about tours coming to us, rather than getting invitations for South Africa to tour, because we all knew that there was still a long way to go in changing the minds of influential people. One worry was that world cricket had become distracted by the dispute with Kerry Packer. The majority of the Boards of Control in world cricket had lost key players to Packer and it looked as if it would become a fight for world dominance in cricket. The establishment thought Packer was just an Australian upstart with no feel for the game who was only interested in television ratings. He had to be taught a lesson, but the establishment knew that would take a lot of money, legal expertise and time. In the end, Packer won in the courts, the official branch of world cricket lost vital revenue and it wasn't until April 1979 that a peace formula was hammered out between the two factions. In the circumstances, it was no surprise that the cause of South Africa's recall was put in the pending tray by the ICC.

There was always the worry that the politicians would move the goalposts and just before the official formation of SACU, they did just that. The Commonwealth heads of state issued the Gleneagles Agreement, which amounted to a major setback for South Africa's hopes of readmission. They said they would take all practical steps to discourage sporting links with South Africa. They were preoccupied with the prospect of the Commonwealth Games, scheduled for Canada, being called off due to political protests, and it was more important to save the Games than reward South Africa for its genuine efforts to beat apartheid. The statement waffled on about the necessity of maintaining 'the harmonious development of Commonwealth sport', yet the 28 African countries who had boycotted the 1976 Olympics because New Zealand had sent a rugby team to South Africa didn't seem all that concerned about such harmony. The Gleneagles Agreement was all about getting those African countries back into line to save the 1978 Commonwealth Games and South Africa was an easy target. For years to come, politicians would look at the small print and find something that justified their latest posturing, while sportsmen were helpless. In the short term, the Gleneagles Agreement meant the countries involved would come under greater pressure to stop organised tours involving South African sport.

By 1977, international opinion had hardened against South Africa for political reasons. The Soweto riots in which hundreds had been killed – including many children – after the government had tried to force the use of Afrikaans in black schools was a major setback, and so was the death of the black leader, Steve Biko, in police detention. In retrospect, against the background of political ferment, the claims of our sporting administrators were bound to fall on deaf ears. The African bloc vote among the Commonwealth Heads of State was well aware that sports isolation was a vital way of pressurising the white South African regime. Gleneagles confirmed that the pressure would be kept up, no matter what we were doing in cricketing circles.

Our administrators had gained the respect of people like Peter

Hain, who acknowledged that cricket in South Africa had done all it could towards normalisation, but that cut no ice with the Commonwealth's leading politicians. Those from England, New Zealand and Australia could only wring their hands and look on, fully aware that they would be outvoted. The ICC would be equally helpless over the next decade. Political considerations wouldn't leave our sporting arena alone. A white government meant Test cricket for South Africa wouldn't be on the agenda. So, on the occasions when our cricket administrators had friendly, informal talks with members of the ICC at their annual meeting in London, they proved to be meaningless. The West Indies officials would be sympathetic and say all the right things, but they knew that with six separate governments back in the Caribbean, the politicians would not fall out with the Afro-Asian bloc at the United Nations over something as trivial as a game of cricket.

I understand that the Australian delegates at the ICC always viewed our cause sympathetically, yet when Boon Wallace of SACA applied for a visa to allow him to enter Australia, so that he could bring officials up-to-date with our progress towards multi-racial cricket, he was refused entry. Twice. Gough Whitlam, the Prime Minister at the time, preached the gospel of free speech and respect for democracy but it didn't apply to South African cricket officials. I don't claim to be an expert on the game of chess but I was amazed when Russia tried to expel us from international competition in 1977 because of apartheid – and this from a country with a shocking record in human rights, where Jews were harassed as mercilessly as any black victim of apartheid. South Africa wasn't the only country where human beings were imprisoned without trial or legal representation, where people disappeared mysteriously.

For every Biko, there was a Sakharov and a Solzhenitsyn in Russia. We didn't want to penalise Russian sportsmen for the policies of their government, so why should our sports – like chess and cricket – be subject to isolation for a political policy we didn't support? On that basis, hardly any country would be playing international sport.

All we could do in South Africa was keep the faith, keep ploughing on to make 'normal cricket' so normal that nobody commented on it any more. We were looking for moral justice from the ICC, so we had to be above moral reproach in cricketing terms. Our conscience had to be clear; we had to promote our cause aggressively, so that the charge of double standards would be laid at other doors, not ours. The rapid progress towards multi-racial sport in South Africa is confirmed by statistics provided by the Ministry of Sport. Between 1971 and October 1976 only 128 'multi-national' sports competitions took place, yet between October 1976 and March 1977 there were 1,304 such events including 71 at provincial level and 57 at national level. And there were hundreds more that weren't official and therefore weren't acknowledged by the department. You couldn't deny that South Africa still had intense political problems, with the government wielding the big stick at various stages – but what could we sportsmen do about that? The welfare of multi-racial cricket was our main consideration even though we were, of course, aware of the political implications on international opinion.

In that first season of 'normal cricket,' eight non-whites played first-class cricket for various provinces, and the trend continued encouragingly. Baboo Ebrahim, who took 6 wickets against Greg Chappell's International Wanderers side the year before, joined up with two other black players to play for the Durban Collegians club, formerly all white. In Transvaal, Ali Bacher joined the all-white Balfour Park who welcomed Edward Habane, probably the best of African cricketers at the time. Then, in October 1977, the 'normal cricket' concept had a major boost when four white players with first-class experience joined the Kohinoor club in the Transvaal Premier League. Kohinoor had been an all-black club but they were delighted to enlist David Dyer, Peter de Vaal, Andre Bruyns and David van der Knaap. Dyer, whose father was a former Test opening batsman and at the time vice-president of SACU, was a very significant capture for Kohinoor. He had proved himself an impressive captain of Transvaal the previous year and he was the sort of high-profile white cricketer ideally qualified to beat the drum for 'normal cricket'. De Vaal had been picked for the tour to Australia in 1971 that never materialised, Bruyns was an experienced batsman who would have been close to a Test place if not for isolation, and Van der Knaap was a fine off-spinner. The decision by these four players to join a black club was even publicised in Indian papers; perhaps the rest of the world was getting tired of nothing but bad news coming out of South Africa.

By the end of the 1970s, progress toward multi-racial cricket had been very solid and encouraging. When I returned to South Africa after playing in Australia or England, I was struck by the relaxed way that cricketers of all races were integrating naturally. Rashid Varachia estimated that in the first two years of normalisation, the scheme had a success rate of 80 per cent. In Western Province alone, there were 250 non-white players affiliated to the cricket union, compared to 20 two years earlier. There was still dissent among hard-liners and Hassan Howa tried now and then to throw a spanner into the works, suggesting that blacks playing alongside whites ought to wonder if they were stooges taking part in a giant public relations exercise. In the Orange Free State, the heartland of the Afrikaner, progress towards normalisation was slow because blacks didn't seem at all interested in the white man's game.

There were also a few disputes in Northern Transvaal and Natal, but no one could deny that by South Africa's standards, progress had been astonishingly rapid. Old wounds were healing, cricketers were talking to each other rather than mouthing slogans. We knew that political reforms were necessary, but what was the point in having a cricketing stand-off between various races when contact on the pitch and socially was proving so valuable? Now black players could prove themselves to be better than white opponents – on merit. That's the only sensible criterion in sport, but it stems from contact, not separation.

Although black adults were getting greater and greater opportunities to develop their cricket skills, it was still a problem bringing the game to the black children. For most of the 1970s there was hardly any mixed-schools cricket, apart from a couple of matches arranged at the white Kimberley School in Griqualand West. There were hardly any black schools with cricket facilities and in general the only way that black kids could develop as cricketers against mixed opposition was to join an adult club. Depending on where they came from, that could be a problem. That background only serves to underline the fantastic work put in by John Passmore in Western Province. He had helped set up a schools week for black kids along the lines of the Nuffield Week, the festival for the best white schoolboys which had become a production line over the years for the best young players in the country. The first such week for black youngsters was held in Cape Town in 1971 and the African Board of Control was so pleased with John's efforts that the new tournament was renamed the John Passmore Schools Week. After that the annual competition was held in Johannesburg, Port Elizabeth, East London, Welkom and Cape Town. The standard of play improved dramatically after the first tournament where, for all their natural athletic talent, most of the kids had no idea about the disciplines needed for cricket. It soon became a life's work for John Passmore, as he wheedled money out of various authorities to improve cricket facilities in the Cape area, and made passionate pleas to SACA's annual meetings to make them realise the importance of catching black kids when young. Soon he began to unearth some genuine talent. It was in the second Passmore Week that the young Xhosa Edward Habane dominated the games, proving a year later that he was the outstanding African cricketer of the '70s by performing well in the Datsun International Double Wicket Competition. If it hadn't been for John Passmore, promising players like Habane would never have graduated further than the plank-and-tennis-ball games that passed for cricket in most African areas. Since then, thousands of black cricketers have come through to test their talents against other coloured players, purely on merit.

Passmore was intelligent enough to realise that an annual week for the best black players wasn't enough, because for the rest of the year those kids might just languish, drift into crime, or move away in search of work. They needed a base where they could play as often as possible and enjoy quality coaching. The raw talent was there, it just needed to be harnessed. So Passmore set to work, pleading with local businessmen in the Western Cape to raise enough money to set up a trust fund to build a centre. Within two years, more than 75,000 rand was raised and the Langa Sports Centre was built in a township near Cape Town.

Passmore first visited Langa in 1970, just after South Africa had been told to do something for non-white cricketers before they could even be considered for Test recall. He wondered what could be done to get some facilities organised so that the blacks could gain some self-respect and grab a lifeline to a better future. He was told that the government wasn't interested, that it was advisable never to let the township-dwellers think they were likely to put down permanent roots. So he dedicated the rest of his life to creating a cricket ground in Langa, transplanting his own love of the game into the local blacks. He was called a *Kaffirboetie* (black-lover) by many unsympathetic whites but he never gave up, and he won the trust of the blacks. During the State of Emergency, he still drove his car into Langa, even though many parts of the township were ablaze, with looting and murder regular occurrences. Once his car was stopped and a black gang demanded he got out. When they saw the driver was John Passmore, their leader smiled and said, 'Mr Passmore, find us more cricket balls, please.'

Twenty years after Passmore's dream started, the centre stands as a monument to his devotion to the cause of black cricket. In 1989,

Rodney Malamba, a fast bowler, became the first product of Langa Cricket Club to play first-class cricket when he represented Natal. It was a proud day for the club and for its inspiration, John Passmore. Rodney's mother sent the following letter to the Cape Times: 'Beneath the excitement, I would like to hail one gentleman, John Passmore. Nothing would have been possible without him. He came into Langa, when this was unthought of by many white South Africans, and worked his way through all the hurdles that stood in the way of his dream. They call him the "Father" of black cricket. I would like to remove the inverted commas.'

John Passmore lived just long enough to see South Africa readmitted into Test cricket before he died in 1991. Yet his great work was done away from the ICC tables and the corridors of international sporting power. He gave countless black kids hope, a love for cricket and the chance of self-respect. When Ali Bacher's dream of a multi-racial South African side finally takes shape, let everyone remember the dedicated pioneering work of John Passmore in the 1970s. It's easy to swim with the tide, but he had the vision and the determination to build something lasting out of nothing at a time when the welfare of young black cricketers wasn't a high priority in our country.

THE REBEL TOURS

Between 1982 and 1990, seven sides drawn from four Test-playing countries came to South Africa to play against us in a series of matches. Those games were unofficial as far as the ICC was concerned but to us they were a godsend. Playing against Englishmen, Sri Lankans, Australians and West Indians of international class was a great shot in the arm for our domestic cricket. Those players who came to South Africa were variously called 'rebels' or 'mercenaries' and they were castigated in many quarters for making money out of the black man. Without apartheid, there would have been no isolation and trying to break free of the effects of isolation cost a lot of money in recruiting players, money that could have gone towards developing black cricket. The other argument is that these players were simply exercising their individual rights to play wherever they pleased, depending on the invitation. I never saw them as rebels: to me they were brave, supportive of multi-racial cricket in South Africa and right to make a stand against the hypocrisy that hangs around the whole question of sporting links with my country. Those tours were the best thing that could have happened to South African cricket at that time.

You have to understand how frustrated we had become. A generation of top players had missed out on testing ourselves at the top level, something that's very important to a sports-mad country like South Africa. Can you imagine how those years of isolation have affected South Africa? There had been consolations for some of us – World Series Cricket and English county cricket, in which we fully participated and which we enjoyed – but it wasn't the same as playing Test cricket for those of us who had experienced it. The Currie Cup was certainly competitive enough, but after a time, you knew all the players involved and there was a staleness, with players going through the motions, and no incentive. Television coverage was minimal, there was no focus on Test cricket elsewhere in the world, and interest in the schools was on the wane. Other sports like rugby and tennis must have seemed more attractive to the kids. If you liked individual sports, you could travel the world and earn a lot of money playing tennis, say, and rugby hadn't suffered the pain of isolation, so the young sporting all-rounder could instead dream of playing against the British Lions for the Springboks. Something needed to be done to rejuvenate interest in cricket. We were drifting so much in our domestic cricket that even if we did get back into the Test arena, our competitive edge would have been so dulled and our youth structure was so under-utilised that we would definitely have struggled for some time against the big guns.

There was no sympathy among our cricketers for the ICC in March, 1982, when Graham Gooch arrived in South Africa with his English team, the first of the rebel tours. We felt the world game's rulers had brought it on themselves by turning a blind eye to the genuine progress made in the previous ten years. Time after time in the 1970s, our leading officials had begged the ICC to come and see at first hand the amount of work being done towards multi-racial cricket. At last, in 1979, eight years after our ban had started, an ICC delegation came to South Africa. They were shown everything they wanted to see and no questions were ducked. They seemed impressed by the fact that five coloured boys from the Port Elizabeth area had been chosen for the Nuffield Schools Week trials, and in another match in Cape Town, they saw a team of 11 Africans take on a side of six whites and five coloureds, one of whom was the captain. No official suggested to the delegation that everything in our garden was rosy – and the militant influence of Hassan Howa wasn't ignored – but there was genuine hope that a gesture of encouragement would act as a reward for our sincerity.

The ICC party reported itself to be impressed, finding that totally integrated cricket was being played on a regular basis at club and provincial level. The delegation recommended that as strong a team as possible should be sent to South Africa, representing the major ICC member countries. In other words, a party of world-class cricketers of mixed race, proud to show their skills to multi-racial audiences and at the same time inspiring black and coloured cricketers to improve their standards in South Africa. There would be problems, of course – some of the world-class players would resent being classified as 'honorary whites' for the purposes of socialising and being booked into hotels, and the respective Boards of Control would possibly be against the tour – but at least it was a constructive proposal and a reward for what we had achieved in recent years. Yet the ICC didn't act on its delegation's recommendations at the annual meeting in 1979. The meeting simply commended South Africa on its progress towards multi-racial cricket and left it at that. Certain countries in the ICC were dead set against our return to Test cricket and would block any attempts to give us any hope. India and Pakistan were particularly hawkish, acting on the instructions of their own governments, and the West Indies, although privately sympathetic, sided with them. That left England, Australia and New Zealand to express pious hopes of a recall in the near future, but we were becoming increasingly pessimistic and cynical. When we were again fobbed off by the ICC at the next two annual meetings, the possibility of a rebel tour became a certainty.

One other decision which came out of that 1981 ICC meeting

hardened South Africa's resolve to take a stand. Sri Lanka was admitted to the list of full member countries, bringing the total of those playing Test cricket up to seven. It also meant that the black member countries now outnumbered the white ones by four to three. Therefore the question of our readmission to Test cricket was likely to be blocked on the majority vote for the foreseeable future. The three white member countries were predictably worried about the ominous prospect of the cricket world falling into two separate divisions – one white, one black – so there was little chance of our old allies fighting our corner. With the Commonwealth Games scheduled for Brisbane in 1982, and healthy profits projected, Australia voted against our readmission at the 1981 ICC annual meeting. Well might Rashid Varachia say to the meeting, 'What more can we do? You ask us to make cricket multi-racial. We have done that and still we are excluded.' He pointed out that no longer did the South African government dictate to the cricketers, whereas it was clear that some ICC member countries were still under the control of their governments.

It wasn't just the political consideration though. Test cricket, particularly in England, was going through a golden period. The two World Cups held in England in 1975 and 1979 had been huge money-spinners while the West Indies had been a major draw on their tours of 1976 and 1980. Glamorous English players like Ian Botham and David Gower had helped underline the appeal of Test cricket and the Test and County Cricket Board was terrified at the prospect of losing all that revenue through the turnstiles and in marketing if the South African question led to a black-white split. With the third World Cup scheduled for England in 1983, why rock the lucrative boat to defend the principle of fairness towards South Africa? We knew that apartheid was an unfair, inhuman policy but that system was now being dismantled after being in place for centuries. If our heartening progress towards multi-racial sport had been recognised it would have given extra impetus to the campaign for an integrated society, with apartheid off the statute book. Sport was proving a catalyst for social change, and it was due to the courage of our administrators and players that all discriminatory laws as they affected sport had been abolished by the time Gooch and his English team came to South Africa. Cricket changed first and our government accepted reality – a remarkable achievement to those who knew the repressed atmosphere in many parts of South Africa before we were isolated. Now it seemed that fear of boycotts was preventing due recognition of our efforts. Gooch's players were banned for three years from international cricket because the Test and County Cricket Board was worried about India and Pakistan pulling out of the 1982 tours to England, and Australia toed the line with the Brisbane Commonwealth Games in mind.

Sport is, of course, an easy target for the hard-liners. The Western world can't afford to cut off trade with a wealthy country like South Africa, so there were never full-scale trade and economic sanctions to set alongside the ban on sporting connections. In 1982, the year English and Sri Lankan cricketers were vilified for doing what any businessman would do – travelling to South Africa to work – the International Monetary Fund loaned a billion dollars to South Africa. The IMF didn't suggest that the Republic should change its official racial policy before the loan was confirmed – that sort of gesture was left to sporting bodies like the ICC. Double standards everywhere you looked. What was the point in withdrawing invitations to me, Graeme Pollock and Eddie Barlow after we had gladly agreed to play in a match at the Oval to raise funds for the Ken Barrington Memorial Trust? A great guy like Kenny, who had played Test cricket in South Africa, and who was a friend to the three of us, must have turned in his grave when our invitations were withdrawn. It was all so petty. What was the justification in the Australian government refusing a visa to Rashid Varachia, when all he wanted to do was visit his son in Sydney? Presumably they felt he was a tool of the evil South African regime rather than a dedicated Indian who had fought tirelessly for all cricketers in South Africa. Such frustrations can't have done a great deal for Varachia's health and he died late in 1981 of a heart attack, worn out by his commitment to the cause of 'normal cricket' and a fairer society. It was sad he didn't live long enough to see our return to Test cricket after he suffered so many ignorant rebuffs from ICC officials who simply didn't want to know about a changing world.

So there was a great deal of excitement in South Africa when those English guys arrived to play us in March, 1982. We were going to play three unofficial 'Tests' and although our opponents didn't see them as having such an important status, we certainly did. We were awarded Springbok colours for all three games and I was pleased that players like Kirsten, Cook, Rice, Kourie, Jennings, Van der Bijl, Hobson and le Roux were at last getting some of the recognition that had been denied them. I was chosen as captain for the first game and I don't mind admitting it was a very emotional moment for me when I tossed the coin with tears in my eyes. During that month of matches, the English side didn't play very well; they were harried by their own press, who had flown out en masse with their minds already made up, and they didn't win a single one-day game. We weren't about to sympathise too much with them, though. A decade of frustration was slowly being eased as we showed that South Africa still had some fair old players. The critics of that first tour pointed out that the atmosphere was unreal, that the English players couldn't give of their best in such trying circumstances, that it didn't feel like the real thing. It's true that nothing in my time has matched the privilege of playing for your country in a properly organised Test match, but it was still rather special to be up against another country's players, even if they weren't supported by their own cricket board.

After that first tour, we had no doubts that more would be in the pipeline, especially after the ICC annual meeting of 1982 held out no hope of our recall to Test cricket. Our officials didn't even get a hearing and the president of SACU, Joe Pamensky, was in no mood to capitulate meekly. He said: 'Maybe that sort of tour was necessary to bring certain people to their senses rather than for them to live in a fool's paradise that South African cricket would do nothing when it was being handed out crumbs. Now that our consciences are clear that we have nothing more to do in South Africa, we must look for something more to happen.' There was renewed interest in South Africa for more international competition after 12 years of starvation. Money was at last rolling into the domestic game, thanks partly to the development of television coverage. At last our television was coming to terms with the practicalities of covering cricket and major sponsors were putting up a lot of money. The great interest in our cricket can be judged by the fact that the 1982 final of the Datsun Shield – our premier limited-overs competition – was sold out a week in advance, despite the presence of live television cameras. The years of stagnation were rolling away, vindicating the decision to make things happen on our own terms, rather than wait for scraps from the ICC table.

The second tour, late in 1982, consisted of 14 Sri Lankan players, five of whom had played Test cricket earlier that year. As a public relations coup, getting coloured players to come to South Africa was a big effort, but the seven-week trip was a cricketing flop. They just weren't good enough, and their highly rated spinners were hammered. Most of the matches were no-contests and the public stayed away in droves. That tour lost the South African Cricket Union a lot of money and confirmed how important it was to have truly competitive matches. We needed stronger opposition than the Sri Lankans to test our strength and we were about to have it.

In January 1983, a side of West Indian players arrived in secrecy to play a series of games that would transform black South African attitudes to cricket. Until this tour, there hadn't been many black supporters watching the English and Sri Lankan teams, but now the grounds were packed for every match and the black fans at last had identifiable heroes. I believe the presence of those West Indies players was a massive blow to the apartheid system. They showed that you can make it to the top whatever your colour, and the live television coverage and blanket newspaper interest meant the tour was the sole topic of conversation for the whole month. It was the first time a South African side had played against a West Indian team and the news created a sensation in the Caribbean and in South Africa. Politicians went scurrying to their copies of the Gleneagles Agreement to see what the proper response ought to be, while black kids in the townships tried to imitate the bowling action of Sylvester Clarke or the spectacular batting of Collis King. In Australia, where the Aborigine is hardly treated nobly, Prime Minister Malcolm Fraser announced that those 14 West Indian players would be banned from ever entering the country. But Lawrence Rowe, the West Indies captain, got it right when he said the tour gave them at least a chance to see for themselves what was going on in South Africa, rather than having to rely on biased information. Some black consciousness groups called for the tour to be boycotted but the sheer novelty of seeing West Indians playing in an organised team in South Africa was too important to miss. Those players also showed the more bigoted whites how more dignified people conduct themselves under a lot of pressure.

From a cricketing point of view, too, the tour was a great success. The West Indian party contained some fine players. Rowe and Alvin Kallicharran had been high-class batsmen at Test level; Collis King was one of the most destructive batsmen in the game, while Colin Croft, Ezra Moseley, Sylvester Clarke and Franklyn Stephenson were class fast bowlers. Bernard Julien had also proved himself as an all-rounder in Test cricket. It was a stronger unit than Gooch's English party, far more powerful than the Sri Lankan one, and the public knew that. At times, the South African players felt they were playing abroad, such was the vociferous support for the visitors from all racial groups, and they saw some vintage batting from Graeme Pollock and Barry Richards, proving to anyone who doubted it that the dominance of fast bowling in modern international cricket would not have troubled those two if they'd been given an extended opportunity. Both sides won a 'Test' and squared the four-game series while South Africa won the one-dayers by 4-2. Yet it wasn't just about playing cricket. The West Indies players admitted that they hadn't known what to expect when they flew in to South Africa. They had heard so much about the downside, that they would be the white man's stooge, yet very little about the positive aspects, that millions of open-minded South Africans wanted them to see the great strides made towards a fairer society. They knew they'd be banned from Test cricket for making the trip, but they also knew that many black businessmen made a fortune from doing business in South Africa. Cricket history was made by their visit and the social and political implications weren't lost on us, either.

The trail had already been blazed for the tourists the year before when Alvin Kallicharran decided to come out and play for Transvaal. Alvin was disenchanted with the West Indies selectors, feeling that as someone of Asian background he wasn't getting a fair deal. He thought that the growth of black consciousness in the Caribbean was doing him no favours, and that his prospects of playing again in Test cricket were negligible. So he agreed to play for Transvaal and for Kohinoor Crescents. He also coached cricketers of all races and soon became a hero to coloured youngsters. Back in his home country of Guyana, he was accused of taking 'blood money' and the West Indies Board of Control said he'd never play for them again. He scored a hundred in his second match for Transvaal, but was then jeered at the Wanderers club by some black spectators who called him 'a racist pig'. Alvin seemed to be able to shrug off those kind of taunts and he was a great success in his three years with Transvaal. After that he made a move that would have astonished anyone who hadn't followed the recent progress of multi-racial cricket. Orange Free State used to be acknowledged as the stronghold of the Afrikaner and the spiritual home of the National government, yet here we had Alvin playing four seasons for them, including an occasional spell as captain. If, when we were banned in 1971, you had told me that a black West Indian would be captaining Orange Free State just a decade later, I would have shook my head and then laughed.

The West Indies were scheduled to return for a second visit early in 1984 and we were pretty sure that they would form our major opposition in the foreseeable future after yet another fruitless visit to the ICC's annual meeting. Yet again, Joe Pamensky wasn't even granted a hearing. It was clear that the existence of the apartheid system in South Africa was now the only stumbling-block to ending isolation, but what could SACU do about that, other than continue to point out that cricket at least was run fairly? The alternative was to keep buying in top players from other countries who would pass up the prospect of playing Test cricket again. In that way, South Africa's best players would get the chance of measuring themselves competitively against internationals, while interest among the public could be maintained. In the absence of the real thing – Test cricket – there seemed little alternative. International tours had to continue.

The second West Indies tour certainly brought home to us more of the realities of international cricket. They had been strengthened by the inclusion of Faoud Bacchus, Monte Lynch and Hartley Alleyne, but it was the sustained aggression of their fast bowling that separated the two sides. Sylvester Clarke in particular was always a handful and those of us who had experienced his pace, bounce and hostility were not surprised at his dominance. It gave food for thought to those one-eyed South Africans who thought we would simply coast to the top spot in world cricket if the magic wand was waved and we were reinstated tomorrow. When you consider that the current West Indies Test bowlers consisted of Michael Holding, Joel Garner, Malcolm Marshall and Courtney Walsh, it was clear that the method of bowling out Test sides had become more ruthless and physically dangerous since we had rolled over Bill Lawry's team. Then it was Peter Pollock and myself who provided the speed, and in my case, the swing, followed by a mixture of medium pace and spin, backed up by brilliant fielding. Now the West Indies fielded equally brilliantly but the secret of their world dominance was an endless supply of punishing fast bowlers who gave you little off the front foot. Those of us who had played in World Series Cricket weren't surprised at this relentless form of attack, and clearly it was here to stay because it was very successful. The two West Indies tours were a rude awakening for many cricket fans in South Africa who hadn't looked further than the Currie Cup scores. When Sylvester Clarke followed up his devastating bowling for the West Indies with a great season for Transvaal – helping them to win the Currie Cup and the one-day final, the Nissan Shield – the value of fast, hostile bowling was obvious. So for those who were concerned about South Africa's long-term prospects if we ever got back into Test cricket, this was an important tour by Lawrence Rowe's side.

They beat us in both the 'Test' series and the limited-overs games. Huge crowds didn't seem to mind that the home team were getting beaten, because the West Indies had captured the imagination of the country. Television broadcast all their matches, with commentaries in native tongues as well as English and Afrikaans, and more and more black kids were getting coaching. Soccer was still the number one sport of the black sportsman, because of the natural talent and enthusiasm of the players and the fact that sophisticated facilities were not needed, but cricket was on the move. Hostile officials like Hassan Howa kept maintaining that the presence of the West Indies created a façade of normality, that underneath it was the same old South Africa, and there was some truth in that. Although the new constitution had offered Indians and coloureds a limited vote, the framework of apartheid was still in place. But youngsters of all races were at last mixing together at cricket matches, playing alongside each other in the intervals on the outfield, just like they do in English county cricket: surely that was a significant sight? That never happened when I was a cricket-mad kid in Durban; we never saw black children at Test matches. The massive public interest in Lawrence Rowe's tourists generated a lot of cash for the SACU to distribute within its coaching programme for disadvantaged young cricketers of all colours. Hassan Howa claimed to represent 10,000 non-white players who had their own leagues and took sanctions against non-whites who went to any of the West Indies games. No doubt Howa was sincere in his motives, but I can't believe that was the best way to foster interest in the game among his players. Cricket was helping to break down social barriers in South Africa and those West Indians had inspired enthusiasm among groups which had never before been interested in the game. The more contact between the races that came through cricket, the more chance of constructive progress towards breaking down apartheid.

That tour also helped to embarrass the government. Colin Croft went shopping in Cape Town and took a train to Newlands afterwards. He was turfed out of his compartment by a fussy ticket collector who pointed to the whites-only carriage. Now our critics seized on that incident with glee, pointing out that it was still an abnormal society, despite all our moves towards 'normal cricket'. But it led to red faces in the government circles and a fulsome apology to Colin Croft. So the injustice of apartheid was publicly demonstrated, giving further evidence to the government that its days as a policy were numbered. For some time, official eyes had been blind to petty regulations about where non-whites could bathe on a beach, sit in a park, book into hotels and eat in restaurants. The reality of apartheid as it applied to a famous West Indian in a railway compartment only made it more likely that one day the government would make such injustices illegal. The game of cricket would then have been a factor in that historic decision.

It would have been much more agreeable to South Africa if we hadn't needed to bankroll the rebel tours, because it meant there was less money to go into the cricket development programme, but there was no alternative at that stage in our isolation. We waited in vain for ICC member countries who played Test cricket to send over some open-minded delegates to see what was happening, but that never happened after the 1979 delegation. It would have been wonderful if one of the countries had decided to defy its government and select a full-strength, official side to tour South Africa, but no one seemed willing to break ranks. There were too many complicated financial and political considerations. Of course, there were contradictions in South Africa itself. A few months after the end of the second West Indies tour, more than 100 sporting bodies in South Africa signed a declaration that committed them to equal opportunities in all sport, whatever race they represented, from school to international level. This followed months of negotiation between the South African Cricket Union, the Rugby Board, the South African Olympic Committee and the South African Sports Federation. It was the first united front shown by so many South African bodies in promoting anti-apartheid policies which weren't espoused by the National government. It called for multi-racial fixtures as well as coaching. Cricket had led the way already, a decade earlier, but it was still a major commitment by other sporting organisations. Yet at the same time blood continued to be spilled in our country: a day after this historic announcement, police killed 19 black demonstrators in Cape Province, and the country was again in ferment. It was difficult to argue that South Africa's image overseas wasn't still being tarnished, despite the good work of sports officials and players.

So the rebel tours went on and next in the frame were the Australians, who arrived in 1985 for the first of two tours, led by Kim Hughes and including 11 men who had played Test cricket. Quality cricketers like Hughes, Rodney Hogg, Carl Rackemann, Terry Alderman and Graham Yallop meant we would be stretched, and the competitive edge was sharp on both tours (the Australians returned the next year). We won the 'Test' series on each occasion and it was fantastic to see Graeme Pollock roll back the years and play so well. The year before, at the age of 40, he had batted superbly against the West Indian fast bowlers. Even though Sylvester Clarke pinged him on the head – a very rare occurrence in Graeme's career – he scored runs in all four 'Tests', including a typical hundred at Newlands. No one could believe after this display that the concentration on hostile, short-pitched fast bowling in world cricket since our isolation would have disturbed him. He was a great player in any era, against all types of bowling, and he again proved that against Kim Hughes' Australians. He warmed up against them for Transvaal in the day-night match – watched by 31,000 at the Wanderers' ground – with an unbeaten 50, and over the next two seasons the Aussies must have been sick of the sight of him. He made runs against them in every game during that period, ending with a brilliant 144 in the final 'Test' at Port Elizabeth. Everyone knew it was his last innings in South African colours and he certainly went out in style. He was a few days short of his 43rd birthday. The effect of that innings on the country was remarkable: television figures went through the roof while Graeme was batting and there was a genuine feeling of national pride.

Graeme used his status as national hero wisely when, in an interview, he again stated his distaste for his government's racial policies. He said: 'I can see the justice of our cricket isolation now, though it was hard at the time. The changes will have to be political because cricket itself has done a great deal. Pressure for change in South Africa will now have to come by way of international trade and political sanctions, rather than through sport.' At the time, the National Party had been going through a great deal of turmoil, with a State of Emergency, a clampdown on media activity and unrest from the right wing over a relaxation of the ban on mixed-race sexual relations. Sanctions were being stepped up against South Africa, and there was a lot of uncertainty and violence. The government let it be known that Graeme shouldn't get involved in political issues and should stick to cricket, but Graeme was right to speak out. He realised that all the pioneering work of players and officials hadn't brought us back into the Test arena. The unofficial tours were necessary to keep the lifeblood of South African cricket flowing, but we had become very frustrated at the deadlock. The politicians had huge problems, trying to inch along the road to reform without alienating traditional support, but what was so wrong about a sporting hero lending vocal support to reforms?

Yet the politicians still tried to have the final word and the Australian players felt the full weight of governmental disapproval of sportsmen who were only doing what countless Aussie businessmen were allowed to do – go to South Africa. The Prime Minister, Bob Hawke (a cricket-lover), threatened life bans and heavy taxation on those players, but there was no prospect that he would break off trade with South Africa. In fact, Australian exports to South Africa had risen by 80 per cent over the previous two years. Much easier to have a go at Kim Hughes' team: you can get some emotive headlines out of that, especially as the defections were weakening the official Australian side that was about to go to England to try to retain the Ashes.

By now, I was a South African selector, along with John Waite, Jackie McGlew and Peter van der Merwe, all former Test players. My knee had finally given out on me and my playing days were over. There was no bitterness on my part: I had enjoyed my career hugely. I had been lucky enough to play Test cricket and perform to a high standard in England and Australia as well. Now I wanted to help our developing players get accustomed to the special demands of international cricket and I assumed my experience of night cricket in Australia as well as other limited-overs games had a bearing on my appointment. The other three selectors were from an earlier, golden era of South African cricket and I hoped to act as a bridge between them and the current players. Night cricket had proved to be very popular as well as a big money-spinner, and now we had six grounds capable of staging international games at night. I thought we did well to beat the Australians on their two tours, when you consider that so many of them had played Test cricket recently and that we were bound to be a little rusty from lack of consistent exposure to that greater pressure. After watching our players at close quarters, it was clear that new blood was needed, that our team was ageing. Players like Graeme Pollock, Garth le Roux and Alan Kourie were going, while Vince van der Bijl, Eddie Barlow, Barry Richards and myself had retired recently. It was also a matter of time for the likes of Clive Rice, Jimmy Cook and Peter Kirsten – or so I thought at the time. I underestimated their drive and desire to keep going. Years later, they were proud to be able to play in official international cricket for South Africa.

Although Transvaal's domination of our domestic cricket in the 1980s wasn't a healthy situation, and though I was also concerned about the lack of motivation among our top players if there wasn't a rebel tour in the offing, there were still grounds for optimism on the playing front. In Graeme Pollock's last appearance at Port Elizabeth in 1987, we blooded the fast bowler Allan Donald and he looked very impressive, clean bowling Kim Hughes twice in the match. I was pleased to hear that he was going off to Warwickshire to learn about bowling on English wickets. He was about the same age as me when I went to Gloucestershire and there was no doubt the experience would make him a better bowler. Among the other fast bowlers I had great hopes for Steve Jefferies, Hugh Page and Corrie van Zyl, while Brian McMillan looked a class all-rounder. Among the batsmen, I was keeping a close eye on Mark Rushmere, Roy Pienaar and the gifted teenager Daryll Cullinan. So the cupboard was hardly bare.

Non-white players were coming through as well. Omar Henry, a Cape coloured, had been selected for South Africa against Kim Hughes' team in 1987, the first non-white to earn Springbok colours. That led to an outburst from Alan Kourie, the left-arm spinner who had been dropped for Henry. Kourie suggested that Henry's selection was just window-dressing, that playing for Boland in the 'B' section of the Currie Cup meant he wasn't good enough. That was ridiculous – Kourie had been given his chance in the first two representative games and hadn't bowled all that well. Henry had turned in consistently good performances in recent years in first-class cricket and was picked purely on merit. It would have been insulting to all non-white players if the call to national colours had gone out to a token individual: we wanted players like Omar Henry to beat down the selectors' door with the quality of their performances, but we would never devalue a selection for South Africa. Kourie was fined 2,000 rand for his remarks and made to offer a public apology. I think that was right – the last thing we needed at that delicate stage was for Hassan Howa to start jumping up and down about tokenism.

We were far more concerned about the flow of good young black cricketers, and it was good to see that many were thriving in the harder competition. A young batsman, Salieg Nackerdien, had become the first coloured cricketer to win a South African Schools cap, and this after being chosen as captain of the Boland Schools side, an area noted for a conservative, Afrikaans background. A year later, two more non-whites (Crain Marais and Shukri Conrad) were picked for the South African Schools, and at the same time as the Boland team included as many as five in several first-class games. The great work being done by John Passmore in the Cape received wider recognition when he brought his Passmore XI to Newlands, where the country's best African schoolboys hammered a full-strength Western Province Schools team. It was clear that Passmore was successfully tapping their natural talent and in Langa at least his boys were catching up on their white counterparts. He saw the next stage as the inclusion of the Passmore XI in the Nuffield Schools Week. That duly happened in the following year, 1987, and so a team representing the cream of non-white young players finally made it to the festival which had turned out so many illustrious Test players. We hoped that exposure to the Nuffield Week would help inspire non-white cricketers to Test cricket.

As we approached the 20th anniversary of our last game in Test cricket, it was clear that another rebel tour was on the cards . SACU had concentrated on building up our domestic cricket after the last of the Australian tours in 1987, and sponsorship kept pouring in. The standard of competition in the Currie Cup had risen, with Transvaal no longer so dominant. Almost every provincial side had a high-class fast bowling attack, with players like Sylvester Clarke, Allan Donald, Corrie van Zyl, Fanie de Villiers and Tertius Bosch and other overseas signings such as Greg Thomas, Neal Radford, Hartley Alleyne and Rod McCurdy. Allan Lamb, Phil Newport, Alan Igglesden and Kevin Curran also brought professionalism from English county cricket and the crowds continued to increase, particularly for the spectacular day-night experience. For the first time in 11 years, Transvaal failed to win one of the three trophies on offer in 1989, and that augured well for our domestic cricket. It meant that there was an even keener edge to the matches, because each side had very good bowlers and the competitions were wide open.

Yet we were still desperate to get back into Test cricket. The South African public and our players had loved the extra competition provided by the various tours since 1982, but it wasn't the real thing. We were curious to see how we would fare against players like Viv Richards, Richard Hadlee, Allan Border, David Gower and Ian Botham. It looked as if no amount of money would tempt such players over. So we'd continue trying to persuade the game's ruling body that we really did deserve to come back in from the cold. The annual humiliation at the ICC meeting in Lord's continued. In 1987, they decided to set up a select committee that would report back the following summer, a decision which ensured the World Cup would go ahead later that year in India and Pakistan. South Africa was again on the back-burner while the international cricket family papered over the cracks and carried on playing each other the while. There was no likelihood that this select ICC committee would do anything as radical as actually visit South Africa to check on our progress. When in doubt, set up a committee to take the heat out of the situation. Predictably, there was nothing of any great importance to emerge from that particular committee when the ICC met the following year.

Two developments made it inevitable that the next team to visit us on an unofficial tour would be an English one. When the England tour to India in 1988-89 was cancelled because of links with South Africa by some of the selected players, it was clear that the strings were being pulled by the Indian government. At a time of elections, it was a popular move to have a go at South Africa and when Graham Gooch was picked as England's captain, his visit to us in 1982 was dragged up, as well as involvement by other players such as John Emburey. So the tour was called off – England couldn't get a replacement organised at short notice – and their top players were left kicking their heels, seething at meddling politicians. We knew the feeling only too well! A few months later, at a special ICC meeting, it was agreed that any English player who coached or played in South Africa would be banned from playing Test cricket. No other country provided as many well-qualified coaches as England and it was hard on those players who still harboured hopes of playing for their country. They faced a cruel dilemma – look somewhere else for off-season work that might not be so fulfilling, or go to South Africa and kiss goodbye to the dream of all first-class cricketers, a Test cap.

England failed to call the bluff of the other Test-playing countries, even though they knew that the West Indies, for one, needed the money from Test cricket because its domestic game was so short of funds. So the interests of English players were sacrificed to keep international cricket alive. South Africa was going to get even less help from the rest of the cricket world: banning qualified coaches was going to do nothing to help the kids in Soweto.

Joe Pamensky and Ali Bacher were in London at the time of that ICC meeting and a few days before they had been allowed to speak to a gathering of English cricket officials, the Test and County Cricket Board. Bacher told the meeting that he didn't want to organise more rebel tours because they cost a lot of money and he would rather divert the cash to developing cricket among the under-privileged. Pamensky said it was illogical to ban county cricketers from South Africa when many other professional workers and businessmen were free to come and go. They were sympathetically received, but Pamensky and Bacher knew that the England representatives at the ICC meeting would be helpless: the hawks would win the day. No wonder current England players contacted Bacher and Pamensky on that London visit; they knew a tour was now inevitable, and they were so fed up with all the hypocrisy that they wanted to confirm their availability. Within a few months, we would all know their names. I was very disappointed that the leaders of English cricket hadn't taken the fight to those countries of the ICC who refused to give any encouragement to South Africa. In 1968, English cricket had been right to stand up to Prime Minister Vorster, who didn't want Basil D'Oliveira to return to South Africa as an England player. That may have led to the collision course that saw us isolated from Test cricket, but the principle of non-interference by another country's politicians was worth defending. Now English cricket was just toeing the line, instead of calling the bluff of others.

I was very sorry that the Test and County Cricket Board didn't see fit to send an official to South Africa for our centenary celebrations a couple of months after that ICC meeting. A hundred years earlier, we had played England for the first time in a Test match, and the celebrations were a marvellous chance not only to meet up again with old friends, but also to show the sceptics just how much we had advanced towards multi-racial cricket. A substantial group of English cricket media came out to see the reforms at first hand, and a host of great names from Test history were there as well. Former England captains Peter May, George Mann and Mike Smith were there, but nobody from the Test and County Cricket Board. They would have heard a message from Sir Donald Bradman, read out at the centenary banquet – 'Keep up your good work in the interests of the game of cricket. It will ultimately bring its reward.' Joe Pamensky gave a stirring speech in which he pointed out that the requirements imposed by the ICC had been met more than ten years before: 'If sanctions are necessary to achieve reform – and they might have been once – then what are the rewards when the reform is forthcoming?' It was hard to find an answer to that question as I sat there listening to Pamensky's speech. I wondered why the big guns like Ian Botham and Viv Richards didn't come and see at first hand what had been accomplished. Why were they apparently content just to believe what they had been told? Could they trust the accuracy of those who had pronounced on South Africa to them? Around 60,000 African schoolboys were now playing cricket, compared to a handful 20 years earlier. Now that was progress. On the political front, rumours were growing that Nelson Mandela was soon to be released, the African National Congress was to be legitimised, and that the Group Areas Act and the Separate Amenities Act, symbols of apartheid, were to be repealed. The pace of reform was quickening, yet here we were, still in limbo, planning another rebel tour.

That tour, under the captaincy of Mike Gatting, was the last one to South Africa before we were brought back into the ICC in 1991, and it was also the most controversial. This was partly because it took a year from its inception for the English players to finally arrive in South Africa. Even though the tour had been inevitable since the ICC's special meeting in January 1989, its announcement the following August unleashed an amazing amount of vitriol towards the players. Yet their hands had been forced and they were faced with a perfectly straightforward decision. Ali Bacher, the main recruiter of Gatting's players, had warned a group of cricket writers and officials at a London dinner in April that another tour was likely. He pointed out that as managing director of SACU, it was his duty to try to foster interest in cricket at all levels in his country. After a couple of years spent developing a comprehensive scheme to launch cricket in the black townships, Bacher felt it was now time to look at the top of the tree again. The international-class players in South Africa had been starved of competition since the Australian tour of 1986-87 and they needed the stimulus of class opposition. That would certainly be provided by Gatting's team, all but two of whom had played Test cricket. Bacher felt confident that this time the tour would not be greatly disrupted because he had worked out a compromise with the National Sports Congress, the newly formed umbrella group for non-white sporting bodies, whereby if the players coached in the townships, the demonstrations against the tourists would be non-violent. But too much time had elapsed between the announcement of the tour and its start six months later. In that time, the new South African President, F.W. de Klerk, had announced that peaceful demonstrations were now legal, and the newly formed Mass Democratic Movement meant the trade unions would be efficiently organised, and in a position to make life very difficult for Gatting's team if they wished. Then the NSC pulled out of its agreement not to harass the English players, and with the time they had to prepare sophisticated disruption, it was bound to be a torrid time for the guys when they arrived in February, 1990.

Almost at once it was clear that cricket was an irrelevance. The police used tear gas and bullets to try to break up the demos, hotel staff refused to serve the English players, stones and beer cans were thrown at Gatting as he met protesters, and a mine exploded outside the Newlands Cricket Ground. It was hopeless to expect the tour to proceed as normally as the earlier ones. In the space of ten days, there were some historic events. President de Klerk lifted the ban on the ANC and released Nelson Mandela and 100 other political prisoners. That sparked off mass celebrations among millions of blacks and violence from white extremists. Even though the President's announcements meant that white minority rule would eventually be a thing of the past, the country was in turmoil. The game of cricket was caught in the crossfire and Ali Bacher acted swiftly. He agreed with the NSC to shorten the Gatting tour to just four one-day internationals in return for a moratorium on demonstrations. Bacher's actions didn't go down too well with some members of the SACU Board and he was reprimanded for exceeding his authority in agreeing to shorten the tour, but it's difficult to know what else he could have done. A series of protracted discussions around the table, with every Board member pitching in, would simply have taken far too long and would have done nothing for the safety of Gatting and his players. So they never got to the townships and they didn't come back for a second tour, as scheduled. The release of Mandela and the unbanning of the ANC were more important to South Africa at that time than a cricket tour, and it was right to call a halt.

Bacher had taken a few chances. He had invested about £1 million in 16 English cricketers when many felt the money ought to have gone to deserving South African cricketers, who were in far greater need of it for equipment, facilities and coaching. With so much ferment in the country, there was a grave danger that the township development programme which had been set up in 1986 would be aborted: where would that leave Bacher in his sincere desire to bring cricket to the disadvantaged? He must have been close to being sacked by SACU for agreeing to the curtailment of the tour – and the cancellation of the second – without referring the prospect to his fellow Board members. But, wisely, SACU realised they couldn't afford to lose someone of his stature, and he survived.

Many felt the Gatting tour was a complete disaster and shouldn't have taken place. I disagree. I believe it was the best thing to happen to South African cricket at the time. It accelerated the unification of cricket and brought the various factions together far quicker than we had thought possible. That tour led to the formation of the United Cricket Board of South Africa and a smooth passage back into Test cricket. Although I felt sorry for the English players, and I particularly admired Mike Gatting's physical bravery, it was clear that events were moving too rapidly in South Africa to allow us to be distracted by another tour, so it was right to cancel the proposed second visit in 1991. It was more important to lay down a proper framework, to get a new structure with a common purpose. Having been forgiven by the SACU Board, Ali Bacher was given the sole responsibility for making recommendations for the future of South African cricket. He said that the day of the rebel tour was now over and that South Africans of all colours had to work together for a unified cricket authority. He had developed a close working relationship with Kris Naidoo of the National Sports Congress. Naidoo could speed up unity talks with the South African Cricket Board. The NSC had concentrated on township sports since it was set up in 1985 and one of its declared priorities was a unified body in all sports. The African National Congress had also let it be known that it viewed cricket as an important unifying element in the South Africa of tomorrow.

It also looked as if Bacher hadn't lost the confidence of the commercial section of the Afrikaner community, who had put up a healthy amount of money to bankroll recent tours. If constructive dialogue was possible between the ANC, the government, SACU, the NSC and the Afrikaner business fraternity, then that was progress on a scale unimaginable in South Africa. With 90 per cent of non-white cricketers operating under the control of SACU, it shouldn't be a massive task for the NSC to deliver the South African Cricket Board to the negotiating table. Ali Bacher made it clear that his aims were one body for all cricketers in South Africa, equal opportunities for administrators as well as players, the absolute necessity for all schools to play non-racial cricket on a home-and-away basis, and that cricket should be used at all times to help eradicate apartheid. He recognised that there was still a deep sense of distrust in the black community, built up over the years by the evils of apartheid, and he promised that better facilities in the townships were a priority. Equality had to start in the schools, he said. He stressed the need to build for the future, a time that would see South Africa in a post-apartheid society, back in Test cricket.

It was an exciting feeling, to talk about the real prospect of a single, united ruling body representing South African cricket, living and working under a democratically elected government. We were entering a period of huge social change, when the pace of events would continue to take us all by surprise. But few of us were ready for the speed with which we were welcomed back to Test cricket, just over a year after the Gatting tour had seemed to publicise our social and political defects to the rest of the world. It may have looked a shambles, but that tour did the cricketers of South Africa a favour. It coincided with the swift dismantling of the wall of repression and it was only sensible that cricket should take a back seat while the political drama unfolded. We would continue to help break down apartheid by showing what could be done on the cricket field when players of all races got together. The sweeping social changes had been felt in our world long before Nelson Mandela was released. We knew the importance of communication in helping to prepare multi-racial cricket for a post-apartheid society. Mike Gatting's aborted tour proved to be the catalyst for a wind of change that blew us back into official international cricket.

ALI BACHER'S TOWNSHIP PROGRAMME

In years to come, when the South Africa Test side includes black players, you can point to the huge benefits of a scheme started in 1986 by the son of a Lithuanian Jew who came to South Africa to escape the Nazis. For Ali Bacher has done an enormous amount of work for black cricketers in South Africa; in particular the township programme he started up has revolutionised the attitude towards cricket in areas where few players of class had previously been unearthed. He has set up a nationwide system which is trying to challenge soccer's traditional hold on youngsters in the townships. Ali says it's the most exciting part of South Africa's cricketing history because a vast reservoir of talent is at last being drained: his dream is that Africans will play for South Africa.

Ali Bacher has a history of making things happen. He was born into a loving family that was short of money after escaping the Nazi regime in Eastern Europe and he knew a lot more about underprivileged people than the rest of the South Africans he later captained. When we faced international isolation, Ali was brave enough to say publicly that we deserved it. He got a few death threats for that statement, but he has always been an emotional, caring man, a champion of the repressed. His principles are rock-solid; after isolation began, he worked as a doctor in a multi-racial hospital in Johannesburg at a time when that wasn't a fashionable thing to do. He never complained about losing out on the glory of leading his country to England and Australia in the early 1970s, he just set his sights on trying to build a fairer South Africa where players of a later generation wouldn't be thrust into the conflict between sport and politics. As a result, he became South Africa's most important cricket administrator. He helped drag our other administrators towards a closer understanding of non-white frustrations at the lack of facilities and hope. He was brave enough to hand out home truths to the government at a time when it was fashionable to keep your head down. He rose up the ladder of officialdom and became accepted as a great reformer, his mind buzzing with all sorts of schemes. The township programme was the best one.

In 1986, many parts of South Africa were almost out of control. The State of Emergency declared by the government had led to even greater unrest and the restrictions on the media indicated that the politicians were badly rattled. With Nelson Mandela still in prison, the ANC seemed to have right on their side in the eyes of many liberal-minded people, and it looked as if South Africa was heading for another damaging period of bloodshed. The prospect of blacks killing whites indiscriminately in the townships was very real. The situation was far worse than after the Sharpeville riots of 1960, or during the Soweto disturbances in 1976. Civil war was squarely on the agenda. Ali Bacher watched in despair and tried to think of some way to defuse the tension in the townships. A great believer in the healing powers of sport, he vowed to take cricket into the most dangerous parts of the townships, to try to break down racial barriers. He contacted several radio stations in Soweto, near Johannesburg, inviting kids to come to a park the following weekend to play cricket. More than 1,000 turned up.

Ali admits he was scared when he arrived on the first day. He knew there was no trust in the white man among the blacks in those sprawling ghettos; he was aware that he might be sacrificed, despite his good intentions. But Ali had a better chance of a rewarding dialogue than other white men of cricket. He had worked in a hospital in Soweto and his reputation as a fair man wasn't confined to white people in prosperous suburbs. He talked to the black leaders, aware that the order to slit his throat might not be too far away. He talked to black teachers, trying to convince them that a properly organised cricket programme would make their jobs easier and give their pupils some hope. Ali talked and talked, something that comes naturally to him. You must remember that in 1986, some of those township areas were as dangerous and as lawless as Beirut. Soldiers, police and black rebels used to slug it out with automatic rifles across playing fields, with no regard for those caught in the crossfire. Any black who was suspected of being sympathetic to the white man was usually 'necklaced' – a car tyre was put around the victim's neck, covered in petrol, then set alight. It was no sensible place for a smooth-talking Jewish idealist who had captained white South Africa at cricket.

Somehow Ali got through to the influential leaders in Soweto. They respected the fact that he and his staff would take risks to try to make the lives of black kids better. This was not the usual attitude of the white man, they thought. He promised better facilities, good equipment, qualified coaching and the chance to play in competitive games that were properly umpired. Within a few weeks, he had set up a fleet of buses to take the kids to a central park where the coaching took place. They handed out oranges and biscuits as well as bats and balls. Soon about 1,500 children were gathering every Saturday morning for the coaching clinics. He sold the idea to some sceptics in the South African Cricket Union, convincing them that the programme could bridge the different groups and widen the appeal of cricket in the South Africa of tomorrow. Large firms like Nissan and Benson & Hedges were wooed and they agreed to plough money into the programme. Within a year, various companies had put up 2 million rand. Half a million went on mini-cricket, aimed at the under-tens, which is played with a soft ball. Mini-cricket began in Soweto and Alexandra, another township near Johannesburg, but it soon spread nationwide. Within a year, 800 kids from Khayelitsha near Cape Town were involved in a primary schools league playing mini-cricket. The soft ball ensures there are no physical worries, and there are no marked-out pitches, so that lots of games can be played on the same field. The idea is to familiarise the kids with the basics of the game, to get them used to swinging a bat or bowling. There is no immediate need to be better than anyone else. It is played for the sheer joy of it. Once the children have mastered the rudiments, you then introduce them to proper cricket. Most of these young black players had never seen a game of cricket in their lives, so it was vital to catch them at an early age, to show them how much enjoyment there could be in hitting a ball with a piece of wood.

Within 18 months of Ali Bacher's first visit to Soweto, the township programme was a viable project nationwide. Ali estimated that 50,000 children between the ages of eight and 11 had experience of the scheme. Seven primary schools from Soweto had started playing white opposition from nearby Johannesburg and in some cases, beating them. Ali proudly pointed out that some black kids had walked seven miles from their township to practise with his son in his back garden. The kids who played had a feel for the game. He became even more certain that great talent would be unearthed, and that cricket was a way of improving their status in life.

Coaching was absolutely vital for the project, and Ali kept busy drumming up sponsorship. He managed to clinch a sponsorship deal of 1 million rand that helped set up the South African Cricket Academy to develop coaching expertise among township people. Ali was very encouraged that a lot of coaching was done by female teachers and that hasn't altered, particularly among the primary schools. Only a year after the programme began, a major sponsorship deal meant that the drive for more coaching could be accelerated. Twenty leading businessmen pledged 50,000 rand a year for the next ten years. Called the South African Executive Cricket Club, it was to be chaired by Mervyn King, a former supreme court judge who had been present alongside Ali Bacher when he took that first dangerous journey into Soweto in October, 1986. It was a terrific boost in the campaign to provide better coaching, facilities and equipment, because it was looking as if demand was exceeding supply.

Initially the township programme was particularly popular around Johannesburg, Port Elizabeth and Cape Town, but soon interest spread to all regions. Early in 1988, Chris Davies became the first full-time paid coach to be appointed by SACU, with a brief to work specifically in the townships. He started a coaching course for 60 black teachers, and after a three-day intensive session, he had a 25 per cent success rate, including six women teachers. Later that year, Chris was able to report 50 more passes from his coaching courses, a third of them women. The township programme was such a success in the East London area that another full-time coach was appointed – Greg Hayes, who used to play for Border. Greg was born and bred in the Ciskei, and his ability to speak fluent Xhosa was very valuable as he communicated so easily with the black kids. Greg said at the time that this was the most rewarding experience of his life, and in the early stages of the programme, he and Chris needed all their dedication and enthusiasm to combat poor facilities – including pitches that were just strips of mud flattened by a heavy roller. But they were knocked out by the enjoyment and keenness of the teachers and children and soon cricket was taking root in the outlying villages as well as the larger townships like Mdantazane.

Bacher also found the way to ensure that white schools agreed to compete against their counterparts from the townships. He persuaded his colleagues on the board of SACA that it should be written into the constitution that if any white schools refused to play township sides, then they would be expelled from the Primary Schools Association and ineligible to play in any organised schools matches. The real test of that commitment came in the Orange Free State, where many die-hards among the Afrikaners didn't approve at all of this latest attempt to appease black people. The township programme had been a great initial success in the Rocklands township just outside Bloemfontein, and five teams from Rocklands had been entered for the Bloemfontein Schools League, previously the exclusive preserve of white schoolchildren. When the news broke, some white schools refused to play against blacks, and those schools were destined to lose the SACU benefits they had taken for granted – coaching, equipment and being eligible for representative schools sides. So the rebellion was short-lived, the township boys played the whites and no one seemed to be too bothered. But it was a very important victory for Bacher and SACU to win the argument on behalf of blacks in a right-wing district like Bloemfontein.

Still the sponsorship money came in for the township programme. Cadbury's agreed to finance 21 black schools in the Transvaal Cricket Council's area, so that they could afford to travel and play against white schools with decent equipment. Gradually, SACU officials began to travel throughout the country, performing various ceremonies to hand over new grounds to the townships. Within three years of the start of the programme, Bacher could proudly point out that townships in the areas of Johannesburg, Pretoria, Bloemfontein, Kimberley and East London all now had cricket fields that were as good as those of any white school nearby.

It's only fair to point out that Ali Bacher's vision was echoing the marvellous work done earlier in the Cape by John Passmore. Nor would Ali want to deny any credit to the man who spent most of his retirement years creating the sports complex in Langa, near Cape Town. Passmore's work was very much the prototype for Bacher.

Today Langa Cricket Club has three pitches, a pavilion, 12 teams (nine of them juniors) and had two players on the South African Youth tour to the West Indies in 1992. Three other local townships are in the process of completing similar sports complexes. The plans for the developments are administered by a trust set up in John Passmore's name after his death in 1991, chaired by the former South African captain and England rugby union international Clive van Ryneveld.

When John Passmore got involved in township cricket, the only sport popular there was football, and even that was played on the most basic of grounds, with rubble and rubbish all over the place. He helped transform the thinking behind the missionary work of cricket, and inspired Ali Bacher to make it a nationwide project. Just before he died, Passmore organised a match at Langa between a local Invitation XI, a mixed side, and an International Golden Oldies team. Afterwards, one of the Golden Oldies, the Australian Ashley Mallett, told him that the pitch and the outfield were good enough for Test cricket. That's a terrific tribute to the work of John Passmore.

He knew the importance of bringing good coaches to Langa. It would take some time before the supply of quality black coaches built up, so every year he would engage English county players to come over and impart their specialist knowledge. He was particularly impressed with the Sussex players John Spencer, Chris Phillipson, Colin and Alan Wells and by Derbyshire's James Graham-Brown and Kevin Lyons of Glamorgan. The English coaches brought authority, experience and organisational skills to township cricket. They did a magnificent 'holding job' as SACU waited for the black coaches to come through a system that was only a few years old. Players like Leicestershire's Russell Cobb were inspirational in the Mammelodi township near Pretoria, where he managed to get 37 primary schools playing well-organised cricket. When he returned to Leicester in the English summer, the kids carried on practising cricket rather than playing football.

Bob Woolmer put in some great work at Avendale, a coloured club in the township of Athlone, near Cape Town. When he first went there in the early 1980s the facilities were very poor: two concrete nets with uneven, dangerous bounce, no roller for the pitch and badly organised coaching. He told Western Province he wouldn't be available for them and set to work trying to modernise Avendale. He had a great deal of opposition from SACOS (the South African Council of Sport), a militant organisation that refused to co-operate with any sporting bodies until apartheid was dismantled. Their stance included refusing offers of better facilities and the chance for black children to play with and against anyone associated with a club that wasn't under the SACOS banner. They believed that SACU was a racialist organisation because they were still prepared to work with the government. A school next door to Avendale was banned by SACOS from using the club's facilities because SACOS saw that as charity. But Woolmer kept doing his best for the club and at the last count, Avendale had 11 teams of mixed race and the senior side recently won the local league. The club had three cricket squares, one artifical wicket, seven grass nets, four concrete nets, and around 150 underprivileged children were getting high-quality coaching throughout the week under the supervision of Bob Woolmer and other well-qualified coaches from England. Officials of the club had raised more than a quarter of a million rand in just a few years to fund the various facilities and Avendale is a shining example of what can be done with goodwill. It's not there just to help underprivileged kids learn how to play the off-drive, it's a symbol of the new South Africa. It's a chance for the non-white players to be treated as the equals of whites, where sporting prowess, not the colour of your skin, gets you promoted to the next team. Clubs like Avendale are there for the whole community, a place where kids of all races can meet, talk and get to understand each other. No coloured or black cricketer is made to feel an 'honorary white' there, they all mix in and talk about the ordinary things all youngsters are interested in.

And the presence of English coaches only served to eradicate any lingering feeling of non-whites being patronised. In turn the English coaches could go back home and spread the essential word – that even though the political situation was still unsatisfactory, at least cricket in South Africa was open to all races at every level.

The great work done in the townships by coaches from English county cricket should never be forgotten. They saw their work as de-racialisation, trying to help the underprivileged, not just those of a darker skin. Because of apartheid, it was inevitable that most of the deprived would be non-white but the will to help all those without facilities was strong. Yet this genuine commitment was threatened by the ICC's decision in 1989, which meant selection for England would be denied to any county cricketers who went out to coach in South Africa. Not only would that put a lot of English players out of work, but it would deprive underprivileged South Africans of the opportunity to learn about the game and improve themselves educationally and socially. The English pros had the practical experience of organising transport to and from games, of running net practice properly, of letting the leaders in the townships know what was happening. In the past, many top South African cricketers had benefited from the expertise of English coaches, but that was solely for the benefit of the white community.

Since the township programme had started, the major beneficiaries of English coaching had been black youngsters. The coaches formed a vital bridge between the first faltering steps in '86 and eventual efficiency under the nationwide tutelage of fully qualified black coaches in great numbers. The ICC decision not only acted as a deterrent to some county cricketers, but it also drove many into considering a lucrative rebel tour that would cost a lot of money from SACU' s coffers. In that way, there would be less money available for the township programme that was vital for the future of South African cricket. It was a relief when the ban on coaching in South Africa was rescinded as we were finally allowed back on to the international scene.

It was a proud day for Ali Bacher and his township programme when an official English side played against a South African team for the first time in 28 years – and it happened in a township. In 1987, 1,200 kids turned up on the first day of township cricket in Alexandra, an area of about a square mile that accommodates a quarter of a million people, just outside Johannesburg. Six years later, in December, 1993, the England 'A' team began their tour with a game against a Transvaal XI. Five of the Transvaal team were from the townships, including the captain, Geoffrey Toyana. He learned his cricket in Soweto and blossomed into a classy left-handed batsman. He also developed his education, attending Johannesburg's Rao University for a degree in commerce. Another township player who impressed the English tourists was Walter Masemola. He didn't play cricket until he was 12, but quickly showed a natural ability to bowl fast. He toured England with the South African Under-17 side and he admitted that cricket and the township programme stopped him drifting into a life of crime. Against the English tourists, he clean bowled Mark Lathwell and looked an exciting, raw talent with genuine speed. Walter is now on the Transvaal Cricket Board groundstaff – on merit – and the day can't be far away when he plays in the Currie Cup. He has already been to Adelaide to be coached by Dennis Lillee and Rodney Marsh, and there is no doubt that without the township programme, Walter wouldn't have been interested in cricket and its opportunities for travel and education in the outside world.

When you consider that 18 months previously there had been daily battles with tear gas, shotguns and automatic weapons, it was a major achievement that Alexandra township could stage that historic match. Back in those lawless days, many of the young cricketers had to stand guard overnight at the clubhouse to make sure the cricket equipment wasn't stolen. Violent death has become a fact of life there, yet somehow a cricket pitch has been carved out of a hillside, built on an old rubbish dump. It stands there as a symbol of hope for those who believe that cricket can help heal the divisions and improve the life of the underprivileged.

When the English tourists played another township game – this time in Langa, in the Cape – it must have been an interesting visit for Alan Wells. The last time he had visited South Africa was in Mike Gatting's tour party and he had soon become aware that the trip was unpopular with the non-white community. But he had coached at Langa for several years before that controversial tour. He was made captain for the Langa match and included in the Western Province XI was Ben Malamba, one of Alan's best pupils from his coaching days at the club. Alan must have had mixed feelings when his talented protégé drove a straight six and batted with great maturity in a low-scoring game, but he admitted that the facilities at Langa were now excellent. The warm welcome he enjoyed from the locals who remembered him confirmed the value of the English county pro in the townships.

That Western Province side included six players from the townships and there were five in the Eastern Province team which played England 'A' in Zwide. They were all there on merit, and their involvement in those games was a great advertisement for the township programme. The gulf of opportunity between white and black youngsters had been huge and something had to be done to provide facilities for those deprived by the apartheid years. If anyone doubts the quality of the township players that were included against England, examine those in the Transvaal side. Four of them played in the trials to pick the Transvaal team for the National Schools Tournament and a fifth, the off-spinner Jacob Malao, practises with the senior Western Province players and has become the first township player to be taken on the MCC groundstaff at Lord's. Just before that historic game at Alexandra, a side drawn from all the country's townships took on the top schools in the country in a tournament in Natal. The township side won two of the four games and I understand that my old school – Hilton College – was saved by the rain. Chasing 280, Hilton were 110 for 6 when rain saved them. I don't suppose any of those young players in that schools tournament talked about window-dressing. Just ask the coaching director of the United Cricket Board, Khaya Majola. Late in 1993 he could state with complete conviction that from junior level all the way up to under-19s, there was no representative side which would not now include on merit players from the township programme. That is a fantastic tribute to something that had only been operational for six years.

This development programme was recognised as the key to South Africa's cricket future by Clive Lloyd, when he at last visited us. During our years of isolation the West Indies had been one of South Africa's sternest critics and it was hard to take issue with Clive's observations on our political structure. If we could manage to win over admired figures such as he, then we were definitely on the move. Clive came over as ICC referee for the India tour in 1992 and we were delighted that he wanted to go to the townships to measure the strength of our development programme. He was impressed by the sight of black kids enjoying their cricket, and at the improving facilities. He thought it was crucial that the country's youth were being encouraged to mix in multi-racial sport, and that at last youngsters of all races had a chance to play for South Africa. But he was right to underline that a great deal of social deprivation still existed. Clive said that there was a life beyond the boundary rope, that decent accommodation tended to produce decent human beings. He praised Ali Bacher and the other administrators who had done so much to bring the races together in cricket, but warned that the pace of reform mustn't slow down. Mixing at school and in the workplace was as important as mixing in the cricket arena. Clive pointed out that sport was a stepping-stone to a fairer society but it couldn't divorce itself from that society. That was something that many of us in South Africa had overlooked in our years of isolation, and it was a good point. The township programme had to push on for the good of those communities, not just to discover promising cricketers.

Another great West Indian cricketer of the past had joined forces with us to promote our development programme. Conrad Hunte, an acknowledged gentleman of the game when he opened for the West Indies in the 1960s, moved to Johannesburg with his family in 1992 to help coach promising black youngsters. He coached the Soweto Under-19 team that did so well against the best schoolboys in Transvaal, and two of those he had tutored made it to the South African Schools squad. Conrad, who for many years was a member of Moral Re-armament and a critic of South African society, had been brought over under a scheme run jointly by the MCC and the United Cricket Board of South Africa and he was not a man to be swayed by cosmetic changes. The presence of someone of Conrad Hunte's stature was a considerable boost to our image and proof that we were travelling at last along the right lines.

It was understandable that Ali Bacher wanted to show off the township programme when so many former players, cricket officials and influential media people gathered in South Africa in 1989 to celebrate the centenary of our first Test. Cynics said that it was all stage-managed, that the trips were organised solely with cameras and notebooks in mind, but that was very unfair. Journalists making that trip were told they were free to go anywhere they wanted to assess the pace of change. It's true that at the time there was still a lot of political tension, with the government perturbed at the build-up of civil unrest, but cricket seemed to have a charmed life in the way that the security forces ignored us. Anything that a visiting journalist wanted to see was laid on for them and no issue was ducked. Yet many influential writers chose not to come. Their minds were made up without giving South Africans the chance to state their case and demonstrate what was being achieved, particularly in the townships. That was the kind of blinkered thinking that had hampered us for so many years.

I know that those who made the centenary trip went away bowled over by the work being done in the townships. Apartheid had existed to keep communities apart, yet here we had black cricketers going to smart cricket grounds in prosperous white suburbs to play against the privileged white boys – and even more significantly, the home-and-away league system meant that the white kids would be in the townships for the return fixture. The Separate Amenities Act and the Group Areas Act proved powerless to stop that flow of cricketing traffic and the barriers of ignorance and fear continued to fall down. The groups of players started getting to know each other. You can learn a lot about someone on the cricket field and the process continues afterwards in the bar. Years ago, if a black kid wanted to play cricket in a fairly enlightened white community, he would probably field all afternoon and not get a bat. He would no doubt end up doing the menial chores, like putting away the gear afterwards. He certainly wouldn't have been treated like an equal. In the more conservative areas of South Africa, that black kid wouldn't even be allowed on the same field as the privileged whites. Now we had township boys playing in Ali Bacher's back garden. Developments like that had to be good for our future.

The development programme was also good for the business community. Bacher and his colleagues worked miracles in getting so much money out of the business sector; no doubt it was good for the corporate image and there were tax advantages, but they still coughed up the money and that was the crucial thing. But those businessmen also started learning about the black community. Ali encouraged them to come into the townships, where their safety would be guaranteed, and they began a dialogue with leaders. After all, the townships provided a great deal of skilled and unskilled labour for those businessmen and they could now understand more about their employees' background, and why some of them appeared to be so militant. There was at least a dialogue and that was something South Africa needed. The programme also helped the educational standards in the townships. Teachers were fully involved in coaching, liaising with the specialist coaches and encouraging parents to let their children play cricket. Football is a far easier game to organise, and it's cheaper, but gradually cricket took hold through the patience and tenacity of teachers. The game is an educational tool, as well as a sporting one: it gives you the chance to exchange views about life as well as instilling the competitive element that is a vital part of getting on in whatever profession you choose. I appreciate that a choice of profession is not something granted many township-dwellers – survival is the main aim – yet cricket was at least helping to bring together the communities; to help them communicate, to understand the pleasure of dressing-room camaraderie and the need to pull together for the sake of the team. That sort of discipline couldn't do any harm, could it?

After a difficult start, the development programme came to be accepted by many black community leaders, who preferred to see their youngsters hurling a ball from the outfield rather than a bomb, with their role models successful cricketers rather than freedom-fighters. As the pillars of apartheid crumbled, there was no point in taking up entrenched positions any more. The post-apartheid future of South Africa was a massive problem and a challenge to those of an open mind. We could only hope that the amount of constructive dialogue between young cricketers of all races which had started through the township schemes would bear fruit in the new South Africa. It wasn't simply designed to spread the base of cricket – although the signs are very encouraging – but it was a deposit on the country's future. The boss of a firm who has to deal with a black trade union leader has surely got a better chance of satisfactory compromise if they discover they once played cricket against each other in a township. Within seven years of Ali Bacher bravely stepping into

Soweto to talk cricket, he could reflect on more than 300 schools in that township alone playing cricket. There would still be violence – the bullet would continue to be more persuasive than the ball – but the progress in bringing cricket to the black community had been remarkable in such a short space of time. I can't think of any other country in the world that has implanted a sport so successfully into a racial group. It will take a long time before mistrust of the whites is eradicated, but due to Ali's personal example and bravery, I believe that a significant proportion of black cricketers accept they have a chance to improve their skills and progress on merit. I know that is a concept which should be naturally in place, but to a country such as ours it is still a novel idea.

Ali Bacher estimates that it will take at least 30 years before the full effects of the township programme are visible. By then the scheme should be institutionalised, with parents and teachers aware of the benefits the scheme brought to them when they were youngsters. Money will still come from the business community and the United Cricket Board, while it is to be hoped that international opinion will have come to accept that it's not window-dressing, but a genuine attempt to heal divisions. Bacher says he's never been more certain that at some stage in the future players from Soweto, Alexandra and other dispossessed areas will be playing Test cricket for South Africa. When that happens – and Ali won't allow the word 'if' – then full credit must be given to the township programme and its inspiration. Ali took some incredible stick from all sides. Many whites thought he was far too soft with black militants, and they couldn't see why he should subject himself to situations where his life was undoubtedly in danger. At the flashpoint of Mike Gatting's tour, outside the De Beers Country Club in Kimberley, it was Ali who stood between the police guns and the ANC supporters who were certainly not there to roar on the English team. Ali knew the tour was leading to much bloodshed in the townships. He was getting death threats from black militants and then, when he called off the tour, he was told by right-wing activists that his life was in danger because he was succumbing to black pressure. Even in his close-knit family he was having problems: his daughter, Lynn, was a strong champion of the underprivileged and, even though she loves cricket, she wouldn't go and see any of the games involving the Gatting team. It was a time of terrible strain for him, but he certainly didn't buckle publicly, even though he had many private doubts. He was the one who applied to all the local magistrates' courts to allow the demonstrators the right to make their protests over the Gatting tour. That shows the measure of the guy – he didn't want to muzzle legitimate complaints about such a controversial event. I'm convinced that anyone other than Ali Bacher would have been helpless to calm down a very emotional, inflammatory atmosphere. His presence helped save lives. It also saved the township programme. As he has said so often, 'We were pretty good when we were an all-white team, so just how good will we be when we're picking from all the people of South Africa?'

BACK AT LAST!

Just as many can still remember where they were on the day President Kennedy was shot, so I can recall precisely the day when South Africa returned to Test cricket. It was July 10, 1991 and I was at the County Ground, Northampton, supervising our preparations for the next day's NatWest match against Leicestershire. I was in my first season as Northants' director of cricket, and thoroughly enjoying the experience, but I'm sure everybody there would understand now when I say I had half an eye on the ICC meeting at Lord's. It was a strange feeling when the news of our readmission came through – a mixture of relief, joy and sadness. I wasn't sad for my wasted opportunities, because I felt I had been lucky, but I did spare a thought for the frustrated generation of players who came after me. I was relieved that the long fight was finally over, convinced we were seeing a new dawn of hope for post-apartheid South Africa and absolutely delighted for Ali Bacher and his dedicated administrators, who had suffered so many rebuffs and still came back for more. It had to happen some time and no one deserved the champagne and the back-slapping more than Ali.

Events had moved so swiftly. Less than 18 months earlier, Bacher's reputation seemed in tatters. He had aborted the Gatting tour in the face of the overwhelming disapproval of the influential black leaders, and everybody seemed to be having a go at him. It looked as if his beloved township programme was in ruins, as the kids started throwing stones rather than attending the nets. When he tried negotiating with the ANC for a resumption of the project, a senior official told him, 'Mr Bacher, we want nothing to do with your cricket and, especially, we want nothing to do with you.' There were threats of a 'necklace' for Ali from some of the more bloodthirsty militants. A lesser man would have packed it in and come to the conclusion that his life's work – the thriving township programme – wasn't going to happen. But he never wavered in his conviction that good intentions would triumph and he kept the dialogue going with the ANC. For seven months, he followed the ANC's advice and stayed out of the townships. Then he had a call to tell him that if he took a plane to East London, he might be able to do a deal with a guy called Steve Tshwete. He was one of the chief ANC leaders who were starting to return home from exile in Lusaka after Nelson Mandela's release and the unbanning of the ANC. Tshwete had spent 15 years on Robben Island, in the same prison as Mandela, and his reputation was so high that he was obviously going to be a major figure in the ANC now that they were negotiating for influence with the government. He sat Ali down and asked him to outline his plans for South African cricket. Ali talked for half an hour about the township programme and his dream of an endless line of talent coming through from those deprived areas. He also admitted he had been wrong to organise the Gatting tour. I can just imagine Ali in full flow, knowing he had to convince this imposing man that they shared the same vision for South Africa. Suddenly, Tshwete shook Bacher's hand and said he'd do what he could. A new partnership had begun.

The ANC's support was absolutely fundamental to our readmission. Without that, we would remain in limbo. Their leaders took the view that sport was an essential healing element. Nelson Mandela had watched South Africa play Australia at Durban more than 40 years before and Steve Tshwete was a big sports fan. They truly believed in the bonding that sport can provide and they pledged to support all those sports that had shown a genuine commitment to a single, non-racial, democratic structure. Cricket had shown the way in that respect and the ANC made it clear that they would support our campaign for readmission. They realised that Test cricket would provide the necessary funds to sustain the township programme and improve the flow of facilities to the underprivileged. Once they were convinced that Bacher's aim was for truly integrated cricket, then we had a partnership. Since then the ANC have been tremendously supportive of our efforts.

Steve Tshwete's first aim was to get the major administrators around the table to talk unity. That was no easy task. In the past, attempts at unification had been dogged by bodies like SACBOC and SACOS, who maintained that SACU had been too soft on apartheid, too willing to toe the government line. So we lost the goodwill and support of some influential officials and players because they came to believe that not enough was being done to speed up political reform. Krish Mackerdhuj had replaced Hassan Howa as president of the South African Cricket Board (the breakaway group from SACU) in 1984 and he had shown himself to be even more trenchant than Howa. When Howa met Ali Bacher for informal talks, Mackerdhuj objected, saying that Bacher shouldn't have been allowed into the ground, which was under the control of the SACB. A tough lawyer of Indian extraction, Mackerdhuj would clearly be a hard nut to crack as talks about unification were discussed. But he had also been an ANC member for 30 years, so perhaps the diplomacy of Steve Tshwete would sway the issue.

Talks started in September, 1990 and within three months, there was agreement in principle on a merged cricket board. A nine-point statement of intent was released, and among the most important conclusions was the commitment to redress the imbalance between separate educational systems and facilities. The statement also undertook to gain recognition from the ICC, paving the way for a return to international cricket. The development programme was to be broadened, and that would need more experienced coaches, especially from England. Soon the fruits of that new understanding began to flow, and 350,000 rand was put up by a furnishing group to fund coaching courses in the township of Lenasia, near Johannesburg. The joint directors of the trust that would oversee the project were to be Ali Bacher and Khaya Majola, and that was another important decision. Majola, a left-arm spinner, had been one of the best players in SACB cricket in recent years, and he was a hard-liner. At the time of the Gatting tour, he had publicly talked about a 'necklace' for Bacher, yet now he was happy to help bridge the gap between SACU and SACB, working for the future. Within a couple of years, Majola was director of national development, working next door to Bacher's office at the Wanderers club. That's progress!

The new partnership wasn't neglecting the outside world, either. Krish Mackerdhuj and the National Sports Congress chairman Mluleki George went to Australia to lobby administrators and tell them about the constructive progress being made. At the time, with the annual meeting of the ICC just a few months away, it didn't seem possible that everything could be in order to table a meaningful bid for readmission, but we were becoming more and more confident it was only a matter of time. In February, president F.W. de Klerk had announced that he intended to start dismantling the remaining framework of apartheid, including the Population Registration Act whereby you were classified a certain race at birth, and the other laws which decree where various racial groups live. Since Nelson Mandela's release almost a year earlier, we had assumed that wide-ranging reforms would happen, but not so quickly. Now, if those apartheid laws were swept away as swiftly as the President had promised, it would mean that South

Africa would conform to the Olympic Charter. Back in the Olympic Games? Back in Test cricket? It was almost too much to take in. We were starting to look at possible scenarios: the International Olympic Commission was due to visit South Africa to assess the progress and its report on our suitability for a return to the Games was due out in June. The following month, we hoped to be able to address the ICC. Could it all happen at once after all these years?

By April, we had our unified cricket body, to be called the United Cricket Board of South Africa. Ali Bacher was to be the managing director, with Geoff Dakin of SACU the first president and the SACB's Krish Mackerdhuj president the following year. Dakin had worked long and hard for the cause of 'normal cricket'. Way back in the mid-1970s, when he was trying to get the concept going in Eastern Province, the Bureau of State Security made it clear that meetings of that type weren't encouraged. Officers took car registration numbers of those who attended meetings at Dakin's house. Now Dakin, Bacher and Mackerdhuj would go to Lord's in July, to plead the case for reinstatement. A lot of work was going on behind the scenes to prepare the ICC delegates for that momentous meeting. Bacher went to London to brief Colin Cowdrey, the ICC chairman, and he also found the time there to lobby the high commissioners of the various Caribbean islands, plus New Zealand and Sri Lanka. He was told by all of them that the matter would be referred to their respective governments, but he was left in no doubt that the response would be warm, now that apartheid was about to be scrapped and there was one official unified cricket body. Bacher also went to Zimbabwe, to lobby the high commissioners of Pakistan and India, two crucial elements in the equation. The foreign ministers of all the full member countries of the ICC and the delegates at the Lord's meeting were briefed by the ANC's Shadow Foreign Minister, Thabo Mbeki. Reactions from the various ministers all seemed favourable.

Back in South Africa, we gained another significant convert. Sam

Ramsamy, the chairman of the South African Non-Racial Olympic Committee, came to see the progress of the township programme. Now SANROC had been a thorn in the flesh of many sportsmen over the years as its chairman compiled a blacklist of those deemed to have been too sympathetic to the government because they played sport in our country, and to have Ramsamy's support was very gratifying. 'This is certainly not the South Africa I knew. It has changed almost beyond recognition,' he said after visiting Soweto. It was a pity that he couldn't have taken up SACU's offer to visit a few years earlier, because the transformation had not been an overnight miracle, but that was just a passing, churlish thought. It was enough to see how moved he was by the sight of the enthusiasm for the programme in Soweto. It was particularly satisfying to see that almost half the coaches were women teachers who were wonderfully enthusiastic.

Less than a fortnight before the ICC meeting, apartheid was formally dismantled and the United Cricket Board of South Africa staged it inaugural ceremony. The news on apartheid was a fantastic shot in the arm for our prospects of readmission, but more importantly, it signposted the start of a new decisive age. It had taken a lot of whites many years to agree that the policy had been indefensible and we cricketers were proud that the politicians had at last followed our lead towards building a multi-racial society. Nobody pretended that all would be sweetness and light overnight. The tribal killings would continue, some of the police would misjudge certain situations and overreact, and the yawning gap between the rich and the desperately poor in the townships wouldn't be bridged. Sport could only do so much in relation to all that, but we'd keep trying to demonstrate that our way – a constructive, healing approach – was the proper one. So, with apartheid officially a thing of the past, the ceremony to launch the new United Cricket Board was an emotional night. Sir Gary Sobers flew over, and Sunil Gavaskar, Richie Benaud, Sam Ramsamy and other respected cricket writers. Some of those attending were on their first visit to South Africa, having refused on principle to come earlier. Nelson Mandela announced that he had instructed Steve Tshwete to go to Lord's with Ali Bacher, adding his weight to the request for admission, and it was great to hear these words from the man who had symbolised black resistance for so many years: 'We have extremists who say there can be no normal sport in a racial society. But it seems to me that sport is sport, and quite different from politics. If sportsmen here take steps to remove the colour bar, then we must take that into account.' And Steve Tshwete caught the mood of optimism when he said: 'If mortal enemies like the State President of South Africa and Nelson Mandela could meet to build a new South Africa, if soldiers on both sides could lay down their weapons while new settlements are being reached, then who are mere cricketers to continue fighting?'

Clearly the presence of Sobers at that inaugural ceremony in Johannesburg wasn't lost on Bacher and the delegation that was to speak at Lord's. After the furore about him playing in Rhodesia in the early 1970s, he had resisted efforts to get him over to South Africa, to lend support to our attempts at reform. He was probably wise to resist, because he could have been sucked into dangerous waters which are unfamiliar to sportsmen. But he would have needed the permission of Caribbean governments to have his passport accepted by South Africa's immigration authorities when he came to that dinner in June, 1991. Surely that meant the West Indian cricket authorities were in favour of our readmission?

In the end West Indies abstained from voting at the ICC meeting but that didn't matter. We were back – 21 years and 122 days since Ali Bacher's catch had won us the Port Elizabeth Test and I had led our team off the field into the wilderness. The motion to readmit us was proposed by India and seconded by Australia, two countries which had taken a hard line towards South Africa during isolation, so that was an encouraging development. No wonder Ali Bacher was close to tears in the Long Room when he faced the media. He had dedicated himself over the previous 20 years to restoring South Africa to international competition, and to create the opportunity for all racial groups to play cricket without any artificiality. He had the vision, the bravery, the perseverance and the personality to achieve the impossible. Who else could have brought the ANC, the NSC, the government, SANROC , the ICC and the two rival cricket boards to the same conclusion – that we deserved to return to Test cricket?

It was only fitting that Steve Tshwete should have stood alongside Ali Bacher that day at Lord's as the champagne was sprayed about. He had been a tower of strength in the previous year, after that initial meeting when he sized up Bacher, then promised him support. Tshwete's lack of bitterness at his prolonged imprisonment impressed everyone and his dignified style of debate and conciliation gave exactly the right impression. Clearly a sports fanatic, he has been tremendously supportive to South African cricket since he joined us, and he has made it clear how much value the ANC has placed on our readmission and success. Looking back on the previous 12 months which had accelerated the process so rapidly, it's clear that the first few days of February, 1990 were absolutely historic: F.W. de Klerk announcing further relaxation of apartheid, the unbanning of the ANC, the release of Nelson Mandela, the collapse of Mike Gatting's tour in the face of so much unrest – all within ten days! We would never have got the breakthrough without the ANC recognising what we had achieved and wished to do in the future, allied to the President's apartheid reforms. Once he had recognised the ANC as a legitimate political entity, they could then take a key role in getting the cricket bodies around the table. Quite simply, the ICC delegates could deliver when they realised that the ANC wanted us back in Test cricket – that was of fundamental importance. The authority and charisma of Nelson Mandela carried so much weight, and the close relationship between the ANC and India was the catalyst in India's decision to propose our readmission. Two years earlier, as Ali Bacher confirmed the details of

Mike Gatting's tour, knowing it would be a controversial time, he said his dream was for the ANC to encourage the township programme, to support international tours to South Africa and to lobby for our re-entry into Test cricket. That had all happened in the space of a few months.

The ANC's vital input confirmed that our return was a political issue. In the past we had been rather naive as we kept on about the fact that we had done everything in cricket terms, and that it was therefore wrong to keep denying us. I hope that frustration is understandable, because we did feel we were just being fobbed off by the ICC, year after year. But eventually it dawned on us that the ICC was just the medium by which we could get back: the outside political world had to accept us as well. Until other countries could see that the political structure in our country was going to change irrevocably, and that multi-racialism was squarely on the agenda, then we were going to stay in isolation. The cricket administrators at the ICC were just rubber-stamping what their governments were making of the current situation. South Africa had laws on the statute book which were offensive to sections of the human race; those laws had to go before we could be accepted by the politicians of the countries we wanted to play in the Test arena. It's not as if we had enjoyed a packed international programme when we were still in that arena. A series against Australia or England at two-year intervals wasn't exactly a schedule designed to burn out our top players, who have always thrived on competition. Now we could think about playing the West Indies, Pakistan, India and Sri Lanka on an official basis for the first time. Apart from the cricketing benefits, it would be a thrill to visit those countries which had always barred us because of politics.

Despite our successful attempts to commit ourselves to integration in our sport, South Africa's cricketers had been helpless in the face of so much implacable political opposition. We did all we could to show what a unifying agent sport can be, but it was a complex political issue for most of the time that we were kicking our heels. We all said some unkind things about the ICC, but a lot of that stemmed from frustration and our inability to change the course of events without a political breakthrough in South Africa. So ultimately the key players had become President de Klerk and Nelson Mandela, as they tried to come to a compromise about South Africa's future. Sport was only a minor consideration in all that, but we cricketers are very grateful that they managed to create the right climate of agreement to allow us to go forward out of the shadows.

A CROWDED SCHEDULE

If the pace of our return to Test cricket stunned us in those last few months, the amount of international cricket we then crammed in was almost as amazing. In the space of two years, we played in the West Indies, India, Australia, New Zealand, Sri Lanka and Australia again – with a series or two thrown in at home. No complaints from us – it had been a long time coming – but inevitably the learning curve would be steep. The fact that we didn't lose a Test series in those two years and got to the semi-finals of the World Cup is a matter of great pride to all of us.

After the euphoria of our day at Lord's had died away, it was time for assessment by South African cricket. The task ahead was clear enough for the top players – get in form, stay in good nick and make the selectors pick you. The one-day game was not too difficult because we played such a lot of it, and because of the competitive streak that is engendered so early in our careers in South Africa. The longer game looked like being a problem for our batsmen, because they weren't used to occupying the crease for session after session, grinding out big totals. Of the likely choices, only Jimmy Cook, Allan Donald and Kepler Wessels had practical experience of overseas pitches, so it would be interesting to see how we would fare in places like India and Pakistan. I thought our strength would be in our seam attack, with Allan Donald, Steve Jack and Richard Snell looking a hostile trio. All in all, I believed we wouldn't be disgraced against any side but the top teams like Australia, West Indies and Pakistan would be a huge test early on in our rehabilitation period. Our leading administrators seemed to understand that the Test match demands necessitated a change of format in the Currie Cup in the first domestic season after our recall. First-class matches were extended from three to four days, bonus points were scrapped and we returned to the old idea of first-innings bonus points and an outright victory. Provinces were to be allowed to field only one overseas player, so the rest of each team knew that a place in the national XI was up for grabs. It seemed that our first-class game was now trying to get as close as possible to the format of a Test match, where you have to be able to bowl a side out twice to win. Fast cameos on a sporting pitch in a three-day game were not the way to learn how to play Test cricket. We needed to get away from 'result' pitches that flattered a bowler and, as near as possible, simulate Test pitches by producing wickets that helped the batsmen prepared to graft, while making the bowlers work for their wickets.

So, as our players wondered just when we would get the chance to play in the international arena, we suddenly found ourselves catapulted into the World Cup. In October, 1991 the Commonwealth heads of state decided to go for South Africa's inclusion after learning that Nelson Mandela was keen. Three months earlier, at Lord's, we had been led to believe that it was too late to include us in the World Cup the following February and March. But a special meeting of the ICC in Sharjah gave us the go-ahead with four months to prepare. We were thrilled, not just because we felt we would do well, but because the World Cup had been a fantastic occasion since it was first staged in 1975, five years after we had gone into isolation. All we needed now was the chance to get some vital big-match experience before the 1992 tournament. That chance came quicker than anybody dared hope. Early in November, I was relaxing at home in Durban one Sunday morning when Ali Bacher called me. He said South Africa was to go to India and asked if I would like to go as cricket manager. The idea was mind-boggling: South Africa playing in India! I jumped at the chance, but then Ali really knocked me for six. We were leaving the following Wednesday. The selectors had picked the tour party already, so we had precisely four days' preparation. Of course, it wasn't enough and we were very underprepared – our domestic season had barely started. So the party was picked on the previous season's form and it included a fair number of experienced players, with four of them in their 30s and the captain, Clive Rice, aged 42. It was right to go for those of proven temperament and experience; the important thing was to represent South Africa in historic circumstances. We were due to play just three limited-overs games against India and I looked on it as a wonderful experience, with the actual cricket not the most vital part of the trip. India had turned out to be our first opponents because the visit by Pakistan had been cancelled and they needed some international cricket at short notice, but in any case, we had been led to believe that India would always have had first crack at us. Ali Bacher and the United Cricket Board had been very grateful to India for proposing us for re-entry at the ICC meeting, and so we were able to show our gratitude earlier than we had imagined.

Yet it was still an apprehensive touring party that landed at Calcutta Airport. It was the first time we had met on the cricket field and we didn't know how the public would react to us. Bacher was his usual optimistic, bubbling self and he was dead right. We were overwhelmed by our welcome. Garlanded by flowers, we were ushered into cars for a journey to our hotel that was supposed to take three-quarters of an hour. It took almost three hours. The Indian press estimated the crowd that cheered us along the way at 1.5 million. There were placards everywhere, announcing how welcome we were, endless garlands piling up around our shoulders, beaming smiles – it was an amazing, moving experience and it meant everything to us that we were so warmly accepted.

Emotions were still running high when we played our first game in Calcutta. The noise and atmosphere were something we'd never experienced. Before the start, we all walked out on to the field to acknowledge the crowd and we couldn't believe its size. The police estimated the crowd at around 96,000 while other local experts put it at 100,000. It doesn't matter.

The occasion and the atmosphere will never be forgotten by any of the South African party. What a way to return to international cricket! I'm sure the circumstances had something to do with the rash shot played by Andrew Hudson as soon as we started batting, and we had to rely on the experience of Kepler Wessels to get us to 170-odd all out. That was never going to be enough, even though the ball swung under the cloud cover for Allan Donald. We ended up losing by 3 wickets, but we weren't too downhearted. The occasion was more important than the result this time.

Before we left Calcutta, we had another memorable experience. We went to see Mother Theresa in her home near Calcutta's worst slums. The poverty was appalling and the saintly presence of Mother Theresa made a deep impression on all of us. The problems she had to deal with every day in those conditions certainly put all our trivial preoccupations into perspective. We used up a fair amount of camera and video film that day, and the same was true of our next port of call, the Taj Mahal in Agra.

To South Africans previously unwelcome in India, this was becoming an unforgettable visit and it was hard to concentrate on the cricket amid all the receptions and wonderful hospitality. It just proved how much our predecessors had missed because of the political structure laid down by previous governments. We felt truly honoured and grateful that the wheel had come full circle and we could now go out into the world, absorbing new cultures, making new friends.

We didn't play at all well in our second match, at Gwalior, where India mastered the slow pitch far better. When we batted, Jimmy Cook was out straight away and Kapil Dev and Prabhakar swung the ball impressively. Only Wessels showed up at all with the bat and as we came to the last match of the tour, I was a little concerned that we weren't doing ourselves justice. It came good, though, under lights in Delhi, in front of 75,000 spectators. They got nearly 300 in their 50 overs and before we went out to bat, I told the guys I was looking for a big improvement, that it was time we really showed India that we could play. All our batsmen played superbly and we ran out winners by 8 wickets, a fantastic performance when you consider we chased 288 and got them inside 47 overs. At last we had won an international match, and in exciting fashion in the unique floodlit atmosphere. I felt we had arrived at last, even if it was just one win in a limited-overs game. We had put a score on the board.

But as I said, cricket was incidental to those memorable eight days in India. We understood why it was one long round of garlands, firecrackers, press conferences, receptions, waving and smiling. I like to think we were good ambassadors for our country on that historic first tour. We certainly pleased our hosts by losing two of the three games! We did pick up some practical experience, though, which was vital with the World Cup in mind. Our fielding wasn't athletic enough, especially inside the circle, where so many runs can be given away in one-day cricket. Our running between the wickets needed to be a lot better, too, and the selectors had food for thought for the World Cup party. The Indian captain, Mohammed Azharuddin, said we should take a younger side to the Antipodes and when our selectors did just that, there was a storm of protest. Clive Rice, Peter Kirsten and Jimmy Cook were all left out, although Kirsten later got back in. This was a big story, because all three were major achievers in South African cricket over a long period – but that was probably the crucial point. I wasn't a selector, merely the cricket manager to the World Cup, but my reading of the decision was that we had struggled in the field in India and that the high-pressure games in the World Cup would expose a few of our creaking bones. Clive Rice called the decision 'idiotic', referring to a personality clash between him and the chairman of selectors, Peter van der Merwe, and the debate rumbled on for a long time. It has to be said that none of the three had been all that impressive, either in India or in our domestic cricket, but it was still a brave decision to dispense with such experience. I also felt sorry for them on a personal level, having got so near to appearing in the World Cup after all those years in the international wilderness.

In defence of the selectors, the guys who came in for those big names did really well in the World Cup, particularly Andrew Hudson, Hansie Cronje and Jonty Rhodes. I had a personal interest in Jonty, whom I had coached in Natal. Before the tournament started, I had said to the Natal guys, 'You watch, Jonty will do something unbelievable in the field in this tournament that'll win us a game,' and he justified my faith in him. He set the standard in the field and that athletic brilliance had a lot to do with us getting to the semi-finals.

I honestly wasn't surprised that we did so well. In our domestic cricket, we play two limited-overs competitions, and we had always been au fait with the special demands involved. We were bound to be competitive – it's in the South African sporting nature – but knowing how good you are is a different matter, and we were in the dark about that one. Our first game was against Australia and their press were at great pains to point out who were the reigning World Cup champions, what a brilliant side they had and how they were awash with batting talent. The game began dramatically when Geoff Marsh edged Allan Donald to our wicket-keeper, Dave Richardson. It was a big nick and Dave took the ball in front of first slip but somehow umpire Brian Aldridge gave him not out. Perhaps the crescendo of noise from the crowd drowned out the sound, but I was pleased that our boys kept cool at what seemed a poor decision. Marsh did us a favour by staying there, actually; he scratched around for a long time, using up valuable overs. We fielded brilliantly, getting two run-outs (the first in the competition for Rhodes) and we had to be pleased with an Australian score of 197 in 49 overs. We needed a good start, and Wessels and Hudson did us proud, putting on 70-odd for the first wicket. I was delighted with the maturity shown by Hudson. He had been picked ahead of Jimmy Cook, to general dismay in the press, and there was a lot of pressure on him as he walked out in a very tense atmosphere. It was an entirely new experience playing under lights in Australia, with their experienced team looking for the slightest sign of nerves, but it was soon clear that we were going to pass the first major test. Wessels and the restored Kirsten showed all their experience to guide us home by 9 wickets. You can't get a bigger victory than that in a one-day match, especially against the defending World Cup champions, and it was an emotional, excited dressing-room that welcomed back Kirsten and Wessels. That win was beyond our dreams, coming as it did in front of a packed Sydney Cricket Ground, with so many cheering South African supporters there. I caught sight of one banner that made me smile – 'South Africa World Champions, 1970-1992 (Unbeaten)' – and it was great to have Ali Bacher and Steve Tshwete there to share our joy. It was such an important win: it gave us great confidence to think we had beaten Australia fair and square in our first game.

So we were on a high when we flew into Auckland to play New Zealand. We should have known better. They beat us easily on a wicket that was like rolled mud, desperately slow and low. All credit, though, to the New Zealanders. It was a bold and imaginative move to open the bowling with the off-spinner, Dipak Patel, and we kept getting out against teasing bowling and good field placings by Martin Crowe. When they batted, chasing 191, Mark Greatbatch played a superb innings, chancing his arm. The ball flew all over the place as he hit over the top, pulled and cut us to ribbons. We lost by 7 wickets and that was a real downer. When we lost the next game – to Sri Lanka in Wellington – we were even more depressed. It was another slow wicket and we gambled by sending in Adrian Kuiper to open. We thought that the strongest hitter would be the best man for the slow pitch, but he and Wessels really struggled right from the start and a total of 195 wasn't enough. Although we had a squeak of a chance near the end of Sri Lanka's innings, their victory by 3 wickets flattered us. They deserved the win.

So we had some honest talking to do. It was gradually getting through to everyone that to do well at international level, you have to be at your best on all types of wicket and in all sorts of conditions: the quick, bouncy wickets in Perth, the slow mud heaps of New Zealand and under the Sydney lights. And that's just in the World Cup. Our next opponents were the West Indies and we simply had to beat them if we had any chance of qualifying for the semi-finals. That was a hell of a task. We had never played them before, but we knew they had been the best one-day side in the world for the past 15 years. OK, Viv Richards and Gordon Greenidge had just retired, but they still had Des Haynes, Richie Richardson, Curtly Ambrose, Malcolm Marshall and Brian Lara. We struggled to get to 200 after being put in, and although I thought that was at least 15 runs short, it had been a gutsy effort by the lower order to get us to the total. We knew that a super fielding performance would be needed and that's what we got. Brian Lara was brilliantly caught at cover point by Jonty Rhodes, then Meyrick Pringle swung the ball so well that he took 4 wickets for no runs in 11 balls! We bowled them out for 136 and the guys were still really fired up when they came off the field.

Beating the two favourites for the World Cup at the first time of asking was amazing, and the way that they had faced up to the extra challenge showed how much character they had. The disappointing feature so far was to lose to New Zealand and Sri Lanka, two sides which we ought to have beaten, if we had been at our best.

Our next game was against opponents we feared – Pakistan. They had great natural talent in batting and bowling and we knew that if it was their day, we could struggle. We also knew that they had a tendency to blow up under pressure, so it was case of maximum concentration and giving nothing away in the field. We won the game by 20 runs, but they were a little unlucky with the rain. Later in the tournament, we were to suffer from the rain regulation, but it seemed odd that when Pakistan lost 14 overs, their asking rate was reduced by only 18 runs. Yet even then, Imran Khan and Inzamam-ul-Haq gave us a fright and it took another brilliant run-out by Jonty Rhodes to seal the game for us. He launched himself at the stumps, knocking all three down to run out Inzamam, and the spectacular photograph of that incident went all over the world, demonstrating Jonty's superb athleticism. He also took a brilliant catch in the outfield. We needed that run-out and at the time, I smiled to myself as I remembered my forecast to the Natal guys that he would change the game with one piece of magic. That moment won us the match.

We built up our confidence even further with an efficient win over Zimbabwe, and with all three departments of our game coming together nicely, we fancied having a go at our next opponents, England, especially with Allan Lamb and Graham Gooch out with injuries. They had other injury problems – Chris Lewis couldn't bowl, Dermot Reeve only managed a couple of overs and Phil DeFreitas wasn't fully fit either. So they did very well to limit us to 236 after an opening stand of 150-odd by Wessels and Hudson. When the rain increased their target from 4.6 to 5.6 an over we had a chance, but Neil Fairbrother played magnificently and they beat us by 3 wickets. I was very impressed by England, and I thought they were the best side we had met so far. They had flexible all-rounders in Reeve, Hick, Lewis and Botham, they could all bat down to number 11, they used their spinners sensibly, and they had some top batsmen. Ian Botham, the great competitor, was desperate to win a World Cup-winner's medal after failing twice. All credit to England for beating us, because they showed real guts and team spirit to overcome their injuries and the revised run-rate after the rain. It was a very depressed South African dressing-room afterwards, though, because we knew that if we had won, we would definitely have been through to the semi-finals.

So our next match was the crunch. If we beat India we were through to the last four. Now fatigue was becoming a bit of a problem: the hectic itinerary, whizzing across two countries to play once every third day, meant it was one long round of airport, unpack, practice then play, pack, airport and so on. We were getting by on adrenaline, the thrill of being back in international cricket, but we needed this win to keep the momentum going. India were a dangerous side, especially in batting. The rain again caused problems, reducing the game to 30 overs a side, and I thought we did well to restrict guys like Kapil Dev, Srikkanth, Tendulkar and Azharuddin to 6 an over. We had to get a quick start in a reduced innings, so we sent Peter Kirsten in ahead of the more stolid Kepler Wessels and it worked. Kirsten played brilliantly but when he was out, we were left needing 14 off the last 2 overs. Jonty Rhodes, fast becoming the man for the occasion, hit a six with a big swing and Hansie Cronje won it with a four to mid-wicket in the final over. A great moment for our younger players in particular – Cronje and Rhodes were both raw and inexperienced. Reaching the semis surprised the cricket world and, to be honest, we surprised ourselves as well. Getting to the last four of the World Cup after 21 years in the wilderness was some achievement and we got there by commitment and devotion to the team rather than the kind of individual brilliance the other fancied sides could offer. There is nothing in sport like winning when you deserve it, and it was a memorable night's celebration in our dressing-room. That feeling of togetherness, pleasure in each other's success, is a terrific experience and we were proud for our country and ourselves. We also had a week ahead of us to prepare for the semi-final, so we could get off the rollercoaster of airports and grounds and settle into our hotel in Sydney, refreshed and ready for the big game. We didn't envy New Zealand and Pakistan having to play the other semi in Auckland because the wicket would be slow and the extra travelling would take its toll.

The record books will show that we lost to England by 19 runs but it was a good deal closer than it appeared. The rain which had hampered the tournament robbed us all of what would have been a very tight finish, and started a controversy that raged for days afterwards. We had 4 wickets in hand, needing 22 to win with 13 balls left when the umpires took the players off for rain. It was a little harsh to come off at that stage, because the rain always looks heavier in night cricket, illuminated by the floodlights. In fact it was only light drizzle that night in Sydney and both set of players would have carried on to get a natural finish. But off they came and out came the rule book. The rain had stopped and we were getting ready for a resumption when we were told that we'd have only 7 balls left to get the runs, not 13. There was another delay while the covers were removed and then the umpires ruled that only one ball was left in the match. The crowd were as baffled as most of us and they made their feelings known as Brian McMillan stroked a single and the players trooped off, very upset. I hate to think what would have happened if other more volatile teams had been in such a situation as the boos rang out. I felt sorry for the England boys: they had played well, and it wasn't their fault that victory had such a hollow ring. They came out to shake our hands, but none of them had the high spirits and pleasure you associate with such an important win. When I went into their dressing-room they were still very downcast, almost as if they had lost. They were embarrassed and frustrated that they hadn't won fair and square.

Basically the rules were tailored to fit into Australian television schedules and left little elbow room. Now, as a former employee of Kerry Packer, I'm bound to be a supporter of live TV coverage of the big cricket games, but I was surprised that the Aussie cricket board didn't think about allowing more flexibility for the biggest tournament in world cricket, transmitted to a domestic audience that loves live sport. I can't think many Aussies would have wanted the action to be finished bang on time, even if the home country wasn't involved. They are far more sensible in England, where the BBC takes account of the fact that in the final tense stages the overs are bowled slower than at the start of an innings. Cricket isn't something that can be covered with a slide-rule and pocket calculator. We didn't help ourselves, though. We took too long to bowl our overs, with an all-seam attack and leisurely walking back by our bowlers. We also bowled too many wides and no-balls, which prolonged our overs. So in the allotted time of three and a half hours, we bowled 45, rather than 50 overs. And Kepler Wessels knew he was taking a risk in deciding to field first after winning the toss. There were dark clouds around at the time and the forecast wasn't very good, but we were gambling on the ball moving about in the muggy atmosphere. It certainly did, and that contributed to the amount of wides we bowled. We could have bowled them out for 150 with a bit of luck and more discipline from our bowlers. The turning point came when Graeme Hick was very close to being lbw first ball, then he was caught at slip off a no-ball just afterwards. He went on to anchor the innings with 80-odd, with Dermot Reeve making valuable runs right at the end. But 253 was within our reach if we kept cool and got off to a reasonable start. Adrian Kuiper, who had disappointed in the series, came good at last with two massive sixes, but then he played a bad shot and got out. But everyone kept chipping in, and Jonty Rhodes in particular revelled in the tense atmosphere, turning ones into twos at the end, and we thought that we had a genuine chance on such a big ground where you could get a lot of twos. The odd boundary, pressure on the bowlers and we were home. But then it rained.

When it was all over, our players swallowed their disappointment and ran round the boundary edge, saluting the crowd. There was a lump in my throat, that's for sure, and I was proud at the dignified way we handled that huge anti-climax. The crowd obviously thought so, too, because we were given a tremendous reception. We knew how close we had come, but we couldn't blame the television executives entirely. We were at least partially guilty, so we just had to accept that the fates were against us. But we had gained enormously from that concentrated spell of pressure games in the past month. We may have lacked the talent of an Imran, a Botham or a Richards who wins a game on his own, but we had shown how much can be achieved by team spirit, dedication, and desire. I never had any doubts that that South African team would fight all the way and being underdogs at various times in the tournament suited us. We weren't at our best in the games we were expected to win, but when we were unfancied, we played very well, against England, Australia, the West Indies and the eventual winners, Pakistan. It's true that one-day cricket was our forte, though. How would we get on in a Test match?

We soon found out. A month after the World Cup, we were in Barbados, playing our first Test since 1970. It was an astonishing sequence of events, speeded up by full support from the politicians and the will of the cricket administrators to make it happen. None of us had been to the West Indies, a group of islands that had been implacably opposed to our country because of apartheid. I had played with and against many cricketers from the Caribbean and admired the way they played the game, and yet I hadn't dared allow myself to think that one day I could be there myself, watching South Africa playing cricket. But it came to pass and it was a remarkable experience. Everywhere we went we were overwhelmed by the hospitality and friendliness. The Prime Ministers of Barbados and Jamaica were at Bridgetown for the historic Test and whenever the political angle was brought up in the various press conferences, it was handled honestly. We were fortunate to have travelling with us Tebogo Mafole, the

ANC's chief representative at the United Nations in New York, and he was able to flesh out our conventional observations about apartheid and its evils. He pointed out that the tour was happening at the right time, and when he mentioned that Nelson Mandela was in full agreement, that seemed to impress the doubters and the conversation returned to cricket. We could also point to the support of Donald Woods, the veteran anti-apartheid campaigner whose escape to Britain and friendship with Steve Biko had been the subject of the film *Cry Freedom*. He had suffered more than many white men during the 1970s when he kept publishing newspaper articles criticising the National Party and in the end he had to flee to Britain. During the World Cup, Donald Woods had travelled with our team and he became a trusted friend to us all. He was with us when news came through from South Africa that almost 70 per cent of the electorate had voted for President de Klerk's reforms in the national referendum, an event of far greater significance than our excellent displays on the cricket field. To have the support of such a respected figure only increased our stature whenever doubters suggested we were lucky to be back. I didn't experience any doubts at first hand when we were in the West Indies – and I made a point of talking to the locals. Whenever I could, I'd get away from the ground and sit in a nearby bar, having a yarn with them about cricket and life. I encountered no resentment at all over South Africa's past sins and it was a lovely experience to have a beer with black people, talking sport and having a laugh. They certainly know their cricket out there and I was struck by the fact that they were grateful for new competition: they reckoned they were getting bored with beating England and Australia so often!

In fact, many Barbadians supported South Africa in that Test, because they were furious that the selectors hadn't picked Anderson Cummins, a local fast bowler. They were also annoyed that the Barbadian Desmond Haynes had been passed over for the captaincy in favour of Richie Richardson, an Antiguan. It meant that the daily attendance never rose above 3,000 in a stadium that's usually packed to the rafters, and on the final morning, there were only 500 there to see a remarkable finish.

It was too remarkable for my liking. We had the better of all four days, yet blew it on the final morning. We had needed just 201 for victory, and at the start of play on the fifth day, we wanted only 79, with 8 wickets in hand. To beat the West Indies on the ground where they had won the last ten Tests in a row on our return to Test cricket was something we could barely imagine – and I think that's what did for us. We knew how excited everyone was back home at the prospect of victory and the pressure just got to us. Even though the pitch was wearing and the bounce uneven, we had Wessels and Kirsten there at the start of play, having batted so well the night before. But Wessels went early and Courtney Walsh and Curtly Ambrose tightened their grip and went up a gear to finish us off. I knew Curtly from the previous year at Northampton and I was aware how dangerous he could be with that extra bounce, while Walsh kept hitting the bare spots, making the ball jag around, giving nothing away. It was high-class bowling, the genuine Test match stuff, and we threw it away. I was shattered at the end, as the West Indies boys went on a lap of honour while we slumped in dejection. We hadn't been positive enough on that final morning, with 8 wickets going for 25 in 20 overs. Someone ought to have taken a chance and tried to disrupt the bowler's line. Losing Wessels to a brilliant slip catch and seeing Kirsten chop on to his stumps was a double blow, but we lacked the temperament to battle back when it was still there for the taking. We had also let them back into the game during their second innings, when they rallied for 196 for 8 to 283 all out, with Jimmy Adams, playing in his first Test, holding the tail together. That at least gave the West Indies some hope, something to bowl at, but when we closed on 95 for 2, we had to be the favourites.

I mustn't be too hard on the lads, though. I think we were undone mainly through a lack of experience. We bowled too many loose deliveries when Adams was organising the resistance in their second innings and we ought to have been more positive on that final morning. But there were many plus points. Andrew Hudson showed he had the right mental approach for Test cricket in making 163 in nearly nine hours, the ideal effort from a Test opener. Allan Donald and Richard Snell lost little in comparison with the West Indies fast bowlers, and as usual we fielded superbly. It was a harsh introduction to the mental demands of Test cricket, the need to keep concentrating from session to session, not to relax when their number 11 walks to the wicket, to keep the opposition down when they're looking groggy. That would come with experience, the exposure to Test cricket. For the moment, that defeat in Barbados proved to be a bit of a blessing in disguise. After our marvellous effort in the World Cup, expectations were running rather too high back home. The press had got carried away as well; many of the writers didn't know much about what it takes to win Test matches and they seemed to think that the disciplines which made you a good one-day side were enough for the longer contest. We were all on a steep learning curve and maybe it was all to the good that the South African public eventually realised after Barbados that we weren't the best side in the world after all, not by a long chalk.

Our next round of international cricket showed that we had learned from that hectic first few months. India became the first country to visit us since our recall, something that had been a certainty since they had proposed us at the ICC meeting the previous year. Beating them 5-2 in the one-day matches and 1-0 in the Test series was a fine effort. By now I had been appointed national team manager, which meant I had to give up my job at Northampton. That was a pity because working in English county cricket is always a pleasure, not least of all because you can watch so many world-class players at close quarters – but you don't turn down the call from your country, especially at such an exciting stage in its international development. I was very encouraged by our fielding and bowling against India. They were one of the best batting sides in the world and I certainly didn't share Geoffrey Boycott's dismissive remark that they were the weakest side he'd seen in Test cricket for more than 20 years. I wasn't at all surprised when they went back home and walloped England 3-0 in the Test series, because their young spinners looked promising in South Africa, while their batting has a touch of genius about it. Perhaps South Africa played rather well, Geoffrey?

Although interest in our return to Test cricket at home was very high, the crowds for the series were disappointing. I don't think we marketed those matches well enough in the media and uninterrupted live television coverage, as well as poor weather, contributed to a disappointing total of 200,000 for the four Tests. I think also the South African public needed to be re-educated about the particular tempo and disciplines of Test cricket. We had seen how important it was to fight for every run in the Barbados Test and Kepler Wessels and I worked hard to impress on the guys that one bad session can lose a Test. In the end, the cricket was a little negative, I admit, and scoring on slow pitches was never all that fast. The only Test to yield a positive result was won at Port Elizabeth by Allan Donald's terrific fast bowling. He took 12 wickets in the match, swinging the ball at speed, and none of the Indian batsmen looked comfortable against him. In our first Test series, we had to be happy with victory, even though we were nowhere near as spectacular a side as in our last series in 1970. I was looking for increased concentration from our players, an awareness of Test cricket's mental demands, and if at times it wasn't riveting stuff, it was successful. Young batsmen like Jonty Rhodes, Daryll Cullinan, Hansie Cronje and Andrew Hudson all learned a great deal in that series, while Brian McMillan was looking a capable all-rounder. We were still struggling in the spin department, though, and India's Kumble and Raju outbowled us. But our fielding was absolutely superb and I believe that we were now the best fielding side in world cricket. The Indian batsmen just seemed to shrivel at the pressure exerted by our fielders and they never seemed to want to take quick singles.

There were other significant matters to consider from that series, though. Around 3 million rand was ploughed back into underprivileged cricket areas from the gates of the international matches. One of the beneficiaries of the grants was the Alexandra township, which was given an artificial strip. I hope that some of those cricket fans in the townships drew strength from the selection of Omar Henry for his first Test for South Africa, thus becoming the first non-white to be picked for a Test. It was a deserved call-up for the Cape coloured slow left-arm bowler who may not be a big spinner but flights the ball well. He was 18 when he watched us play in the Newlands Test in 1970. Omar grew up living in one room with six brothers and sisters and his parents. His hero was another Cape coloured, Basil D'Oliveira, who coached him at school. He played in the Lancashire League, then angered SACBOC's Hassan Howa by going to the Kingsmead ground in Durban to watch Natal play; he then refused to apologise for patronising what SACBOC deemed to be racialist cricket for the white man. He was banned from SACBOC games and received death threats but he stuck to his guns. After a time, people accepted that he was in Currie Cup teams on merit, not through tokenism, and from 1978 onwards he became a fixture, with Western Province, then Border and finally Orange Free State. We had taken Omar to the World Cup with us and he was picked to play Test cricket at Durban for his country because he was the spinner in form at the time, having taken 17 wickets in the three previous first-class games. He might even have played in Barbados six months earlier, but he was ill after playing in two of the three one-day internationals. A very fit man for someone coming up to 41, he was a very popular selection and it's difficult to imagine his emotions when you realise he'd watched Richards and

Pollock back in 1970, penned into the non-white section of the ground without any shade. Omar was a symbol of what could be achieved in the new South Africa, but no way was he in the team just so it would look good. Don't forget that at the end of the 1992-93 season he was named the Man of the Match in the Currie Cup final after guiding Orange Free State to their first title in the club's history.

For the Indians, that tour to South Africa was a gruelling one off the field, never mind in cricketing terms. We had been royally treated out there the year before, and now it was one long reciprocal whirl of garlands, kisses and motorcade tours through the Indian suburbs of our cities. India had been the first country to sever diplomatic relations with us in 1948 after the legalisation of apartheid and it was especially symbolic that they were now our first guests back in international cricket. The relationship between the players was excellent despite a couple of highly publicised spats on the field that came in the heat of the moment. You only had to see the easy leg-pulling and spontaneous laughter between the two sides at various receptions to appreciate what a power of good this tour was doing for multi-racialism.

The same applied when Pakistan and West Indies came over immediately afterwards to play a triangular series of exclusively one-day cricket. It meant that in the space of a few weeks, the three countries which had been most implacable to our readmission in the recent past had been welcome guests and happy visitors. Again the spirit between all three sides was excellent – as it had been in the World Cup – and the crowds flocked to see all ten games, even when South Africa weren't playing. West Indies won the tournament easily enough, with South Africa not even getting to the final. We fielded brilliantly throughout, our bowling was efficient enough, but our batsmen lagged behind the talented Pakistanis and West Indians because we never managed to accelerate quickly enough. Food for thought there, although I was pleased with the progress of young Daryll Cullinan in the middle order.

I was also aware that the South African public seemed more keen on the one-day game than the longer version. I've always believed that Test cricket is like chess, the most satisfying part of our game, but a whole generation had grown up loving the spectacle of flying stumps, spectacular fielding and huge sixes. When all that happened under the lights, it was an even better spectacle. It was also a great money-spinner and it was marketed very well indeed in South Africa. For the triangular games, we were getting crowds of 30,000 at the Wanderers for West Indies against Pakistan. We needed to broaden the appeal of Test cricket to an audience that had got used to the instant game, a brand of cricket that is definitely exciting and in which South Africa was very efficient. But I wanted us to be equally good at Test cricket, because that is where the real satisfaction lies. Good Test cricketers are usually good at the one-day game as well; we needed to be able to adapt naturally to whatever brand of cricket was being played on any day. A prolonged spell of Test victories would be a good start, that would get the crowds in. They're keen on winners in South Africa.

Having said that, I wonder if the South African sporting public realised what a great performance it was to beat Sri Lanka in their own backyard. Just a few months earlier, they had hammered England in the Test at Colombo and we had to go there and play three Tests in August-September, which is three-quarters of the way through our winter. What is more, it was the hottest place I've ever experienced for playing cricket and I was absolutely delighted that the hard work we'd put in during our time at the training camp paid off. It was very hard for our seam bowlers, who did most of the bowling. Brett Schultz in particular impressed with his left-arm pace. He'd come on in leaps and bounds, and he won the second Test for us in Colombo, whipping the ball across the right-hander, keeping our slips and wicket-keeper busy. Twenty wickets in three Tests was a great effort by Schultz and he was a fine support for Allan Donald in such intense heat and humidity. Our other young players acquitted themselves excellently,

Daryll Cullinan scoring a fluent maiden Test hundred, Andrew Hudson looking secure at the top of the order and Hansie Cronje showing great maturity at number 3. The most important innings in the series for us was played by Jonty Rhodes. Jonty had come in for a fair amount of criticism for the ungainly style of his batting, and some had hinted that he was simply the best fielder in the world who was a handy enough batsman, but not worth his place in the side for anything but his fielding. I was convinced that he had the right batting qualities to come through all that, and he showed his marvellous temperament when he scored his maiden Test hundred at Moratuwa. We had been set a victory target of 365 that was never on with the pitch taking spin. We were in trouble at 126 for 5, just after lunch, and Jonty needed to stay in to shield a tail that was rather long. There were 90 minutes left and we had just 3 wickets to fall when Jonty was joined by Clive Eksteen, who was playing his first Test. They stayed together for the rest of the day and Clive made just 4 in that time. Jonty got to his hundred just before the close and everyone agreed it was a top effort. And it was an authentic Test match battle, with men crowding around the bat, the spinners wheeling away and a good defensive technique needed. Fans of the instant one-day game might have been bored but I loved it. Just a year earlier, we had folded up in Barbados when the pressure was on. Five of that side were on duty in Moratuwa and they showed that lessons were being learned. There are times when you just have to tough it out in the middle and make it difficult for the opposition to prise you out.

We drew the one-day series 1-1 and so we had to be very happy with that short tour of Sri Lanka. We'd been told that the ball would turn a lot and I remembered how uncomfortable several English batsmen had looked a few months earlier. So I was very encouraged at the way our young batsmen put the time in out in the middle, trying to work out the spinners. There's simply no substitute for that kind of practical experience, and when you consider that we don't have a great deal of decent spin in our current first-class scene, it's no wonder that this generation of South African batsmen might have been vulnerable against spin.

With our tour to Australia coming up, we knew that a major contest would be between our batsmen and Tim May and, in particular, Shane Warne. I had seen enough of them in the summer's Ashes series to know just how good a bowler Warne had become: you don't see great players of spin like Mike Gatting and Graham Gooch getting bowled unless that spinner is a bit special. So those hours spent battling away against the Sri Lankan spinners would be very worthwhile when we faced the Australians. Different conditions and a different type of bowler, I agree, but there is no substitute for experience, and you don't get that in the nets. The nine Tests played against Sri Lanka and Australia over the next six months were a valuable lesson in playing the spinners.

So in our first 18 months of Test cricket the learning curve had been steep, but we were getting to grips with Test cricket's special demands. Out of eight Tests, we had lost just one – and we ought to have beaten West Indies – and won two. The only two series to be played had gone to us, but the major challenges lay ahead.

Two back-to-back series against the Australians would test our mettle, especially after they had hammered England. With the West Indies in a transitional period after the retirement of so many great players and the Pakistanis under a bit of a cloud, there was a case for saying that the Australians were the strongest current Test team. They had great batting depth, with so many exciting young players and quite a few others unable to force their way in. Their bowling contained two match-winners in Craig McDermott and Shane Warne. Above all, they approached Test cricket in the way I respected: tough, giving nothing away, always fighting to stay in the game.

When I played for South Africa, victories against the Aussies were always very enjoyable because we had similar attitudes to the way the game should be played. I was going to be very interested to see over the next few months just how far we'd progressed. If we could beat the Aussies, then we could say we were on the move.

THE FUTURE FOR SOUTH AFRICAN CRICKET

One of the first things any prominent South African cricketer is asked these days is: 'When will we get a black man playing for South Africa?' It's a measure of how far we've come that the question can be posed. It was never asked when I played Test cricket. The short answer is some day, but not soon. Within ten years, certainly. You can't rush these things, or make them happen. It has to be a natural process, so that the player knows he's in on merit and everyone accepts the situation. It would be awful if that player felt he was being patronised, patted on the head for doing well. That sort of attitude devalues our desire for multi-racial cricket and selection purely on merit, and if that player failed, you'd get the inevitable hard-liner saying, 'I told you so, they're not up to it.' The black players are no different from any other group when it comes to the desire to feel comfortable in a dressing-room, secure in the knowledge that you're in the side because you're up to the job – not because it looks good, or because it helps post-apartheid South Africa to ease its conscience for all that's gone before.

I put a ten-year span on the matter because the development programme needs time. Its aims need to seep through all sections of society, so that everyone realises that youngsters of all races start out with an equal chance of representing South Africa. After that, it's a matter of opportunity, desire and luck. In relation to the black players, I realise that opportunity is the most vital consideration. Facilities must be improved, particularly for net practice, before you can rely on a consistent flow of good players into provincial sides like you can with white youngsters coming out of our best schools. We need to build on the great work of dedicated men like John Passmore, who died just a few months before a significant milestone in the development of black young cricketers. During the Nuffield Week of 1992, when the best schoolboy cricketers in the country showed their quality, three black lads were picked for the South African Schools XI against the senior Western Transvaal side. One of them, an off-spinner called Morgan Mfobo, was a player at the Langa Club near Cape Town, and all he could say when he knew he'd been picked was 'John Passmore'.

So Ali Bacher's development programme remains the key to any desire that our national side should eventually reflect more accurately the make-up of our population. If only cricket could become the national game of South Africa, the black youngsters would roll off the production line. It's happening, certainly; after our successful World Cup, kids in the street were impersonating the white players, Jonty Rhodes becoming a particular hero because of his flamboyant fielding. The more success we get in the national team, the more we'll influence the young through the medium of television. At the moment, though, there's no denying that soccer is still the favourite sport of the blacks. The national football team is dominated by blacks, there are 1 million registered black players in the various leagues, and you regularly get crowds of 50,000 for the big club matches. When Arsenal played in Johannesburg in 1993, 60,000 came to see them and a few days earlier, 1,000 fans welcomed Manchester United when they flew in. The best English games are featured live on South African television and the explosive nature of football seems to appeal to black sports fans. Cricket is a longer, more thoughtful game in which concentration is an important element and natural athleticism doesn't automatically mean you'll be a good player. So cricket needs to teach black youngsters more than just how to hold a bat, it has to instil the necessary mental disciplines.

That's why the development programme is vital. A percentage of gate receipts and money from future tours is now earmarked by the United Cricket Board of South Africa for that purpose. That's why the former West Indian Conrad Hunte agreed to come over to help in the scheme. Conrad is one of many highly qualified coaches who will select every year 50 underprivileged youngsters who have the most potential. They will be awarded bursaries to the best schools in South Africa, where they'll enjoy excellent facilities as well as a good education. It's only a drop in the ocean, I agree, but it's a start. Until as many underprivileged people as possible get equality of opportunity, there will remain a vast, untapped area of cricket potential. We need to consistently penetrate that area, not just to nurture the players but also to reassure parents that cricket is no longer just the white man's game, it's there for all South Africans. In our isolation period, most of us bemoaned our luck at some stage, complaining that we had been denied the chance of staying on top of the world cricket ladder by the politicians. I hope that frustration was understandable, but let's get one thing straight – it was a white South African's complaint. The black player wasn't part of that equation, he had always been isolated. Only Basil D'Oliveira among non-whites managed to break through, and that was because he went to England at an advanced age to see if he could make it. It's all very well to feel sorry for Richards, Pollock and the rest, but what about the non-white players? They wouldn't have been picked for their country if we'd stayed in the international arena, so spare a thought for them. When you see the amount of natural talent in township cricket, you realise sadly how much waste there was before the township scheme started in 1986. It took isolation to make us understand what had to be done, so it's understandable that years of mistrust and bitterness have to be considered now that genuine efforts are being made to absorb cricket into underprivileged areas. All of this takes time, you can't suddenly propel a black player into the Test team because of a favourable result in the 1992 referendum, or the staging of our first democratic general election. You're dealing with impressions, images, folk tales and experiences that have grown up through the decades, handed down through families. It's not enough for white cricket administrators to say 'trust me' and assume that everything will be fine.

Black kids need to come to the Tests in greater numbers, to experience the thrill of seeing top players in the flesh, something that television only hints at. There's nothing like sitting on the boundary's edge, watching someone like Jonty Rhodes hurling himself around, stopping the ball, then throwing it back in the same movement, or seeing Allan Donald uproot the stumps with a fast delivery. When you see it at first hand, it's inspiring – and I speak as someone who felt that way in the 1950s and early '60s when I watched Test cricket. The desire must be there in a black kid who wants to play top-class cricket; unfortunately, he often doesn't get the chance when he leaves school, because the job situation is so desperate and he has to go wherever there's work. That was the fate of many of the best non-white players who came through in the early years of normalisation in the late 1970s – guys like Edward Habane couldn't afford to play cricket for long periods despite great natural talent. It's been suggested that the best players would benefit from having something like the Cricket Academy which Australia runs under the supervision of Rodney Marsh. Already Michael Slater and Shane Warne have graduated from the Academy, but they were in their late teens when they enrolled, learning about the disciplines of cricket, its history, the way to deal with the media and all the other aspects of the modern game. They had been picked out, along with the other students, because they needed a little fine tuning; they were already class performers, with a solid record of achievement behind them. The Academy was there to refine their techniques and mental attitudes, not show them how to bowl the leg-cutter. I think that in South Africa the need isn't for a finishing school for the élite teenager, it's to catch the underprivileged when they are very young. Dedicated coaches are needed in great numbers, so are improved facilities. Until that becomes a fact, there's still inequality with the white schoolboys favoured. Look at the experience of Herschelle Gibbs. He is a very talented young black batsman who has played first-class cricket for Western Province, and he was included in the South African Schools side in the 1992 Nuffield Week. But he didn't come through the development programme system – he was lucky enough to be educated at the Diocesan College in Cape Town, one of the best private schools in the country. When you are equipped with the necessary talent, and then get the chance to fine-tune that talent in an environment that caters for your every cricketing need, then you are well on the way.

I can speak from experience about the good fortune to be coached at an excellent school. At Hilton College, I lacked for nothing in my sporting facilities. The practice wickets were superb, we were taught discipline early on and the coaching we received was tremendous, and all that undoubtedly helped my development. It was the same for Allan Lamb, who went straight into the Western Province team from playing for South African Schools. Barry Richards was equally fortunate at Durban High School. The Nuffield Week has been a fantastic breeding-ground for most of South Africa's top cricketers since Lord Nuffield, an English businessman, made a grant to the South African Cricket Association after the England tour in 1939. The idea of bringing together the best schoolboy cricketers in an annual tournament, in the hope that the standard of our cricket would be raised in the intense competition, has certainly been proven, and the best schools in the country turned out an array of talent that hasn't decreased. Among recent South African Test players, the likes of Allan Donald, Hansie Cronje, Jonty Rhodes, Mark Rushmere, Daryll Cullinan and Richard

Snell have played in the Nuffield Week. I can only think of Jimmy Cook, Dave Richardson and Brian McMillan who haven't come through that system, yet have managed to play for South Africa recently. The discipline at the top schools is very strong: if you don't turn up on time for nets, or lark around at practice, then you don't play, simple as that. The wickets are very good, the coaching thorough and you are instilled with a will to win at a very early age. In other words, you get a very good start to a cricket career if you have the ability and the good fortune to be at a good school. It's not quite the same in the townships!

The talented township player needs a lot of luck if he graduates to better things. It also helps if cricket is in his family. Take Kenneth Mahuwa, a promising all-rounder who played for Western Province after touring the West Indies with the Under-19 development team. He comes from Kwazakele, a township near Port Elizabeth, and he started with mini-cricket, then played for his club's under-16 team when he was only 12. But he was lucky in that his natural ability was spotted by his father, who was a groundsman at the Eastern Province cricket ground. He instilled a love of the game into Kenneth, and though he is now dead, his widow is equally proud of their son. Geoffrey Toyana, who captained a Transvaal XI against England 'A' in 1993, owes his progression not just to the development programme in the Alexandra township, but also to his father's keenness and desire to see his son realise his potential as a batsman. Another Alexandra boy, Walter Masemola, has the potential to be a fast bowler of first-class standard, as he showed against the England 'A' tourists. He needed an interpreter when he first started playing cricket with white boys. If his mother hadn't nagged away at him, telling him he could make the grade, Walter admits he would have been dragged into crime, because there was little else that appealed.

So it's unfair to put too much pressure on youngsters like Walter Masemola and Geoffrey Toyana. They should be left alone to hone their skills, develop concentration, mental hardness and all the other aspects that make you good enough to play Test cricket. If too many start building them up into potential Test players, they will be under enormous pressure from their own black communities to produce the goods. They'll feel the burden of all those great expectations and possibly fail to realise their potential. Let them progress in their own time – naturally, just like the best white cricketers. If they prove themselves to be good enough for South Africa in Test cricket, then they'll be picked.

The growing involvement among black players isn't the only example of South African cricket broadening its base. The Afrikaner is also coming to cricket in a big way. That is a major change in attitude since I first played for South Africa in 1967. Only Peter Heine and Peter van der Merwe among the Test players of that era was an Afrikaner and in 1970, our last series before being banned, all 15 players used were English-speaking. Now the current Test squad contains four who speak Afrikaans as their first language – Allan Donald, Kepler Wessels, Hansie Cronje and Fanie de Villiers. But previously, the Afrikaner viewed cricket as the game brought to our country by British colonials, and with old memories of the Boer War taking a long time to fade away, many didn't want to know about cricket. Afrikaner schools played rugby in the winter and athletics was the main summer sport. When South Africa became a top Test team towards the end of the 1960s the Afrikaners became more interested because they love to see our country as a winner. With the government at the time full of Afrikaners, there was a feeling that cricket was now acceptable because sporting success somehow symbolised the efficiency of a political philosophy that was unpopular in many parts of the world. When we were banned, many Afrikaner schools started to play cricket. Grey College in Bloemfontein was particularly efficient in establishing excellent cricket facilities, with Kepler Wessels and Corrie van Zyl illustrious pupils. Eventually, Grey College was responsible for many Orange Free State players, and the fortunes of the province have been transformed in recent years. Free State won the Castle Currie Cup for the first time in 1993, and there is an encouraging number of non-white players coming through their youth system. When you consider that Omar Henry plays for Free State and that the West Indian Franklyn Stephenson captained them, with Hansie Cronje away on Test duty in Australia, then the progress towards multi-racial cricket in what used to be the heartland of the Afrikaner is remarkable. It just shows how much cricket has advanced in recent years in South Africa. Television has also helped the keen Afrikaner cricketer, with commentaries in the language alternating with other tongues every half an hour. The Afrikaner sportsman brings a fantastic pride and passion to his game – a bit like the Welsh with their commitment to rugby – and that was only too obvious in the way that Fanie de Villiers kept going in sapping heat to win us the Sydney Test against all odds. He just wouldn't give in, and that inspired the other guys. You need that pride in your country to give yourself the best chance in a Test match.

Mind you, the Afrikaans language can be a bit of a problem – things do get lost in translation sometimes. On our tour to Sri Lanka in 1993, Fanie de Villiers was his usual sociable self, getting on well with everyone and enjoying all the sightseeing. A man who plays hard and still enjoys life, he's a great tourist. One day, though, he got himself in trouble with me. We had arranged a compulsory practice session just before the last Test, and this was after some of the guys had taken part in an optional session the day before. We were due to leave the hotel at 8.30 to get the compulsory practice out of the way before the heat got too unpleasant. Only one man was missing when everyone gathered at the hotel reception – Fanie de Villiers. Our physio told me that Fanie had sent word that he was staying in bed. He wouldn't get up for anyone, so we went on to the ground and our tour manager returned to the hotel to drag Fanie along. Kepler Wessels and I discussed whether to fine him, drop him or even send him home, because we took his offence very seriously. If one drops out, that is useless for team morale and we were angry, especially as Fanie had worked so hard the day before in the optional session. But when he came to the ground, ready to face the music, he completely floored us when he said: 'What's the problem? Yesterday was optional, so I thought it was OK to stay in bed today, because I didn't need to come.' He was totally genuine about it, and we had to point out what 'optional' and 'compulsory' really meant!

The growth in interest among the Afrikaners and the black population is one good reason why we can be optimistic about South Africa's prospects. So is the continuing support among the coloureds, who have thrown up quality players for many years. The schools system will continue to provide class cricketers, and the natural advantage of our climate will always help the development of young cricketers: it's much easier to coach when the sun is shining and you're not spending the day ducking the showers. The intensity of delight at our World Cup success, then our victory in the Sydney Test early in 1994 brought home to us how hungry our country is for sporting glory. On each occasion, we were in Australia, but the amount of phone calls, faxes and telegrams we received was incredible. Heaven knows what it would have been like if we had beaten West Indies in Barbados in April, 1992! The live television coverage is now comprehensive in South Africa, and now that it's dawned on the media that we can't be expected to win every Test, I can honestly say that our cricket writers and commentators do a good job for the game.

The domestic structure has also brought us in line with the demands expected of international cricket. Four-day matches on good wickets are as near as you will get to what is expected in a Test match, and are a far better guide to the right qualities than the three-day games we used to have on 'result' pitches. For the 1993-94 season, our administrators gave the players a maximum of 32 days of first-class cricket, compared to 24 the previous season, by promoting Boland to the Castle Currie

Above The ICC meeting at Lord's in 1991 was followed by a press conference in the Long Room. Behind the microphones were (l to r) Steve Tshwete, Geoff Dakin, Krish Mackerdhuj and Ali Bacher. **Below** The return to international cricket – Ali Bacher, Clive Rice and Mike Procter in Calcutta.

Facing page An emotional moment for South African cricket as Clive Rice and Mohammed Azharuddin shake hands before the one-day game in Calcutta.
Above Ali Bacher looks on as Steve Tshwete greets Mike Gatting, when the two met during the World Cup in Australia in 1992.
Below Anxious moments for Kepler Wessels, Mike Procter and the South African party during the World Cup semi-final against England.

Above The two teams line up for the photographers before the first-ever Test between the West Indies and South Africa in Barbados in April 1992.
Right The two captains, Richie Richardson and Kepler Wessels, get the proceedings under way.
Below Mike Procter and Curtly Ambrose, after Curtly had the spoilt the party for South Africa with a devastating spell on the final morning.

Cricket and politics reconciled **Above** Nelson Mandela with Colin Cowdrey, Krish Mackerdhuj and Ali Bacher at the Durban Test against India in 1992, the first Test on South African soil for 22 years.
Below President F.W. de Klerk meets Australian captain Allan Border during the Johannesburg Test in March 1994.

Above Allan Donald (left) and Fanie de Villiers make similar enquiries during the final Test against Australia at Durban in March 1994.
Right Runs off the Australians for Daryll Cullinan at Sydney and Jonty Rhodes (below) at Durban
Facing page Hansie Cronje sports the insignia of the United Cricket Board of South Africa.

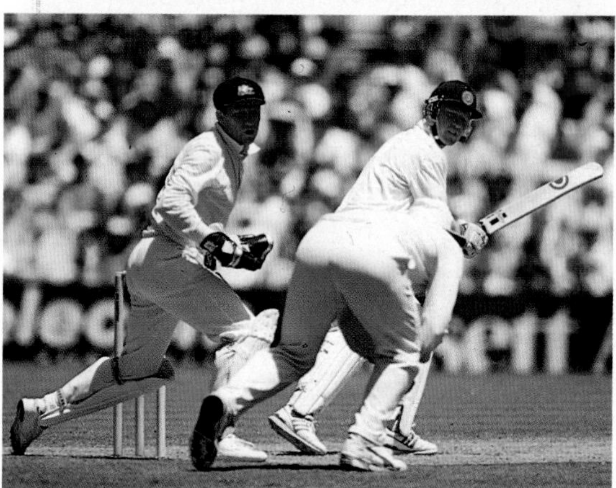

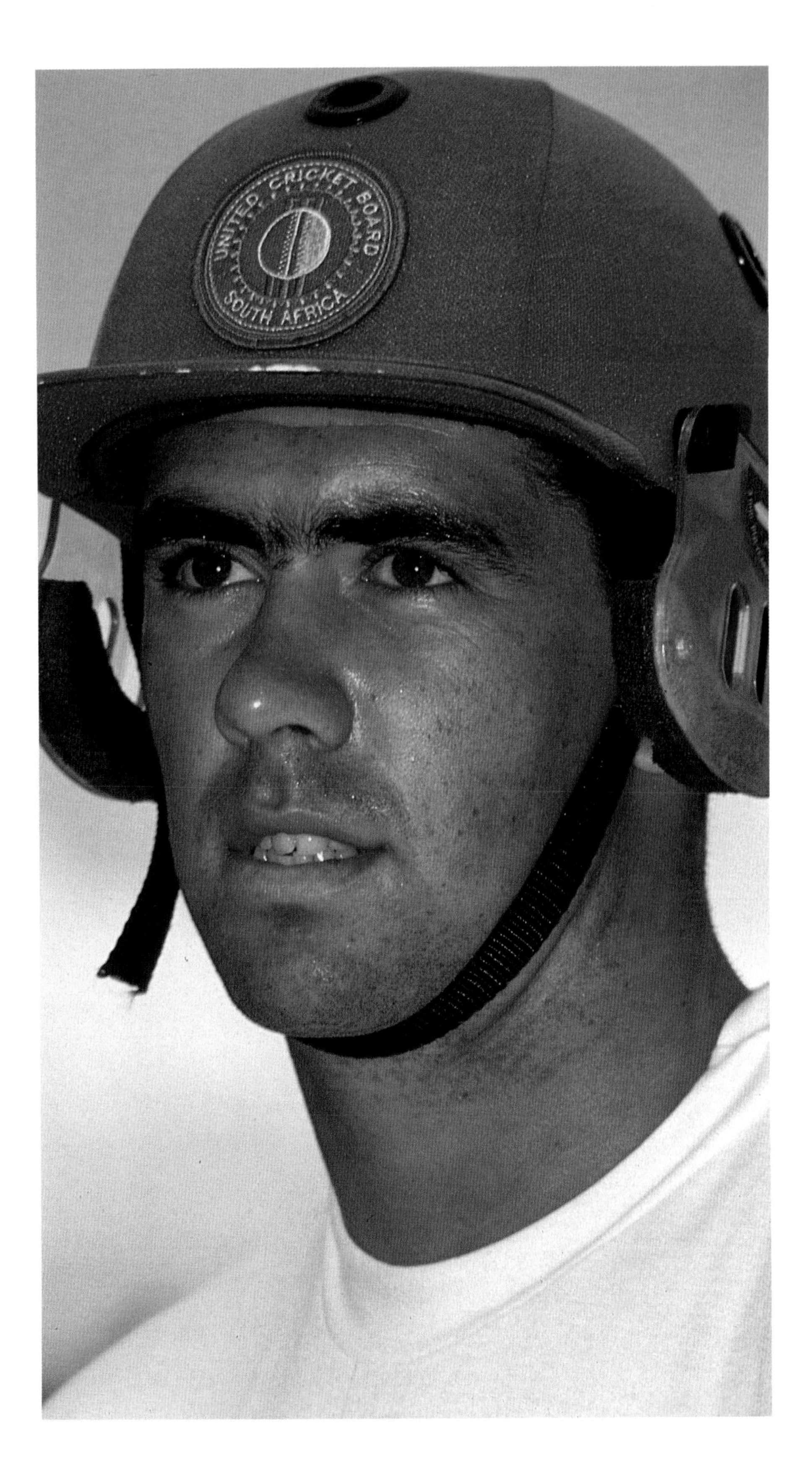
UNITED CRICKET BOARD
SOUTH AFRICA

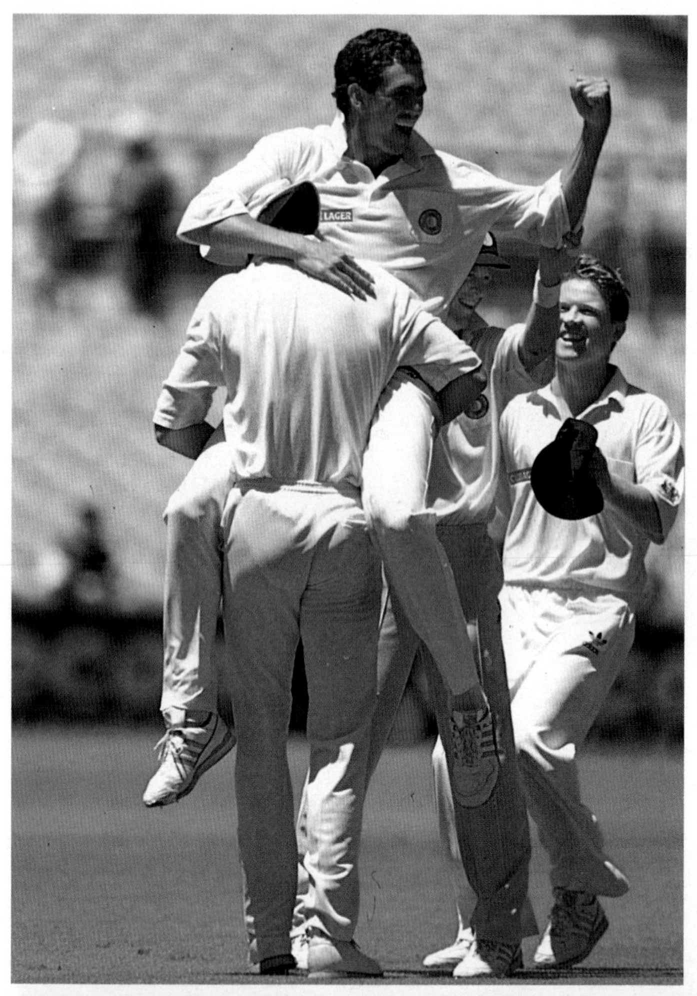

Moments of victory. Two memorable wins against Australia in 1994 : Sydney (left) and Johannesburg (below).

Cup League and ensuring that every province would play a four-day game against either England 'A' or the Australians. The daytime limited-overs competition was shelved for the season and the night-time Benson & Hedges series was extended from 45 to 50 overs, with unrestricted run-ups for bowlers, to mirror what goes in international cricket. On paper at least, the competitive standard ought to be high in our domestic cricket because so many West Indian players were being signed up. Malcolm Marshall, Franklyn Stephenson, Ottis Gibson, Carlisle Best, Eldine Baptiste and Clayton Lambert were all involved in the 1993-94 season in South Africa and exposure to those guys must have done some of our players a power of good in their continuing cricket education. Added to that, we seem to have gathered a healthy crop of young fast bowlers to coincide with our return to Test cricket. Hostile fast bowling remains the most common method of dismissing a Test team twice in a match and I had to be happy with a list headed by Allan Donald, Brett Schultz, Stephen Jack, Tertius Bosch, Richard Snell and Fanie de Villiers. It was probably our best group of young fast bowlers for 15 years and the prospect of seeing them firing on all cylinders was very exciting.

Everything seems in place for South Africa to rise up the international ladder, but we need more flair to keep attracting the public. I don't think we have a great deal of depth to our pool of Test-class players. I look at Australia and wonder what I'd give for someone like Dean Jones, Matthew Hayden or Damien Martyn, none of whom have nailed down a regular place in the Test team in the past year. We haven't anyone of their class available. Our spinners won't trouble many top batsmen on good Test wickets and the scarcity of class spin bowling in South Africa means that our batsmen lack much practical experience when they come up against a Shane Warne or a Phil Tufnell. I was disturbed at the success of the England 'A' team on their tour of South Africa. At the time we were touring Australia with the senior party, but I looked closely at the scores and talked regularly to

Ali Bacher back home. England lost only one game on the tour and we should have pushed them harder than that. It was a great chance for those left behind on the fringes of international selection to perform, to make the selectors notice them, with the tour to England and the Australian visit in mind. We seem to be short of batsmen in their mid-20s who want to push open the door. When Kepler Wessels was injured in Australia and returned home, the replacement was 38-year-old Peter Kirsten because he was still a class player and, in the absence of any close rivals, the best man for the job. He also played in the return series in South Africa. Clive Rice scored a hundred for Natal in the Castle Currie Cup – and he's 44! I looked at the South Africa side that played England 'A' in the unofficial 'Test' and noticed that Jimmy Cook (aged 40) and Adrian Kuiper (34) were in the middle order: where were the young batsmen demanding selection because of consistency and talent? It looks as if Daryll Cullinan might be the only young batsman to have blossomed into a Test player in the last year or so. But he was a disappointment in the Test series in Australia and as yet, he's certainly no Tendulkar or Lara or Slater, even though he has the same natural ability.

The strength of our schools cricket might be a factor here. I know that sounds contradictory, given the excellence of our coaching and facilities at so many schools, but I think our best young players don't get into first-class cricket as quickly as they should. Guys like Graeme Pollock, Daryll Cullinan and Peter Kirsten are an exception, having played in the Currie Cup when they were 16 or 17, but that's not unusual in Pakistan, India or the West Indies. In grade cricket in Australia, it's common to come up against current Test players. I remember Kim Hughes telling me that at 16 he played against Dennis Lillee, and that kind of experience is very valuable. In South Africa, the talented schoolboy gets locked into the schools network of under-13s, under-15s and under-19s and I think that hinders them. They may be outstanding in their age group, but by the time they're 19, having left school for work or university, many of them haven't cut their teeth in adult cricket against players of first-class experience. In other parts of the world, youngsters are thrown in at the deep end in good quality club cricket, but our schools structure, culminating in the Nuffield Week, is so good that perhaps many of the best youngsters settle for doing well in that. Then they are exposed when they leave school. That's why you don't have someone as young as Sachin Tendulkar or Inzamam-ul-Haq playing Test cricket for South Africa.

I suppose one-day cricket also has to bear some responsibility. Now I don't want to decry the one-day game, not only because I loved playing it myself, but also because it is a tremendous spectacle in a place like South Africa, where the climate is ideally suited to it, especially at night-time. You can go to the beach during the day, wander into the cricket as it gets darker, get the barbecue organised, and watch exciting action with a definite result under the lights on a lovely, balmy evening. It's a social occasion and terrific fun. We played night cricket in South Africa before it was tried by Kerry Packer in Australia and within a few years, all our major grounds had facilities for floodlit cricket. Traditionalists saw it as 'gimmick cricket' but I won't dismiss it, because it increased the base of support for the game. It helped raise the standard of our fielding, brought in a lot of money, which helped the township programme, and gave us some much-needed excitement during the depressing period when we looked like being out of official international cricket for a very long time. Yet there was too much one-day cricket, whether day or night, at the expense of the longer game. There was a danger that our standards would be lowered, particularly in batting, as improvised shots with an angled bat replaced the full face of the bat, and there was a lack of mental discipline to occupy the crease all day. The debate over the influence on technical standards has raged for years in England and I can see both sides, but there's no doubt that the ability to build an innings has been eroded by the popularity of one-day cricket in South Africa. That's why it was important to introduce four-day cricket into our domestic structure, but it'll take some time before I can say that it is proving to be a satisfactory breeding-ground for the ultimate in cricket, a Test match.

The wickets aren't helping batsmen either. There was a lot of criticism of the slow scoring in the series against India, where the average rate was 2 runs an over, and I understand the England 'A' tourists were very unimpressed by the turgid wickets and low bounce when they toured South Africa. When we then played three Tests here against the Aussies, it was the same story. But I think it's a worldwide problem. I was surprised at the slowness of the pitches when we toured the West Indies, and during the World Cup most were very disappointing, especially in New Zealand. Having toured Australia again, for the Test series, I would say that only Perth comes up to scratch in terms of even, lively bounce. Perth is the fastest wicket we've encountered so far in world cricket and I wish there were more of them, especially in South Africa. The extra bounce helps bowlers and batsmen alike, but if the pitch rolls out slow and low, the cricket will almost certainly be dull. I have no idea why pitches throughout the world seem to be slowing up, especially when you consider the scientific strides that are being made in all other areas of society. Why can't some expert come up with a treatment that'll give us better wickets? During World Series Cricket, the head groundsman, John Maley, produced some fantastic pitches which helped the matches as a spectacle. If he could manage that at short notice, why can't the groundsmen employed at the major Test grounds? I think Harry Brind at the Oval had the right idea when he dug up several wickets every year. He reckoned that wickets are like people – they get old and tired out – so he decided on radical surgery. As a result the Oval pitches are now the truest and fastest on the England Test circuit and you usually get an excellent game there.

So at the moment, South African cricket isn't really utilising the talent that exists. It was inevitable that during the isolation years there would be some deterioration in standards and the depth of ability, and no one should believe that the magic wand will wave all that away overnight now that we're back in the frame. We desperately need class players at number 4 or 5 in the order, guys who can play either game – attacking safely or blocking it out with good technique to avoid defeat. I'm sure we'll find those players again, but for the moment I try to ensure that we make everything count on the field, that we give our all to the cause. I know Graham Gooch and Micky Stewart were heavily criticised by the English press for being over-keen on physical fitness, but I think they were right. Under Gooch and Stewart, their great players like Botham, Lamb and Gower were in decline and so they needed to paper over the cracks by insisting on hard work, fitness and dedication to make them difficult to beat. That's the way I see it for South Africa in this transitional period, as we try to pick up the feel of Test cricket after so many years out of it. It's like a game of chess where, if you're outwitted, you can easily lose the game in one session and spend the rest of the time trying to claw your way back. The one-day game is so instant that players tend to react spontaneously. Any side can win a one-day game, whereas the best team usually wins the Test and the series. We do think about the opposition – we watched hours of Shane Warne on video before we first faced him – but I tend to concentrate on our own assets so that we can do our job properly. Self-belief, concentration, awareness of your team-mates: these are the qualities I look for at the moment. My ambition is to have all 11 guys concentrating 100 per cent of the time when they're out on the field, but I know that'll never happen, because I'm dealing with human beings.

Test cricket in the modern era is very hard. On our tour to Australia, the pressure was immense on and off the field; the Aussies were a battle-hardened outfit, who were clearly going to give us nothing and grind us to defeat if they saw the glimmer of a chance, so we had to make everything count. Physically it was also very demanding - we made 38 flights on the tour. So I think we deserve enormous credit for drawing that series and also the return one back in South Africa. When Shane Warne and Merv Hughes were fined and condemned for some over-the-top behaviour in that first Test at Johannesburg, many commentators missed the most significant point to those controversies - the Aussies were rattled. They had lost that crucial first Test, and they were under great pressure, much more than England had exerted in the recent Ashes series. Fair play to the Aussies, they did well to come back and draw the series, beating us in Cape Town and batting out the final day in Durban, but we pushed them all the way. They looked physically drained at the end of that series and their captain Allan Border was good enought to pay tribute to the guts we had shown out on the field. We proved that we were the best fielding side in the world, while young batsmen like Rhodes, Cronje and Hudson enhanced their reputation. Our wicket-keeper, Dave Richardson impressed Border. I think Dave is now as good as any 'keeper in world cricket, he never seems to miss a beat and, although he's not flashy, he is very reliable. As a batsman he is invaluable coming in at number 8 - as good a player as Ian Healy in Tests, although he lacks Healy's flair in the one-day games. Border also agreed that our pace quartet of Allan Donald, Craig Matthews, Fanie de Villiers and Brian McMillan was as good as any on the Test scene. I was pleased with that, because even though Donald in particular ended up exhuasted, they all kept going, showing dedication and professionalism.

That is the key to our cricket at the moment: one hundred per cent commitment. Someone like Darryl Cullinan is very important to South African cricket because he has so much flair, but until we see that consistently at the top level, we have to rely on everyone pulling together and giving their all. That's why our performances against Australia were so encouraging. On paper their first six batsmen had more talent and experience, but that's not always as decisive as people think. The right attitude is now so vital in Test cricket.

On our tour of Australia, we had several valuable sessions with Alan Jones, the former coach of the Wallabies rugby team, and he was fascinating on the psychology of sport. We went to his house and he talked pure common sense about the need for positive thinking, the value of forgetting a previous error, the need to concentrate on the next ball, the necessity for a game plan, rather than just trusting to inspiration and luck. So much of it was blindingly obvious but he was a great help. I find South African sportsmen are quite open-minded about psychology in sport, compared to England, where many of the players dismiss it as mumbo-jumbo. We tend to believe that you can actually make things happen, impose yourselves on opposition that may be more talented, but less resilient. You must have a plan, though, and I drum into our bowlers the old-fashioned virtues of line and length. That doesn't necessarily apply to our fastest bowler, Allan Donald, because I am well aware that genuine speed leaves a fair margin for error. The fast-medium bowlers are constantly told that giving a Test batsman room to cut, pull or drive is a cardinal sin. Give them nothing to hit: if they miss the ball, you hit the stumps. The 'corridor of uncertainty' was a phrase that haunted Micky Stewart when he was England's cricket manager, but he was right to stress the point. In the absence of raw speed, you look to bowlers like Angus Fraser and Terry Alderman to frustrate the batsmen and induce a mistake in them. That philosophy worked a treat against the Indians when they came to South Africa in 1992-93, and I was delighted that their strong batting line-up never reached 300 in any innings in the Test series. Our fielding, which we worked so hard at, was wonderful and that, combined with tight bowling and Donald's hostility, meant the Indians could never break free. The fielding has to be aggressive, not just spectacular – you must make the batsman hesitate, doubt if there's a single when there really is one if they react positively. Manjrekar and Azharuddin were particularly vulnerable in their calling for singles in that series, and the way we pressurised them in the field had a lot to do with it.

So hard work has to be the basis for our approach to Test cricket, because we have a lot still to do before we can think about being in the top bracket. It may not be very exciting at the moment as our batsmen grind down the bowling and our guys bowl to a set plan, but if you look at the way we support each other in the field, you'll at least appreciate how glad we are to be back in Test cricket, and that we'll do all we can to keep on improving. And it's not as if we're the only Test country to apply the work ethic. The Australians are very competitive and dedicated and when the West Indies were invincible under Clive Lloyd, their practising before each day's play was highly impressive. They had immense natural talent as well, and if you ally that to professionalism, you have a formidable unit. Any South African who thinks that we would have been more than a match for that West Indies side if we hadn't been banned is sadly deluded. Of course, we had some top players, but the fast bowlers that they kept turning out were an awesome sight.

The West Indies would still have ruled the roost even if we had been eligible to play them. Truly great players like Graeme Pollock and Barry Richards would have had to concentrate extra hard against an unrelenting battery of top fast bowlers, operating hour after hour, slowing down the over-rate, giving them very little that was loose. Because of that attack, the opposition was rarely in a position to force victory because the batsman didn't get the chance to score quickly enough.

So I veer towards realism when I'm asked about our prospects at Test level. The overwhelming feeling is one of relief and pleasure that we're back in the frame and it's tremendously exciting to look at the forthcoming tours and speculate about how we'll do. But let's be sensible about our assets and our weaknesses. We have a great deal going for us. Our top players are now professional, they're like the

Aussie élite – working about ten months a year, employed by the cricket board, and fully aware that the financial rewards are considerable. Unlike in England, our players in domestic cricket aren't worked into the ground. There's still around ten days before the next first-class game, time in which the players can recharge their batteries or even return to their other professions before getting back to the cricket. The game is aggressively marketed now and extensive redevelopment work on most of the major grounds means that attendances of 30,000 are possible at every Test match arena. That's more than England can match, with the exception of Lord's, and only Australia can top that, at Sydney and Melbourne.

I also think that South African cricket administrators are more open-minded than in other countries. We led the way in providing video evidence for umpires in the event of a close decision. When Sachin Tendulkar was correctly given run out after a half-minute's delay in the Durban Test of 1992 everyone was satisfied. It was clearly a very close decision and waiting for the replay meant there would be no bitterness on either side. It was fair to everyone and the only surprise was that it had taken so long for some authority to try the experiment in the case of stumpings and run-out decisions. Within a few months, it seemed as if all cricket fans had welcomed the use of video, apart from the die-hards. We also experimented for one season with a 14-man squad for matches in the Nissan Shield, which are 55 overs a side. That was my idea, readily accepted by Ali Bacher. To me, one-day cricket was getting very samey; if you could introduce substitutes, you could have the best bowlers against the best batsmen, backed up by the best fielders. The captain could make up to six changes during a match, so that he could replace a batsman who was struggling, or substitute a bowler who was getting hammered. A player who was substituted could also return to the game if the captain wanted. The whole idea was to give the captain more flexibility in a format that had become rather stereotyped, and to reward the specialist, rather than the bits-and-pieces player who was suited to the one-day game but exposed in first-class cricket. It would allow the top player who wasn't fully fit to play in the important parts of the match, ensuring that the spectators weren't disappointed by his absence. I can't think of another cricket board in the world that would have been so positive about such an experiment, but we tried it out for the 1990-91 Nissan Shield games. I can't honestly claim that the scheme was a raging success and it was shelved – but at least we tried something different, something that might have benefited the quality of the cricket while interesting the paying customers. That was the thinking behind night cricket, behind painting logos on the pitch, revolving sightscreens and rock jingles to celebrate wickets and boundaries in day-night games: to some, these are an intrusion into the stately pace of a great game, and I have some sympathy with that. But cricket has to move with the times in some of its competitions, and we have to keep trying different things to sell the game to the public. One-day cricket was a great success during our years of isolation, keeping interest going when the sport might have faded away. All we need now is to get the balance right between the instant brand and the more satisfying version that is Test cricket.

The interest in cricket in South Africa reached a new high during that series against Australia. The crowds for the one-day games were fantastic; for the first group of four matches we had 100,000 turning up to watch in the space of a fortnight. After the game at the Wanderers ground in Johannesburg, Allan Border said that the noise made the crowd of 30,000 was greater than he had heard from 80,000 at the Melbourne Cricket Ground. I believe that cricket is now very close to taking over from rugby as the white South African's favourite sport, even among the Afrikaners. Everyone I spoke to during the Aussie tour wanted to talk of nothing but cricket. We must build on that massive enthusiaism.

I'm often asked if I was jealous that rugby in South Africa didn't suffer as prolonged a spell of isolation as cricket. After all, we were out of it for 21 years, whereas the rugby isolation didn't start in earnest until 1984. There had been two British Lions tours in 1974 and 1980 and 22 Tests against England, Ireland, France, New Zealand and Australia, 14 of them in our country. I don't feel at all bad that they kept going longer than us in the international arena – good luck to them. It's true that cricket seemed to react quicker to the outside world, beginning the process towards normalisation soon after our ban started, but as I know from personal experience, you don't give much thought to reforms when you're still lucky enough to be playing international sport. After rugby isolation began in earnest, their top officials realised that they were operating in a changing environment, that they couldn't keep political considerations at bay. Dr Danie Craven, 'Mr South African Rugby' in everyone's eyes, was criticised for talking to the ANC in 1988 two years before they were unbanned. He started criticising the government in public, pointing out that apartheid had caused so much violence, rather than the ANC for reacting to the discrimination. That was a brave thing to say to a rugby community fearful of a black backlash and resentful that their familiar pattern of internationals was now under threat. In the end, the white South African Rugby Board merged with the black South African Rugby Union in 1992, with the blessing of the ANC. The new South African Rugby Football Union was told it could stage the 1995 World Cup, but again, that was due to the support of the ANC. Danie Craven, who died early in 1993, was entitled to say he had been vindicated in his willingness to talk to the ANC. Steve Tshwete, a keen rugby player in his youth, is watching the rugby situation very closely, pointing out now and then that cricket has pioneered the way ahead with its development programmes, and that rugby needs to do more in that direction. Certainly, the game seems slow to catch on in the townships and the ANC will expect a fair proportion of the World Cup money to go to the game's development programme.

I wonder what odds we would get on a South African World Cup double – the rugby in 1995, and in cricket a few months later? There must be a chance of that. Our cricketers will certainly have packed in a lot more practical experience before we go to India, Pakistan and Sri Lanka at the start of 1996. Consider this itinerary: a tour to England in the summer of 1994, then a limited-overs series in Pakistan and a tour to South Africa by New Zealand. In October 1995, England visit us for a full Test series, so by then the crash course in exposure to international cricket will be complete and we'll know the true extent of our capabilities. I believe we're mid-table at the moment, but I have to be content with drawing Test series home and away against Australia, winning in Sri Lanka and beating India. Just three defeats in the first two years of whizzing around the world is something to build on. There are still flaws in our cricket and no one should pretend we are world-beaters yet, but four wins and seven draws out of 14 Tests is a good start. The South African sports fans are a bit like the Aussie version: convinced their team is the best around and that defeat is a national disaster. We need to be little more humble, concentrate on our strengths – team spirit, fitness, hard work and organisation – and continue developing a wider base for our cricketing talent of the future. When you miss out on two decades of practical experience of Test cricket, you can't expect to reign supreme within a year or two, especially when you're lacking a genius like Graeme Pollock or Barry Richards. But we'll give everything to the fight, something you expect from a South African sportsman, and we'll be difficult to beat. And if by the end of this century we are thrashing the other sides in the world with a team that doesn't contain 11 white faces, that'll be even better.

SOME PLAYERS TO WATCH

The current South African squad prides itself on being a group without stars. That's a realistic attitude, because we are still feeling our way into the international scene and you can't expect a player to dominate the Test arena just like that. Players like Botham, Gower, Lillee, Richards and Ambrose don't grow on trees and in the absence of greats like them, you have to concentrate on getting everything possible out of your squad of players. Consistency of performance is the hallmark of the great Test cricketers and I wouldn't pretend that any current South African had achieved that yet. In a few years, time, though, I reckon one or two of the following might be able to call himself world class.

ALLAN DONALD

At times Allan bowls as quickly as any fast bowler in the world, but he's lacked consistency. He needs rhythm to be at his best, to time the delivery of the ball, to streamline his approach to the wicket. I speak from personal experience about the importance of rhythm, because there were days when I just couldn't get it all in working order. The end product is frustrating fast-medium that threatens nobody and the bowler is left wondering just what he's doing wrong. Other days, it just flows and you don't know why. When Allan is motoring, he's a terrific sight and his strike-rate in Tests – 63 wickets in 14 Tests – is up there with the best. I think he could be more hostile out in the middle; he ought to impose himself on the batsman like a Lillee or a McDermott. A bit of snarling aggression from a genuine fast bowler is always good to see, as long as it stays within legitimate areas, and yet Allan is a quiet guy who just gets on with his bowling. Perhaps a bit more devil would get him more wickets. He's tough, though. Three years in the South African Defence Force hardened him up mentally, as well as instilling the virtues of physical fitness. He's a natural athlete, the ideal lean and tall shape for a fast bowler, and he's a brilliant fielder anywhere. A great trier who never holds back, he was severely tested physically in Sri Lanka, when we played in temperatures of around 37 degrees in unbelievable humidity. It took a lot of out of him, and that's going to be a problem for him over the next couple of years. That's why he had a long rest between the end of the home Test series gainst Australia, missing the remaining one-day internationals, and the start of the tour to England.

How much does he give to his county, Warwickshire, who have treated him well and used him sparingly? How much will be left over for South Africa? Allan feels a great deal of loyalty to Warwickshire, having been given the chance of county cricket in 1987 and being preferred as overseas player ahead of Tom Moody when the club faced a tricky problem. He has also married a Birmingham girl and looks forward to going back to England. But he has to beware of burning himself out. If all goes according to plan, he will have played in 12 Tests and 43 internationals between leaving Warwickshire in August, 1993 and returning to Edgbaston in April, 1995. That is a hell of a lot of cricket for your strike bowler, especially one who tries as hard as Allan. I know what's involved in bowling fast in English cricket, season after season, and my instincts are that two to three years is enough for an overseas fast bowler. You could say I'm watching Allan's position very closely, because he's very valuable to us.

ANDREW HUDSON

Andrew is a very talented opening batsman who is technically correct apart from one blemish that appears when he's out of form. I was his coach at Natal when I noticed that at times he tended to move his back foot slightly towards leg-side, instead of the approved method of back-and-across to the faster bowlers. To try to get him out of the habit, I put a stump behind his heels, but there wasn't enough time to work on it before we went to the World Cup in 1992. Many wrote off his chances because of that technical fault, but he played very well. Andrew is the type of player who needs his confidence boosted, but when he's going through a bad patch, he tends to move away from the ball a little. That's something that fast bowlers spot, but he fights it out. That hundred in our first Test, in Barbados, was a fantastic effort in the circumstances from someone so inexperienced in such an historic situation. He later impressed against the Aussie quicks early in '94. He is a very good player of fast bowling when his self-confidence is strong, so he must keep tapping into his record of success, rather than his failures. So much of top-class cricket is played in the mind.

HANSIE CRONJE

I suppose Hansie is South Africa's equivalent to Mike Atherton of England – destined to be his country's captain from a few years back. Certainly Hansie has impressed us all with his maturity and obvious leadership qualities. He was groomed for the job, captaining the Under-24 side, then becoming vice-captain of the senior team to Sri Lanka and leading Orange Free State to the Castle Currie Cup at the age of 22. He was the youngest player in the tour party to Australia, but you wouldn't have known it when he took over from Kepler

Wessels as captain during the desperate closing stages of the Sydney Test. He didn't miss a trick in that final Australian innings. I'd discussed the options with him on that last morning, before he led the boys out, and I was impressed at his grasp of detail, at his awareness that we would have to make them really work to chisel out every run. Pressure had to be exerted on the batsmen to make them aware of the possibility of defeat. I don't think anybody could have captained the side better, and his example in the field was wonderful. Hansie is a superb fielder because he works at it, putting in lots of extra time after practice has officially ended. He expects the rest of the side to be sharp at their ground fielding and no one can say he doesn't lead the way. Hansie is a very disciplined batsman, the most efficient of the younger batsmen. He has a similar mental toughness to Kepler Wessels, although Hansie is a freer batsman than Kepler. He played Shane Warne better than anyone in world cricket when the Aussies toured South Africa, hitting him regularly over long-on. Above all, Hansie has a very strong mind, and he is the ideal type of dedicated captain for our emerging side in the years ahead. He makes people play for him and his youth doesn't matter.

BRIAN McMILLAN

We need to get more out of Brian. He has the potential to be a very fine all-rounder, but I'm concerned about whether he has the drive and self-motivation to thrive under the pressure of international cricket. At his best he's a hostile bowler, using his height to get bounce from slow pitches, but at other times he looks a little plain. He has had back and knee problems in the past, and that sort of nagging pain isn't ideal for a bowler who is also expected to bat in the middle order, but when it's going well for Brian he really looks the part. For such a big guy, he ought to be looking to crash the ball around harder, but he prefers to stroke it, and he's a very stylish player. He played one season of county cricket with Warwickshire and he batted very well, but didn' t get many wickets. It was probably best for him that he didn't go back, because he might have burned himself out. A brilliant slip fielder, he can give us vital balance in our side as the all-rounder, but at the age of 30, time is running out for him. Perhaps deep down he lacks self-confidence, but with his ability, he shouldn't. I hope his improvement in the home series against Australia proves a good omen.

DARYLL CULLINAN

Another enigma. Daryll is definitely the most talented batsman in South Africa, but people haven't done him any favours by comparing him with Graeme Pollock. Like Graeme he was a teenage prodigy, becoming the youngest to score a first-class century when two months short of his 17th birthday, but Graeme built on his youthful brilliance and kept hammering hundreds. Daryll is now 26, the age at which Graeme played his last Test. Apart from that, Daryll is a right-hand bat, so enough of silly comparisons. Anyone who can score 337 not out, the highest score ever in South Africa, has to be a considerable talent and this chap's certainly that. But he still isn't doing himself justice. We played him at Cape Town in his first Test in 1992 and I told him that the number 4 spot was there for the taking. He played brightly in his first Test, showed good technique in the following one-day series against the West Indies and impressed in Sri Lanka, scoring his maiden Test hundred. Yet he struggled in Australia, and I started wondering not for the first time about his big-match temperament. His technique is not a problem – the best among young South African batsmen – but you wonder why he has failed so often in those ten years since he graduated from the Nuffield Week, looking a tremendous prospect.

Daryll is a quiet man and sometimes he has been labelled a loner, moody and a poor team man. His relationship with management and players at Western Province deteriorated, culminating in actions by Daryll that constituted matters of principle to him, but to the rest of the dressing-room looked petulant. He objected to being moved around the batting order, was passed over for the captaincy and once he got himself out late in the day when he felt he ought to have been protected in favour of a nightwatchman. His move to Transvaal was a good one for both him and his Western Province colleagues and Eddie Barlow, the Transvaal coach, brought the best out of him by insisting on hard work and discipline. It looked as if Daryll was at last realising his talent, especially after that unbeaten triple hundred against Northern Transvaal in October, 1993. The worry now is that his Test career might follow the pattern of his domestic career in the Currie Cup: under-achievement for someone of his great talent, with too many silly dismissals. He should now be churning out big hundreds with a technique and ability like his. Perhaps he needs more reassurance and sympathy. South Africa needs to see the best of Daryll Cullinan because we are vulnerable in the middle order.

JONTY RHODES

Now here's one chap who makes everything count. When I first coached him at Natal, some people took one look at his unusual technique and decided he'd never make a batsman. Yet he has some assets that are priceless to a batsman – he plays very late, his head is over the ball all the time, he has a great eye and huge heart. Jonty manages to forget about the previous ball and he's never bothered if the bowler tells him he's lucky still to be there. He's become a very good player, a Test-class batsman. He now plays very straight after getting out too often by hitting across the line. I put that down to the influence of one-day cricket and he's worked very hard at correcting the fault. When Jonty first played for South Africa, he was dismissed as just a useful batsman who fielded brilliantly, but they reckoned without his self-belief. He really wants to be a top batsman and I wasn't at all surprised that he topped our batting averages in the series against India and batted very well in Sri Lanka, followed by that gutsy innings in Sydney that helped us win the Test and another in the first innings at Johannesburg which again helped to set up victory against the Aussies. His wicket became much valued by the Aussies in both series.

Jonty's a quiet chap, modest and self-critical, but he really winds up the guys in the dressing-room before they go out to field. He's bouncy and a great motivator once he focuses on his cricket and he has a terrific temperament. I couldn't think of many men who, facing a target of 7 to win, with just one ball left, managed the victory. It happened in a Benson & Hedges day-night semi-final when Transvaal's Richard Snell only needed to bowl a legitimate delivery and they were through to the final. But he bowled a high full toss which Jonty pulled for six, and Snell was no-balled for sending one down that was above stump height. With the scores level, Jonty hit the last ball to the boundary. He just loves that kind of situation.

As a fielder he is remarkable for the way he stops the ball and gets it back over the stumps in one swift movement. He can be on his knees, yet he can still run someone out in an instant. This is where he's different from Colin Bland. Colin had a wonderful arm and used to shell out batsmen with his accurate, strong throw, but he could never have rivalled Jonty's amazing athleticism. Jonty's lucky that he's a brilliant hockey player and used to bending down close to the ground, with eyes on the ball, so he can get to it quicker than a bigger guy who would have to stoop. Somehow Jonty's on to it in a flash. He also has a great pair of hands, and he seems to be able to stop the hardest hit.

He's well on the way to becoming our biggest draw-card, and he's a big hit with non-white cricket fans in South Africa as well. A recent survey of kids conducted by the United Cricket Board voted Jonty way ahead of any other as the favourite player in the country – among all colours. I think that's terrific and if it means that kids are going to throw themselves around in the field like Jonty Rhodes, that's good for the game. They ought to have seen him in Sri Lanka. The outfields were bare and hard, with hardly any grass at all, yet he still dived all over the place, stopping certain boundaries, reducing the amazed batsman to just a single. He had cuts and bruises all over his body, but not once did he pull out of a chance for a catch or to save a run. He is an inspiration and I think world cricket is going to love this fellow.

BRETT SCHULTZ

When fit, Brett is an ideal partner for Allan Donald. He is fast, strong and big-hearted. When we toured Sri Lanka, our boys thought he was quicker than Donald and he gave a tremendous performance in the hottest conditions you could find anywhere in cricket. He bowled 11 overs on the trot in one of the Tests, when Donald, a very fit guy himself, could only manage five over spells.

Brett bowls left-arm and gets the ball to leave the right-hander as you'd expect, but he can also bowl over the wicket and that's when he's a real handful with his extra bounce. When he gets his line right, the ball keeps coming in at the right-hander, and that often gets him catches at bat or pad. He's not a natural swinger of the ball, but anyone who can get bounce on Port Elizabeth's placid pitch has my respect! Brett is disciplined, a big believer in driving himself to peak fitness, but he's a little bit of a worry with a vulnerable knee. We missed him against Australia in both Test series, but he wasn't right after an operation, and we just hope he'll come through. We couldn't take a chance on him for the England tour, but if he can get fully fit, he'll surprise a lot of Test batsmen over the next year or so.

THE ENGLAND TOUR PARTY

If Schultz can regain peak fitness, he will have an important part to play over the next hectic year of our international calendar, but for now, we shall see how young Aubrey Martyn gets on. Like Schultz, he is a left-arm seamer, though not so fast, and he was chosen for the England tour as part of the learning process. At 21, he has time on his side and he gives us variety with his different line of attack. We want him to be pushing our four other experienced seamers, because competition for places always strengthens a squad.

The rest of the tour party to England was a vote for experience. It was felt that the players who did so well in the two series against Australia deserved the chance to represent us on our first tour to England since 1965. Some felt that Jimmy Cook might have forced his way in because of his great experience and success on English wickets but he didn't have a terrific domestic season and Peter Kirsten and Kepler Wessels were felt to have enough know-how to help an emerging group of players. After all, the likes of Hansie Cronje, Jonty Rhodes and Andrew Hudson have pakced an enormous amount of practical experience into the last two years at international level. We know the selectors have taken a bit of a chance on Daryll Cullinan, after he was left out of the home series against the Aussies. Shane Warne had troubled him in Australia, but hopefully the period away from the pressure will have helped him sort out his game and his stroke selection. We have a lot of faith in Daryll, but at 27 he must now start to play consistently. He has all the shots and we wait to see just how strong he is psychologically. We need the flair of Daryll Cullinan, he has the ability take apart Test attacks.

It is obvious that our bowling strength will revolve around our quickers bowlers, and I believe that Allan Donald's prolonged rest will have him fit and raring to go. In the slow bowling department, we have again gone for experience - the left-arm spinner, Tim Shaw and the off-spinner Pat Symcox are both in their thirties, and they have served their time in Currie Cup cricket over the years. They are both over six feet, so they should get some bounce on English pitches that can help the spinners. Having played in that gripping Sydney Test - and bowling tightly - Symcox is now aware of the special pressures of Test cricket, and Shaw has played in a few recent one-day internationals.

One thing I can guarantee about this South African party, we will never stop trying, helping each other out on the field, and we should confirm to English supporters that we are now the best fielding side in the world. That sort of inspiration will make a huge difference to our bowlers when we're up against it. The photographers will love Jonty Rhodes, and so will the crowds!

APPENDIX

ACKNOWLEDGEMENT

The publishers would like
to express their thanks
to Richard Lockwood who
has provided all the
match details and averages
in this section

THE REBEL TOURS 1982-1990

Scorecards and averages

for the international matches

against teams from

England, Sri Lanka,

West Indies and Australia

SOUTH AFRICA vs. ENGLAND XI

at Johannesburg on 12th, 13th, 14th, 15th March 1982
Toss : South Africa. Umpires : P.R.Hurwitz and B.C.Smith
South Africa won by 8 wickets

SOUTH AFRICA				
B.A.Richards	c Amiss b Underwood	66	(2) lbw b Lever	4
S.J.Cook	c Gooch b Taylor	114	(1) c & b Old	2
P.N.Kirsten	c Gooch b Taylor	88	not out	20
R.G.Pollock	not out	64	not out	9
C.E.B.Rice	c Knott b Taylor	1		
M.J.Procter *	c Knott b Lever	1		
A.J.Kourie	lbw b Old	14		
R.V.Jennings +	c Knott b Lever	24		
G.S.le Roux	not out	6		
S.T.Jefferies				
V.A.P.van der Bijl				
Extras	(lb 17,w 4,nb 1)	22	(lb 2)	2
TOTAL	(for 7 wkts dec)	400	(for 2 wkts)	37

ENGLAND XI				
G.A.Gooch *	b le Roux	30	c Jennings b van der Bijl	109
G.Boycott	c Cook b van der Bijl	5	lbw b van der Bijl	36
W.Larkins	lbw b van der Bijl	2	c Kourie b van der Bijl	20
D.L.Amiss	not out	66	c Procter b Jefferies	24
R.A.Woolmer	c Jennings b Kourie	14	lbw b le Roux	21
P.Willey	lbw b Jefferies	1	lbw b le Roux	24
D.L.Underwood	c Cook b van der Bijl	8	(10) lbw b van der Bijl	6
A.P.E.Knott +	c Richards b van der Bijl	5	(7) lbw b van der Bijl	9
C.M.Old	c Kourie b van der Bijl	1	(8) b le Roux	11
J.K.Lever	b Kourie	9	(9) not out	10
L.B.Taylor	b Jefferies	0	c Pollock b le Roux	0
Extras	(b 1,lb 5,w 2,nb 1)	9	(b 4,lb 3,w 2,nb 4)	13
TOTAL		150		283

ENGLAND XI	O	M	R	W	O	M	R	W
Taylor	31	7	73	3				
Old	28	10	76	1	6	1	8	1
Lever	32	3	122	2	5.4	1	27	1
Underwood	23	1	92	1				
Gooch	2	0	15	0				

SOUTH AFRICA	O	M	R	W	O	M	R	W
van der Bijl	22	8	25	5	31	9	79	5
Jefferies	20	5	59	2	27	4	88	1
Kourie	11	2	19	2	16	7	53	0
le Roux	10	2	38	1	22.2	5	44	4
Procter					6	3	6	0

FALL OF WICKETS	SAF	ENG	ENG	SAF
1st	117	38	119	8
2nd	278	38	174	14
3rd	286	42	179	
4th	290	73	207	
5th	295	80	229	
6th	331	90	252	
7th	388	124	258	
8th		130	267	
9th		142	278	
10th		150	283	

SOUTH AFRICA vs. ENGLAND XI

at Cape Town on 19th, 20th, 21st, 22nd March 1982
Toss : England XI. Umpires : O.R.Schoof and B.C.Smith
Match drawn

ENGLAND XI				
G.A.Gooch *	hit wicket b Kourie	83	c Kourie b Hobson	68
G.Boycott	c Kuiper b Kourie	16	c Jennings b Jefferies	1
W.Larkins	c Richards b Kourie	29	lbw b Kirsten	95
D.L.Amiss	c Jennings b Jefferies	13	not out	73
R.A.Woolmer	c & b Kourie	2	not out	1
P.Willey	c Kourie b van der Bijl	39		
A.P.E.Knott +	b van der Bijl	16		
C.M.Old	c Jennings b Jefferies	1		
J.K.Lever	b Jefferies	8		
D.L.Underwood	c Richards b van der Bijl	0		
L.B.Taylor	not out	10		
Extras	(lb 2,w 2,nb 2)	6	(b 4,lb 7)	11
TOTAL		223	(for 3 wkts dec)	249

SOUTH AFRICA				
S.J.Cook	c Knott b Lever	18		
B.A.Richards *	lbw b Taylor	8		
P.N.Kirsten	lbw b Lever	114		
R.G.Pollock	c Knott b Lever	0		
C.E.B.Rice	lbw b Taylor	12		
A.P.Kuiper	c Willey b Underwood	1	(2) not out	9
A.J.Kourie	c Knott b Lever	18		
R.V.Jennings +	c sub b Lever	32	(1) not out	28
S.T.Jefferies	c Knott b Lever	3		
V.A.P.van der Bijl	not out	4		
D.L.Hobson	b Taylor	2		
Extras	(lb 6,w 1,nb 16)	23	(lb 1)	1
TOTAL		235	(for 0 wkts)	38

SOUTH AFRICA	O	M	R	W	O	M	R	W
van der Bijl	33	12	61	3	21	6	53	0
Jefferies	24.4	9	56	3	14	5	39	1
Hobson	13	3	48	0	30	7	86	1
Kourie	32	15	52	4	16	4	38	0
Kirsten					4	2	7	1
Kuiper					8	2	15	0

ENGLAND XI	O	M	R	W	O	M	R	W
Taylor	27	8	49	3				
Lever	37	11	86	6	3	0	22	0
Old	18	6	33	0	4	0	15	0
Underwood	22	9	36	1				
Willey	4	1	8	0				

FALL OF WICKETS	ENG	SAF	ENG	SAF
1st	27	11	8	
2nd	104	43	112	
3rd	140	43	231	
4th	144	85		
5th	148	87		
6th	189	144		
7th	199	212		
8th	205	218		
9th	207	232		
10th	223	235		

SOUTH AFRICA vs. ENGLAND XI

at Durban on 26th, 27th, 28th, 29th March 1982
Toss : England XI. Umpires : D.D.Schoof and O.R.Schoof
Match drawn

SOUTH AFRICA				
S.J.Cook	c Gooch b Lever	11	not out	50
B.A.Richards *	c Knott b Hendrick	41	retired hurt	17
P.N.Kirsten	c Gooch b Hendrick	11	c Knott b Lever	14
R.G.Pollock	b Taylor	15	c Hendrick b Larkins	12
C.E.B.Rice	c Gooch b Hendrick	9	not out	39
A.P.Kuiper	b Taylor	0		
A.J.Kourie	not out	50		
R.V.Jennings +	c Knott b Taylor	22		
G.S.le Roux	c Knott b Taylor	0		
V.A.P.van der Bijl	c Knott b Taylor	0		
W.K.Watson	not out	4		
Extras	(lb 11,w 7)	18	(lb 4,nb 7)	11
TOTAL	(for 9 wkts dec)	181	(for 2 wkts)	143

ENGLAND XI		
G.A.Gooch *	c Kourie b le Roux	48
G.Boycott	c Jennings b van der Bijl	31
W.Larkins	lbw b van der Bijl	39
D.L.Amiss	c Cook b van der Bijl	50
R.A.Woolmer	c Kourie b Watson	100
P.Willey	b Watson	15
A.P.E.Knott +	c Kirsten b van der Bijl	6
C.M.Old	c Rice b van der Bijl	10
J.K.Lever	not out	4
L.B.Taylor		
M.Hendrick		
Extras	(lb 7,w 1)	8
TOTAL	(for 8 wkts dec)	311

ENGLAND XI	O	M	R	W	O	M	R	W
Taylor	25.3	5	61	5	8	2	23	0
Lever	13	1	53	1	16	9	25	1
Old	11	3	21	0	6	2	18	0
Hendrick	21	9	28	3	12	3	37	0
Larkins					5	0	24	1
Knott					1	0	5	0

SOUTH AFRICA	O	M	R	W	O	M	R	W
van der Bijl	40	14	97	5				
Watson	25.1	4	79	2				
le Roux	24	5	71	1				
Kourie	17	3	43	0				
Kuiper	3	1	8	0				
Kirsten	2	1	5	0				

FALL OF WICKETS	SAF	ENG	SAF	ENG
1st	48	67	61	
2nd	61	95	91	
3rd	77	137		
4th	92	217		
5th	92	259		
6th	111	270		
7th	168	301		
8th	170	311		
9th	170			
10th				

SOUTH AFRICA vs. SRI LANKA XI

at Johannesburg on 19th, 20th, 22nd, 23rd November 1982
Toss : Sri Lanka. Umpires : C.J.Mitchley and O.R.Schoof
South Africa won by an innings and 24 runs

SRI LANKA XI				
N.D.P.Hettiaratchi	c Jennings b le Roux	1	lbw b le Roux	1
B.de Silva	c Jennings b Jefferies	70	c & b Kourie	3
B.Warnapura *	lbw b Jefferies	15	c Jennings b Jefferies	31
G.J.A.F.Aponso	lbw b le Roux	12	c Jefferies b Kirsten	44
J.B.N.Perera	c Jennings b Kuiper	2	c Pollock b Jefferies	0
J.F.Woutersz	lbw b le Roux	51	c Kuiper b Kourie	0
P.L.J.Fernando	c Rice b van der Bijl	21	absent ill	
L.W.Kaluperuma	c Rice b le Roux	2	(7) c Richards b Kourie	39
H.M.Goonatillake +	not out	15	(8) b Kourie	2
A.R.Opatha	c Jennings b le Roux	9	(9) c & b Kourie	4
G.R.A.de Silva	c Jennings b le Roux	0	(10) not out	8
Extras	(lb 5,w 9,nb 1)	15	(b 4,lb 3,w 2)	9
TOTAL		213		141

SOUTH AFRICA		
S.J.Cook	b Perera	169
B.A.Richards	b Opatha	1
S.T.Jefferies	c Fernando b Kaluperuma	45
P.N.Kirsten *	c Goonatillake b Opatha	3
R.G.Pollock	c & b Kaluperuma	79
C.E.B.Rice	b Kaluperuma	19
A.P.Kuiper	c Opatha b Kaluperuma	11
A.J.Kourie	lbw b Opatha	11
R.V.Jennings +	lbw b Kaluperuma	2
G.S.le Roux	c Kaluperuma b Perera	6
V.A.P.van der Bijl	not out	4
Extras	(b 6,lb 3,w 16,nb 3)	28
TOTAL		378

SOUTH AFRICA	O	M	R	W	O	M	R	W
le Roux	18.3	1	55	6	8	1	22	1
van der Bijl	21	4	51	1	14	8	22	0
Jefferies	14	3	44	2	14	4	29	2
Kourie	15	2	42	0	22	6	54	5
Kuiper	4	0	6	1				
Kirsten					4.1	2	5	1

SRI LANKA XI	O	M	R	W	O	M	R	W
Opatha	29	4	111	3				
Fernando	7	1	24	0				
Woutersz	2	0	11	0				
Kaluperuma	45	7	123	5				
de Silva G.R.A.	5	0	33	0				
Perera	18.5	2	48	2				

FALL OF WICKETS	SRI	SAF	SRI	SAF
1st	10	4	6	
2nd	34	93	46	
3rd	73	96	46	
4th	76	261	49	
5th	134	291	51	
6th	176	317	103	
7th	179	348	123	
8th	193	357	131	
9th	213	373	141	
10th	213	378		

SOUTH AFRICA vs. SRI LANKA XI

at Cape Town on 9th, 10th, 11th, 13th December 1982
Toss : South Africa. Umpires : D.D.Schoof and B.C.Smith
South Africa won by an innings and 100 runs

SRI LANKA XI				
N.D.P.Hettiaratchi	c Jennings b le Roux	4	(3) b Hobson	10
H.H.Devapriya	c Seeff b Kuiper	29	st Jennings b Hobson	53
B.Warnapura *	c Pollock b Kuiper	21	(1) b Jefferies	14
G.J.A.F.Aponso	c sub b Kirsten	81	b Kuiper	7
A.N.Ranasinghe	c Hobson b Jefferies	54	b Kuiper	9
J.B.N.Perera	c Seeff b Hobson	13	c Rice b Jefferies	102
J.F.Woutersz	c Jennings b le Roux	31	c Jefferies b Hobson	32
H.M.Goonatillake +	b Jefferies	19	c Pollock b le Roux	10
L.W.Kaluperuma	b Jefferies	9	(10) not out	1
A.R.Opatha	not out	5	(9) lbw b Jefferies	20
G.R.A.de Silva	b le Roux	0	st Jennings b Kirsten	0
Extras	(lb 6,w 4,nb 6)	16	(lb 15,w 4,nb 4)	23
TOTAL		282		281

SOUTH AFRICA		
S.J.Cook	b Ranasinghe	112
L.Seeff	c Woutersz b Perera	188
P.N.Kirsten *	run out	27
R.G.Pollock	c Goonatillake b Perera	197
C.E.B.Rice	c Perera b Opatha	37
A.P.Kuiper	st Goonatillake b Woutersz	66
R.V.Jennings +	not out	11
G.S.le Roux		
S.T.Jefferies		
A.J.Kourie		
D.L.Hobson		
Extras	(b 2,lb 12,w 2,nb 9)	25
TOTAL	(for 6 wkts dec)	663

SOUTH AFRICA	O	M	R	W	O	M	R	W
le Roux	18.5	5	69	3	12	3	39	1
Jefferies	18	5	43	3	19	6	76	3
Kuiper	13	3	37	2	12	3	33	2
Kourie	6	0	12	0				
Hobson	25	2	77	1	34	9	87	3
Kirsten	10	1	28	1	4.2	0	23	1

SRI LANKA XI	O	M	R	W	O	M	R	W
Opatha	42	5	150	1				
Ranasinghe	36	3	123	1				
de Silva	7	0	41	0				
Kaluperuma	16	0	110	0				
Perera	42.3	3	154	2				
Woutersz	16	0	60	1				

FALL OF WICKETS	SRI	SAF	SRI	SAF
1st	4	250	48	
2nd	47	328	83	
3rd	77	344	90	
4th	150	449	102	
5th	174	623	109	
6th	229	663	186	
7th	268		236	
8th	268		271	
9th	281		280	
10th	282		281	

SOUTH AFRICA vs. WEST INDIES XI

at Cape Town on 21st, 22nd, 24th, 25th January 1983
Toss : South Africa. Umpires : O.R.Schoof and B.C.Smith
South Africa won by 5 wickets

SOUTH AFRICA				
S.J.Cook	c Murray b Stephenson	73	c Rowe b Moseley	6
B.A.Richards	c Rowe b Moseley	49	c Parry b Clarke	7
P.N.Kirsten *	lbw b Parry	2	b Parry	13
R.G.Pollock	b Moseley	100	not out	43
C.E.B.Rice	lbw b Parry	16	lbw b Clarke	6
K.A.McKenzie	lbw b Parry	4	lbw b Parry	0
A.J.Kourie	c Murray b Moseley	69	not out	12
R.V.Jennings +	b Parry	15		
G.S.le Roux	c & b Stephenson	30		
V.A.P.van der Bijl	c Stephenson b Parry	10		
S.T.Jefferies	not out	40		
Extras	(b 18,lb 13,w 2,nb 8)	41	(b 8,lb 5,w 5,nb 3)	21
TOTAL		449	(for 5 wkts)	108

WEST INDIES XI				
R.A.Austin	c Jennings b van der Bijl	93	b Kourie	23
A.T.Greenidge	b Jefferies	4	lbw b le Roux	23
E.H.Mattis	lbw b le Roux	0	c Jennings b le Roux	19
A.I.Kallicharran	b van der Bijl	21	st Jennings b Kourie	89
L.G.Rowe *	c Kourie b van der Bijl	9	lbw b Jefferies	26
C.L.King	c Jennings b van der Bijl	19	b Jefferies	13
D.A.Murray +	b Kourie	3	c Jennings b le Roux	27
D.R.Parry	b Kourie	18	lbw b Jefferies	29
F.D.Stephenson	run out	56	b Jefferies	16
E.A.Moseley	st Jennings b Kourie	8	c Kirsten b van der Bijl	25
S.T.Clarke	not out	5	not out	0
Extras	(b 1,lb 7,nb 2)	10	(b 3,lb 9,w 3,nb 4)	19
TOTAL		246		309

WEST INDIES XI	O	M	R	W	O	M	R	W
Clarke	34	9	88	0	15	4	22	2
Moseley	25	3	87	3	8	1	25	1
Stephenson	23.4	0	93	2				
Parry	43	10	117	5	7	1	40	2
Austin	7	1	23	0				

SOUTH AFRICA	O	M	R	W	O	M	R	W
le Roux	17	4	56	1	21	5	71	3
Jefferies	9	4	28	1	35.4	17	58	4
van der Bijl	20	6	44	4	22	4	46	1
Kourie	28	6	101	3	31	4	94	2
Kirsten	1	0	7	0	13	3	21	0

FALL OF WICKETS

	SAF	WI	WI	SAF
1st	85	8	43	14
2nd	98	9	70	18
3rd	201	46	73	65
4th	264	66	127	82
5th	270	86	177	85
6th	276	89	198	
7th	351	129	253	
8th	371	212	280	
9th	382	232	308	
10th	449	246	309	

SOUTH AFRICA vs. WEST INDIES XI

at Johannesburg on 28th, 29th, 31st January, 1st February 1983
Toss : South Africa. Umpires : C.J.Mitchley and O.R.Schoof
West Indies XI won by 29 runs

WEST INDIES XI				
R.A.Austin	c Pollock b van der Bijl	4	c McKenzie b van der Bijl	14
A.T.Greenidge	not out	42	c Jennings b le Roux	48
E.H.Mattis	lbw b le Roux	3	b Jefferies	21
A.I.Kallicharran	b Kourie	37	b van der Bijl	13
L.G.Rowe *	b van der Bijl	0	b Jefferies	0
C.L.King	lbw b Kourie	101	lbw b Kourie	39
D.A.Murray +	c Pollock b van der Bijl	8	c Cook b Jefferies	4
D.R.Parry	b Kourie	20	b Kourie	15
F.D.Stephenson	c Pollock b Kourie	0	c Pollock b le Roux	4
S.T.Clarke	c Rice b Kourie	25	c Kourie b le Roux	0
R.A.Wynter	b Kourie	9	not out	0
Extras	(lb 9,w 2,nb 7)	18	(b 4,lb 4,w 5,nb 5)	18
TOTAL		267		176

SOUTH AFRICA				
S.J.Cook	c Wynter b Stephenson	0	c King b Clarke	27
B.A.Richards	c Kallicharran b Clarke	0	b Parry	59
R.V.Jennings +	c Parry b Clarke	0	c Murray b Clarke	0
P.N.Kirsten *	b Clarke	56	b Clarke	7
R.G.Pollock	b Stephenson	73	c King b Clarke	1
C.E.B.Rice	c Austin b Parry	38	c Austin b Clarke	12
K.A.McKenzie	c Rowe b Wynter	27	not out	26
A.J.Kourie	lbw b Clarke	17	c Murray b Clarke	5
G.S.le Roux	lbw b Wynter	0	lbw b King	2
S.T.Jefferies	b Clarke	11	run out	31
V.A.P.van der Bijl	not out	1	b Clarke	2
Extras	(lb 7,w 1,nb 2)	10	(b 1,lb 4,w 1,nb 3)	9
TOTAL		233		181

SOUTH AFRICA	O	M	R	W	O	M	R	W
le Roux	17	2	58	1	15.1	3	46	3
Jefferies	16	3	62	0	22	8	66	3
van der Bijl	16	3	74	3	16	7	24	2
Kourie	29	9	55	6	9	2	22	2

WEST INDIES XI	O	M	R	W	O	M	R	W
Clarke	23.3	4	66	5	22.2	10	34	7
Wynter	11	3	26	2	9	0	33	0
Stephenson	18	1	68	2	18	3	47	0
King	7	2	29	0	1	0	3	1
Parry	17	5	25	1	20	3	51	1
Austin	2	0	9	0	1	0	4	0

FALL OF WICKETS

	WI	SAF	WI	SAF
1st	13	1	33	87
2nd	16	1	56	97
3rd	39	8	56	97
4th	104	122	57	100
5th	164	151	65	111
6th	185	199	70	117
7th	185	203	70	119
8th	222	204	105	124
9th	233	230	176	179
10th	267	233	176	181

SOUTH AFRICA vs. WEST INDIES XI

at Durban on 23rd, 24th, 26th, 27th December 1983
Toss : South Africa. Umpires : D.H.Bezuidenhout and D.D.Schoof
Match drawn

WEST INDIES XI		
S.F.A.F.Bacchus	retired hurt	19
E.N.Trotman	c Pollock b le Roux	21
M.A.Lynch	c Hobson b Kourie	26
A.I.Kallicharran	c Hobson b le Roux	103
C.L.King	c Jefferies b Rice	0
L.G.Rowe *	lbw b Jefferies	157
D.A.Murray +	c Kourie b le Roux	32
F.D.Stephenson	b Hobson	53
D.R.Parry	not out	63
E.A.Moseley	not out	33
S.T.Clarke		
Extras	(b 5,lb 9,w 2,nb 6)	22
TOTAL	(for 7 wkts dec)	529

SOUTH AFRICA				
S.J.Cook	c Murray b Clarke	69	not out	30
H.R.Fotheringham	lbw b Moseley	0	not out	22
P.N.Kirsten *	c Murray b Moseley	84		
R.G.Pollock	b Parry	62		
K.S.McEwan	c sub b Moseley	11		
C.E.B.Rice	c & b Parry	7		
A.J.Kourie	b Clarke	32		
R.V.Jennings +	b Clarke	18		
G.S.le Roux	c Stephenson b Clarke	11		
S.T.Jefferies	b Clarke	0		
D.L.Hobson	not out	12		
Extras	(b 4,lb 9,w 1,nb 13)	27	(b 2,nb 5)	7
TOTAL		333	(for 0 wkts)	59

SOUTH AFRICA	O	M	R	W	O	M	R	W
le Roux	27	2	88	3				
Jefferies	31	3	132	1				
Kourie	36	5	123	1				
Rice	21	4	65	1				
Hobson	19	1	95	1				
Kirsten	1	0	4	0				

WEST INDIES XI	O	M	R	W	O	M	R	W
Clarke	32.1	11	105	5	3	0	9	0
Moseley	26	5	76	3	4	2	8	0
Stephenson	21	5	61	0	6	1	16	0
Parry	25	7	62	2				
King	2	1	2	0	6	2	13	0
Kallicharran					5	2	6	0

FALL OF WICKETS	WI	SAF	SAF	WI
1st	34	2		
2nd	86	132		
3rd	87	219		
4th	241	239		
5th	311	249		
6th	392	257		
7th	468	302		
8th		313		
9th		313		
10th		333		

SOUTH AFRICA vs. WEST INDIES XI

at Cape Town on 30th, 31st December 1983, 2nd, 3rd January 1984
Toss : South Africa. Umpires : C.J.Mitchley and S.G.Moore
South Africa won by 10 wickets

WEST INDIES XI				
E.N.Trotman	c Jennings b Kourie	28	c Jennings b Jefferies	1
E.H.Mattis	lbw b Jefferies	6	c Rice b Kourie	26
M.A.Lynch	c Jennings b Kourie	2	run out	23
A.I.Kallicharran	c Fotheringham b Kourie	8	lbw b Kourie	17
C.L.King	c Kourie b Jefferies	83	c Pollock b Jefferies	26
L.G.Rowe *	c & b Kourie	0	c Cook b Hobson	31
D.A.Murray +	lbw b Rice	39	c Fotheringham b Kourie	40
F.D.Stephenson	c Pollock b Kourie	7	lbw b le Roux	7
B.D.Julien	not out	33	c Kirsten b le Roux	18
D.R.Parry	c & b le Roux	30	c Pollock b Rice	58
S.T.Clarke	lbw b Jefferies	0	not out	3
Extras	(b 4,lb 7,w 1,nb 4)	16	(b 4,lb 7,w 6,nb 1)	18
TOTAL		252		268

SOUTH AFRICA				
S.J.Cook	c Murray b Clarke	45	not out	40
H.R.Fotheringham	c Julien b Stephenson	20	not out	71
P.N.Kirsten *	c Parry b Julien	88		
R.G.Pollock	c Murray b Parry	102		
K.S.McEwan	c Murray b Clarke	32		
C.E.B.Rice	not out	71		
A.J.Kourie	lbw b Clarke	1		
R.V.Jennings +	lbw b Parry	8		
G.S.le Roux	c Mattis b Clarke	11		
S.T.Jefferies	c Julien b Parry	1		
D.L.Hobson	c & b Clarke	1		
Extras	(lb 17,w 6,nb 1)	24	(lb 5,w 1)	6
TOTAL		404	(for 0 wkts)	117

SOUTH AFRICA	O	M	R	W	O	M	R	W
le Roux	17	6	34	1	17.3	5	50	2
Jefferies	20.4	6	63	3	16	6	62	2
Kourie	22	6	66	5	27	11	61	3
Hobson	20	5	49	0	15	2	36	1
Rice	8	1	24	1	15	8	21	1
Kirsten					6	1	20	0

WEST INDIES XI	O	M	R	W	O	M	R	W
Clarke	37.5	13	92	5	6	0	23	0
Julien	24	5	71	1	2	0	11	0
Stephenson	27	5	95	1	2	0	11	0
Parry	36	8	79	3	8	0	36	0
King	5	1	21	0	3	0	22	0
Kallicharran	3	0	22	0	0.2	0	8	0

FALL OF WICKETS

	WI	SAF	WI	SAF
1st	31	61	5	
2nd	38	84	53	
3rd	46	267	63	
4th	49	273	86	
5th	49	315	100	
6th	156	317	178	
7th	183	364	206	
8th	183	393	232	
9th	247	398	260	
10th	252	404	268	

SOUTH AFRICA vs. WEST INDIES XI

at Johannesburg on 13th, 14th, 16th, 17th January 1984
Toss : South Africa. Umpires : S.G.Moore and D.D.Schoof
West IndieS XI won by 1 wicket

SOUTH AFRICA				
S.J.Cook	lbw b Clarke	7	c Greenidge b Alleyne	17
H.R.Fotheringham	b Moseley	8	lbw b Moseley	4
P.N.Kirsten	c Murray b Alleyne	67	c King b Moseley	61
R.G.Pollock	c Moseley b Alleyne	41	b Stephenson	46
K.S.McEwan	c Murray b Alleyne	0	c Stephenson b Alleyne	0
C.E.B.Rice *	c Trotman b Stephenson	4	c Murray b Clarke	47
A.P.Kuiper	lbw b Alleyne	16	c Mattis b Alleyne	10
A.J.Kourie	not out	7	b Alleyne	31
R.V.Jennings +	c sub b Moseley	1	lbw b Alleyne	0
W.K.Watson	lbw b Moseley	0	not out	6
R.W.Hanley	c Murray b Moseley	0	c Stephenson b Clarke	0
Extras	(lb 4,nb 5)	9	(b 3,lb 5,w 4,nb 2)	14
TOTAL		160		236

WEST INDIES XI				
E.N.Trotman	c Fotheringham b Hanley	3	c Pollock b Watson	4
A.T.Greenidge	c Jennings b Kuiper	20	c Kourie b Kuiper	43
E.H.Mattis	lbw b Watson	0	b Watson	32
M.A.Lynch	lbw b Rice	9	c Jennings b Rice	7
C.L.King	c Jennings b Watson	54	c sub b Rice	42
D.A.Murray +	c Pollock b Kuiper	43	c Pollock b Rice	3
A.I.Kallicharran *	lbw b Hanley	18	c Pollock b Watson	7
F.D.Stephenson	not out	30	c Jennings b Kuiper	20
E.A.Moseley	c Pollock b Kuiper	0	c Hanley b Watson	14
S.T.Clarke	lbw b Kuiper	9	not out	23
H.L.Alleyne	c sub b Kuiper	0	not out	0
Extras	(lb 3,w 1,nb 3)	7	(lb 3,w 2,nb 5)	10
TOTAL		193	(for 9 wkts)	205

WEST INDIES XI	O	M	R	W	O	M	R	W
Clarke	13	6	17	1	24.3	5	74	2
Moseley	10.4	2	45	4	14	1	55	2
Alleyne	12	1	54	4	14	1	62	5
Stephenson	9	2	34	1	4	0	31	1
King	1	0	1	0				

SOUTH AFRICA	O	M	R	W	O	M	R	W
Watson	16	5	42	2	16.2	3	63	4
Hanley	13	4	26	2	9	1	27	0
Rice	6	1	46	1	12	0	50	3
Kuiper	11.5	0	50	5	11	0	32	2
Kourie	6	1	22	0	5	1	23	0

FALL OF WICKETS	SAF	WI	SAF	WI
1st	16	6	6	4
2nd	24	11	44	72
3rd	91	23	127	86
4th	92	69	149	94
5th	102	106	169	97
6th	151	142	169	99
7th	154	154	169	143
8th	160	154	216	172
9th	160	189	236	200
10th	160	193	236	

SOUTH AFRICA vs. WEST INDIES XI

at Port Elizabeth on 27th, 28th, 30th, 31st January 1984
Toss : South Africa. Umpires : H.R.Martin and C.J.Mitchley
West Indies XI won by 6 wickets

SOUTH AFRICA				
S.J.Cook	c Murray b Stephenson	26	c Murray b Clarke	2
M.Yachad	c Murray b Moseley	6	lbw b Alleyne	31
P.N.Kirsten	c Murray b Clarke	0	b Clarke	4
R.G.Pollock	c Mattis b Clarke	0	c Murray b Clarke	42
K.S.McEwan	c Kallicharran b Moseley	120	c Murray b Alleyne	0
C.E.B.Rice *	c Murray b Clarke	23	c Clarke b Stephenson	12
A.P.Kuiper	c Murray b Stephenson	5	c Alleyne b Clarke	14
A.J.Kourie	not out	63	c Murray b Stephenson	4
D.J.Richardson +	lbw b Alleyne	13	b Stephenson	3
W.K.Watson	c Murray b Clarke	8	not out	4
R.W.Hanley	b Clarke	0	b Clarke	0
Extras	(b 2,lb 8,w 3)	13	(b 3,lb 4,w 2,nb 2)	11
TOTAL		277		127

WEST INDIES XI				
S.F.A.F.Bacchus	c Kirsten b Rice	66	c sub b Watson	76
E.N.Trotman	c Pollock b Hanley	43	c Kuiper b Kirsten	77
E.H.Mattis	c Kourie b Kuiper	15	lbw b Hanley	1
A.I.Kallicharran	c Cook b Watson	16	not out	32
C.L.King	c Kuiper b Watson	0	c sub b Kourie	1
L.G.Rowe *	lbw b Kuiper	16	not out	10
D.A.Murray +	run out	8		
F.D.Stephenson	not out	19		
E.A.Moseley	c Kourie b Kuiper	4		
S.T.Clarke	c Kuiper b Watson	0		
H.L.Alleyne	lbw b Kourie	4		
Extras	(b 1,lb 5,w 1,nb 1)	8	(lb 4,w 2,nb 3)	9
TOTAL		199	(for 4 wkts)	206

WEST INDIES XI	O	M	R	W	O	M	R	W
Clarke	23	7	36	5	13.4	3	32	5
Moseley	20	2	93	2	8	1	22	0
Stephenson	18	2	61	2	15	2	47	3
Alleyne	16	2	55	1	10	3	15	2
King	5	1	19	0				

SOUTH AFRICA	O	M	R	W	O	M	R	W
Watson	24	10	46	3	9	0	46	1
Hanley	15	4	30	1	8	0	38	1
Kourie	11	1	23	1	19	5	65	1
Kuiper	18	3	57	3	4	0	25	0
Rice	13	2	35	1	3	0	9	0
Kirsten					6	1	14	1

FALL OF WICKETS

	SAF	WI	SAF	WI
1st	11	83	4	130
2nd	16	113	9	133
3rd	16	136	66	182
4th	54	136	87	186
5th	100	160	103	
6th	117	170	109	
7th	205	176	117	
8th	264	180	122	
9th	277	185	124	
10th	277	199	127	

SOUTH AFRICA vs. AUSTRALIA XI

at Durban on 26th, 27th, 28th, 29th December 1985
Toss : South Africa. Umpires : D.H.Bezuidenhout and O.R.Schoof
Match drawn

SOUTH AFRICA				
S.J.Cook	lbw b Hogg	52	c Haysman b Hogg	2
H.R.Fotheringham	c Rixon b Hogg	70	(6) not out	100
P.N.Kirsten	c Rixon b Hogg	2	(2) c Rixon b Hogg	5
R.G.Pollock	c Hughes b Rackemann	108	b Rackemann	6
K.S.McEwan	c Rixon b Rackemann	4	(3) c Haysman b Rackemann	5
C.E.B.Rice *	c Dyson b Hogg	11	(5) c Hogan b Rackemann	9
A.J.Kourie	c Haysman b Hogg	1	run out	44
G.S.le Roux	c Rixon b Rackemann	9	c Haysman b Hogan	28
R.V.Jennings +	c Rixon b Rackemann	46		
S.T.Jefferies	not out	43		
H.A.Page	c Hogan b Rackemann	10		
Extras	(b 11,lb 17,w 5,nb 4)	37	(b 3,nb 1)	4
TOTAL		393	(for 7 wkts dec)	203

AUSTRALIA XI				
J.Dyson	c Jennings b Jefferies	29	(2) c Cook b Page	4
G.Shipperd	b Kourie	59	(1) lbw b le Roux	6
M.D.Haysman	lbw b Jefferies	0	not out	3
K.J.Hughes *	c Pollock b Page	38	not out	17
M.D.Taylor	c Jennings b Jefferies	109		
T.V.Hohns	c Kourie b Rice	10		
S.J.Rixon +	c Rice b Jefferies	20		
T.G.Hogan	c Rice b Kirsten	53		
J.N.Maguire	c Kirsten b Page	10		
C.G.Rackemann	c Jennings b le Roux	8		
R.M.Hogg	not out	12		
Extras	(lb 5,w 3,nb 3)	11	(lb 1,nb 1)	2
TOTAL		359	(for 2 wkts)	32

AUSTRALIA XI	O	M	R	W	O	M	R	W
Hogg	32	13	88	5	13	6	26	2
Rackemann	42.1	6	115	5	15	4	28	3
Hogan	16	4	62	0	14.4	1	77	1
Maguire	24	2	79	0	9	1	22	0
Hohns	5	2	21	0	8	1	38	0
Haysman					4	1	9	0

SOUTH AFRICA	O	M	R	W	O	M	R	W
le Roux	24	1	77	1	6	2	24	1
Jefferies	34	10	100	4				
Page	25.3	6	84	2	5	2	7	1
Rice	8	1	21	1				
Kourie	27	6	72	1				
Kirsten	1	1	0	1				

FALL OF WICKETS	SAF	AUS	SAF	AUS
1st	124	51	2	4
2nd	130	51	7	12
3rd	133	115	16	
4th	148	160	23	
5th	184	185	30	
6th	186	236	130	
7th	237	315	203	
8th	327	331		
9th	359	343		
10th	393	359		

SOUTH AFRICA vs. AUSTRALIA XI

at Cape Town on 1st, 2nd, 3rd, 4th January 1986
Toss : South Africa. Umpires : D.A.Sansom and D.D.Schoof
Match drawn

SOUTH AFRICA				
S.J.Cook	lbw b McCurdy	91	c Rixon b Rackemann	70
H.R.Fotheringham	c Rixon b Rackemann	10	b Rackemann	31
P.N.Kirsten	b Rackemann	72	c Haysman b Rackemann	20
R.G.Pollock	b Hogg	79	c Dyson b McCurdy	3
C.E.B.Rice *	c Haysman b McCurdy	21	not out	27
K.A.McKenzie	lbw b Hogg	20	(7) not out	18
A.J.Kourie	c Rixon b Rackemann	8		
G.S.le Roux	c Dyson b McCurdy	45	(6) c Haysman b Rackemann	15
R.V.Jennings +	c Dyson b McCurdy	9		
S.T.Jefferies	c Hughes b Rackemann	22		
H.A.Page	not out	33		
Extras	(b 5,lb 8,nb 7)	20	(lb 15,nb 3)	18
TOTAL		430	(for 5 wkts dec)	202

AUSTRALIA XI				
J.Dyson	c Jennings b Kirsten	95	(2) c Jennings b Page	33
G.Shipperd	b Jefferies	17	(1) lbw b le Roux	8
M.D.Haysman	b Jefferies	4	lbw b Rice	33
K.J.Hughes *	b Kirsten	53	not out	97
R.M.Hogg	c Jennings b Page	0		
M.D.Taylor	c & b Kirsten	22	(5) c McKenzie b Kourie	17
G.N.Yallop	b le Roux	51	(6) not out	24
S.J.Rixon +	b le Roux	11		
T.G.Hogan	lbw b le Roux	28		
R.J.McCurdy	not out	4		
C.G.Rackemann	b le Roux	2		
Extras	(lb 10,nb 7)	17	(lb 10,w 1,nb 1)	12
TOTAL		304	(for 4 wkts)	224

AUSTRALIA XI	O	M	R	W	O	M	R	W
Hogg	29	6	85	2	14	2	43	0
Rackemann	37.2	3	118	4	26	1	106	4
McCurdy	30	1	133	4	12	2	38	1
Hogan	30	6	81	0				

SOUTH AFRICA	O	M	R	W	O	M	R	W
le Roux	20.3	3	56	4	13	3	23	1
Jefferies	19	3	59	2	13	4	32	0
Page	16	3	39	1	11	2	41	1
Kourie	16	3	58	0	23	7	54	1
Rice	10	3	21	0	13	3	30	1
Kirsten	17	3	61	3	17	4	34	0

FALL OF WICKETS

	SAF	AUS	SAF	AUS
1st	37	25	86	31
2nd	169	30	121	54
3rd	204	135	128	106
4th	287	142	156	185
5th	287	171	176	
6th	308	230		
7th	352	255		
8th	367	260		
9th	384	302		
10th	430	304		

SOUTH AFRICA vs. AUSTRALIA XI

at Johannesburg on 16th, 17th, 18th, 20th, 21st January 1986
Toss : Australia XI. Umpires : D.D.Schoof and O.R.Schoof
South Africa won by 188 runs

SOUTH AFRICA				
S.J.Cook	b Hogg	5	lbw b Alderman	21
H.R.Fotheringham	lbw b Alderman	19	c Rixon b Rackemann	5
P.N.Kirsten	c Rixon b Rackemann	12	b Faulkner	10
R.G.Pollock	c Rixon b Rackemann	19	not out	65
C.E.B.Rice *	c Faulkner b Rackemann	9	c Rixon b Rackemann	50
K.A.McKenzie	c Rixon b Rackemann	72	c Alderman b Rackemann	110
A.J.Kourie	c Rixon b Rackemann	14	lbw b Alderman	0
G.S.le Roux	c Alderman b Rackemann	23	c Rixon b Rackemann	18
R.V.Jennings +	c Rixon b Rackemann	0	run out	0
H.A.Page	not out	14	lbw b Alderman	2
C.J.P.G.van Zyl	c Rixon b Rackemann	13	c Rixon b Alderman	2
Extras	(b 2,lb 8,nb 1)	11	(lb 17,w 2,nb 3)	22
TOTAL		211		305

AUSTRALIA XI				
S.B.Smith	c Pollock b van Zyl	116	c Jennings b van Zyl	14
J.Dyson	c Rice b Page	9	not out	18
G.Shipperd	b le Roux	44	b le Roux	3
K.J.Hughes *	lbw b van Zyl	0	c Jennings b le Roux	0
M.D.Taylor	c Jennings b Page	21	lbw b le Roux	0
G.N.Yallop	c Jennings b van Zyl	20	b Rice	6
P.I.Faulkner	c McKenzie b Rice	25	c Fotheringham b Rice	7
S.J.Rixon +	lbw b van Zyl	3	b Page	2
C.G.Rackemann	lbw b Rice	8	b Rice	2
T.M.Alderman	not out	3	c Jennings b Page	1
R.M.Hogg	b Rice	0	c Jennings b Page	0
Extras	(lb 13,w 1,nb 4)	18	(b 2,lb 5,nb 1)	8
TOTAL		267		61

AUSTRALIA XI	O	M	R	W	O	M	R	W
Hogg	4	3	3	1				
Alderman	28	6	68	1	37	6	116	4
Rackemann	26.4	3	84	8	30.1	6	107	4
Faulkner	13	4	46	0	19	0	65	1

SOUTH AFRICA	O	M	R	W	O	M	R	W
le Roux	25	6	68	1	7	2	11	3
van Zyl	27	4	83	4	8	3	16	1
Page	26	8	37	2	7.4	0	19	3
Rice	24	8	43	3	6	2	8	3
Kourie	4	0	23	0				

FALL OF WICKETS	SAF	AUS	SAF	AUS
1st	12	45	25	24
2nd	31	159	31	29
3rd	51	159	80	29
4th	69	192	204	29
5th	86	214	207	36
6th	155	230	242	48
7th	166	237	242	53
8th	166	263	258	60
9th	191	267	274	61
10th	211	267	305	61

SOUTH AFRICA vs. AUSTRALIA

at Johannesburg on 24th, 26th, 27th, 28th December 1986
Toss : Australia. Umpires : D.D.Schoof and F.E.Wood
South Africa won by 49 runs

SOUTH AFRICA				
B.J.Whitfield	b Rackemann	17	lbw b Maguire	23
S.J.Cook	b McCurdy	28	c Rixon b McCurdy	1
P.N.Kirsten	c Wessels b McCurdy	14	c Rixon b Maguire	19
B.M.McMillan	c Rixon b McCurdy	1	lbw b Maguire	30
C.E.B.Rice *	c Rixon b Rackemann	61	c Rixon b Maguire	18
K.A.McKenzie	c Wessels b Rackemann	12	lbw b Maguire	40
A.J.Kourie	lbw b McCurdy	3	c Haysman b Maguire	1
D.J.Richardson +	c Rixon b McCurdy	29	c Rixon b Rackemann	33
G.S.le Roux	lbw b McCurdy	42	c Rixon b Rackemann	0
H.A.Page	c Rixon b Faulkner	5	not out	7
S.T.Jefferies	not out	27	c Rixon b Rackemann	0
Extras	(lb 5,w 4,nb 6)	15	(b 1,lb 6,w 2,nb 1)	10
TOTAL		254		182

AUSTRALIA				
S.B.Smith	c Richardson b Rice	29	c McKenzie b McMillan	36
J.Dyson	b Jefferies	5	b Kourie	16
K.C.Wessels	c McMillan b le Roux	0	c Richardson b McMillan	49
K.J.Hughes *	lbw b le Roux	34	not out	54
M.D.Taylor	c Richardson b Rice	9	c Richardson b Rice	8
M.D.Haysman	b Page	25	c Kourie b Page	17
P.I.Faulkner	b Page	9	c McKenzie b McMillan	8
S.J.Rixon +	lbw b Page	0	b Page	16
J.N.Maguire	c Richardson b Rice	3	c Richardson b Rice	3
R.J.McCurdy	not out	2	b Jefferies	0
C.G.Rackemann	b Rice	2	c McKenzie b Rice	12
Extras	(b 7,lb 9,w 1,nb 7)	24	(lb 15,w 2,nb 9)	26
TOTAL		142		245

AUSTRALIA	O	M	R	W	O	M	R	W
McCurdy	24.5	7	67	6	19	4	58	1
Rackemann	25	3	70	3	19.4	3	54	3
Maguire	18	4	54	0	29	12	61	6
Faulkner	21	2	58	1	2	0	2	0

SOUTH AFRICA	O	M	R	W	O	M	R	W
le Roux	11	4	25	2	14	3	39	0
Jefferies	8	0	29	1	17	5	42	1
Page	17	3	39	3	20	3	53	2
Rice	16	6	19	4	18.1	4	37	3
McMillan	9	3	14	0	15	2	44	3
Kourie	2	2	0	0	11	6	15	1

FALL OF WICKETS

	SAF	AUS	SAF	AUS
1st	36	20	2	49
2nd	56	24	34	57
3rd	63	51	49	107
4th	66	93	92	143
5th	103	99	103	156
6th	125	125	115	169
7th	154	125	153	199
8th	188	137	173	219
9th	210	137	182	224
10th	254	142	182	245

SOUTH AFRICA vs. AUSTRALIA XI

at Cape Town on 1st, 2nd, 3rd, 5th, 6th January 1987
Toss : Australia XI. Umpires : D.H.Bezuidenhout and O.R.Schoof
Match drawn

SOUTH AFRICA				
S.J.Cook	c Rixon b McCurdy	6	c & b Hohns	40
B.J.Whitfield	st Rixon b Hohns	77	c Hughes b Maguire	23
P.N.Kirsten	c Hughes b Hohns	173	not out	105
R.G.Pollock	c sub b Maguire	66		
C.E.B.Rice *	lbw b Maguire	72		
K.A.McKenzie	c Rixon b Maguire	24	(4) lbw b Wessels	52
B.M.McMillan	run out	30	(5) not out	17
G.S.le Roux	c Rixon b McCurdy	13		
D.J.Richardson +	lbw b Maguire	1		
H.A.Page	c Smith b McCurdy	7		
A.J.Kourie	not out	2		
Extras	(b 5,lb 10,w 1,nb 6)	22	(b 4,lb 14,nb 2)	20
TOTAL		493	(for 3 wkts)	257

AUSTRALIA XI		
S.B.Smith	c McKenzie b le Roux	2
J.Dyson	run out	198
K.C.Wessels	lbw b le Roux	36
K.J.Hughes *	c Richardson b le Roux	48
M.D.Taylor	c & b le Roux	0
M.D.Haysman	c Kirsten b le Roux	153
T.V.Hohns	c Kirsten b McMillan	0
S.J.Rixon +	c Richardson b McMillan	1
J.N.Maguire	c Kirsten b McMillan	20
C.G.Rackemann	c Whitfield b Rice	8
R.J.McCurdy	not out	11
Extras	(lb 19)	19
TOTAL		496

AUSTRALIA XI	O	M	R	W	O	M	R	W
McCurdy	43	8	133	3	10	1	42	0
Rackemann	28	7	113	0	19	3	54	0
Maguire	46.4	8	116	4	16	3	53	1
Hohns	40	6	116	2	26	6	63	1
Wessels					12	6	18	1
Smith					2	0	9	0
Dyson					1	1	0	0

SOUTH AFRICA	O	M	R	W	O	M	R	W
le Roux	42	13	85	5				
Page	43	8	118	0				
Kourie	39	10	87	0				
McMillan	36	10	83	3				
Rice	31	8	60	1				
Kirsten	11	0	44	0				

FALL OF WICKETS

	SAF	AUS	SAF	AUS
1st	16	4	48	
2nd	177	78	99	
3rd	288	166	194	
4th	341	170		
5th	407	395		
6th	449	399		
7th	480	401		
8th	483	453		
9th	491	478		
10th	493	496		

SOUTH AFRICA vs. AUSTRALIA XI

at Durban on 17th, 19th, 20th, 21st, 22nd January 1987
Toss : Australia XI. Umpires : K.E.Liebenberg and L.J.Rautenbach
Match drawn

AUSTRALIA XI				
S.B.Smith	c Page b Henry	137	b Page	5
J.Dyson	c Richardson b le Roux	1	c McMillan b Rice	101
K.C.Wessels	c Richardson b le Roux	0	c Richardson b Page	2
K.J.Hughes *	c & b le Roux	25	lbw b Page	9
G.N.Yallop	c Page b Henry	36	(7) c Henry b le Roux	26
M.D.Haysman	c McKenzie b Kirsten	5	(5) b Rice	115
T.V.Hohns	c McKenzie b Kirsten	26	(6) lbw b le Roux	10
S.J.Rixon +	c Richardson b Page	13	not out	42
J.N.Maguire	c Richardson b le Roux	2	run out	2
R.M.Hogg	c Richardson b Page	6	c McEwan b Kirsten	9
R.J.McCurdy	not out	0	c Whitfield b Kirsten	0
Extras	(lb 3,w 1,nb 9)	13	(b 2,lb 14,nb 2)	18
TOTAL		264		339

SOUTH AFRICA				
S.J.Cook	b Hohns	44	c Rixon b Hogg	23
B.J.Whitfield	c Rixon b Hohns	59	b Hogg	26
P.N.Kirsten	c Yallop b Hohns	13	lbw b Maguire	33
K.S.McEwan	b McCurdy	101	b Hohns	27
C.E.B.Rice *	c Dyson b Hohns	22	lbw b Hogg	0
K.A.McKenzie	lbw b Hohns	14	b Hohns	3
B.M.McMillan	c Haysman b McCurdy	15	not out	18
D.J.Richardson +	not out	44	c & b Hohns	0
G.S.le Roux	c Rixon b McCurdy	6		
O.Henry	c Yallop b Hogg	7		
H.A.Page	c & b Hohns	2		
Extras	(b 8,lb 7,w 1,nb 7)	23	(b 1,lb 7,nb 5)	13
TOTAL		350	(for 7 wkts)	143

SOUTH AFRICA	O	M	R	W	O	M	R	W
le Roux	13.3	1	33	4	29	5	63	2
Page	17	1	57	2	35	6	87	3
Rice	10	2	32	0	19	4	38	2
McMillan	10	0	57	0	17	3	55	0
Henry	23	4	58	2	26	11	44	0
Kirsten	15	4	24	2	14.4	3	36	2

AUSTRALIA XI	O	M	R	W	O	M	R	W
Hogg	28	5	87	1	16	4	33	3
McCurdy	22	2	76	3	17	3	59	0
Maguire	28	7	74	0	7	3	16	1
Hohns	47.4	13	98	6	17.5	6	27	3

FALL OF WICKETS	AUS	SAF	AUS	SAF
1st	4	100	7	29
2nd	7	127	11	89
3rd	80	130	25	93
4th	148	177	50	102
5th	198	197	253	115
6th	220	237	260	130
7th	256	309	301	143
8th	256	319	304	
9th	264	341	337	
10th	264	350	339	

SOUTH AFRICA vs. AUSTRALIA XI

at Port Elizabeth on 30th, 31st January, 1st, 3rd, 4th February 1987
Toss : South Africa. Umpires : K.E.Liebenberg and D.D.Schoof
Match drawn

AUSTRALIA XI				
S.B.Smith	lbw b le Roux	77	b Rice	113
G.Shipperd	c Whitfield b Donald	53	b le Roux	0
J.Dyson	lbw b le Roux	1	c Kirsten b le Roux	8
K.J.Hughes *	b Donald	42	b Donald	44
K.C.Wessels	b Henry	135	not out	105
M.D.Haysman	c Rice b Donald	19	not out	53
T.V.Hohns	hit wicket b Rice	37		
S.J.Rixon +	c Page b Henry	61		
R.M.Hogg	lbw b Henry	0		
R.J.McCurdy	not out	6		
T.M.Alderman				
Extras	(b 2,lb 11,nb 11)	24	(b 4,lb 2,w 1,nb 3)	10
TOTAL	(for 9 wkts dec)	455	(for 4 wkts)	333

SOUTH AFRICA		
S.J.Cook	c Dyson b McCurdy	84
B.J.Whitfield	c Rixon b Hogg	4
P.N.Kirsten	lbw b Hogg	34
R.G.Pollock	b Hogg	144
K.S.McEwan	not out	138
H.A.Page	b Hohns	9
C.E.B.Rice *	lbw b Hogg	26
D.J.Richardson +	lbw b Hogg	7
G.S.le Roux	lbw b McCurdy	20
O.Henry	c Hohns b Alderman	13
A.A.Donald	c Haysman b Hohns	21
Extras	(b 2,lb 24,w 1,nb 6)	33
TOTAL		533

SOUTH AFRICA	O	M	R	W	O	M	R	W
le Roux	27	6	67	2	16	0	61	2
Donald	32	7	94	3	19	4	71	1
Page	27	4	95	0	19	1	64	0
Rice	19	5	43	1	10	1	25	1
Henry	36.5	10	96	3	35	14	63	0
Kirsten	22	6	47	0	15	4	42	0
Cook					2	1	1	0

AUSTRALIA XI	O	M	R	W	O	M	R	W
Hogg	39	7	97	5				
Alderman	37	3	142	1				
McCurdy	40	5	159	2				
Hohns	51.2	12	109	2				

FALL OF WICKETS	AUS	SAF	AUS	SAF
1st	123	9	26	
2nd	131	64	26	
3rd	191	211	142	
4th	192	312	198	
5th	255	329		
6th	308	382		
7th	442	394		
8th	442	446		
9th	455	477		
10th		533		

SOUTH AFRICA vs. ENGLAND XI

at Johannesburg on 8th, 9th, 10th February 1990
Toss : South Africa. Umpires : K.E.Liebenberg and J.W.Peacock
South Africa won by 7 wickets

ENGLAND XI				
B.C.Broad	c Jennings b McMillan	48	c Jennings b Donald	0
C.W.J.Athey	b Donald	3	lbw b McMillan	16
R.T.Robinson	c Snell b McMillan	31	c Jennings b McMillan	17
M.W.Gatting *	c McMillan b Snell	22	b Kuiper	0
A.P.Wells	b Snell	4	c Wessels b Donald	11
K.J.Barnett	c Fotheringham b Donald	0	c Donald b Snell	24
B.N.French +	c Jennings b Donald	1	c Jennings b Donald	0
J.E.Emburey	c Jennings b Snell	1	c Jennings b Snell	2
R.M.Ellison	b Donald	6	c Cook b Rundle	12
N.A.Foster	b Snell	11	c Jennings b Donald	21
P.W.Jarvis	not out	1	not out	0
Extras	(b 4,lb 17,nb 7)	28	(b 4,lb 11,w 2,nb 2)	19
TOTAL		156		122

SOUTH AFRICA				
S.J.Cook *	c Robinson b Ellison	20	c & b Gatting	15
H.R.Fotheringham	lbw b Jarvis	8	lbw b Ellison	38
K.C.Wessels	st French b Emburey	1	lbw b Gatting	2
P.N.Kirsten	c French b Jarvis	4	not out	17
R.F.Pienaar	c French b Ellison	13	not out	1
A.P.Kuiper	b Foster	84		
B.M.McMillan	b Ellison	0		
R.V.Jennings +	c Emburey b Ellison	23		
D.B.Rundle	c French b Foster	23		
R.P.Snell	c French b Jarvis	7		
A.A.Donald	not out	7		
Extras	(lb 7,w 5,nb 1)	13	(w 3)	3
TOTAL		203	(for 3 wkts)	76

SOUTH AFRICA	O	M	R	W	O	M	R	W
Donald	21	10	30	4	18	5	29	4
Snell	22.5	11	38	4	15	5	28	2
McMillan	15	2	41	2	11	6	18	2
Kuiper	6	1	21	0	14	4	23	1
Rundle	1	0	5	0	5	2	9	1

ENGLAND XI	O	M	R	W	O	M	R	W
Jarvis	22.5	7	71	3	6	2	25	0
Foster	21	6	54	2	4	0	20	0
Ellison	15	6	41	4	7	1	13	1
Emburey	14	5	30	1				
Gatting					6	1	17	2
Athey					1.1	1	1	0

FALL OF WICKETS

	ENG	SAF	ENG	SAF
1st	15	23	2	56
2nd	96	28	33	56
3rd	106	40	34	71
4th	118	40	42	
5th	119	77	69	
6th	123	77	73	
7th	132	148	78	
8th	138	180	85	
9th	152	189	122	
10th	156	203	122	

AVERAGES

SOUTH AFRICA
(Unofficial 'Test' matches, 1982-1990)

BATTING AVERAGES - Including fielding

Name	M	Inns	NO	Runs	HS	Avge	100s	50s	Ct	St
L.Seeff	1	1	0	188	188	188.00	1	-	2	-
R.G.Pollock	16	25	4	1376	197	65.52	5	7	20	-
K.S.McEwan	7	11	1	438	138*	43.80	3	-	1	-
S.J.Cook	19	34	3	1320	169	42.58	3	7	8	-
P.N.Kirsten	19	32	3	1192	173	41.10	3	7	10	-
H.R.Fotheringham	7	14	3	406	100*	36.90	1	2	5	-
K.A.McKenzie	7	14	2	422	110	35.16	1	2	9	-
B.J.Whitfield	4	7	0	229	77	32.71	-	2	3	-
B.A.Richards	6	10	1	252	66	28.00	-	2	4	-
A.A.Donald	2	2	1	28	21	28.00	-	-	1	-
S.T.Jefferies	11	11	3	223	45	27.87	-	-	3	-
C.E.B.Rice	18	28	3	679	72	27.16	-	4	10	-
A.P.Kuiper	7	10	1	216	84	24.00	-	2	5	-
A.J.Kourie	16	22	5	407	69	23.94	-	3	19	-
D.B.Rundle	1	1	0	23	23	23.00	-	-	-	-
B.M.McMillan	4	7	2	111	30	22.20	-	-	3	-
D.J.Richardson	5	8	1	130	44*	18.57	-	-	14	-
M.Yachad	1	2	0	37	31	18.50	-	-	-	-
G.S.le Roux	15	19	1	285	45	15.83	-	-	3	-
R.V.Jennings	14	18	2	239	46	14.93	-	-	46	4
H.A.Page	7	9	3	89	33*	14.83	-	-	3	-
R.F.Pienaar	1	2	1	14	13	14.00	-	-	-	-
W.K.Watson	3	5	3	22	8	11.00	-	-	-	-
O.Henry	2	2	0	20	13	10.00	-	-	1	-
D.L.Hobson	4	3	1	15	12*	7.50	-	-	3	-
C.J.P.G.van Zyl	1	2	0	15	13	7.50	-	-	-	-
V.A.P.van der Bijl	6	6	3	21	10	7.00	-	-	-	-
R.P.Snell	1	1	0	7	7	7.00	-	-	1	-
K.C.Wessels	1	2	0	3	2	1.50	-	-	1	-
M.J.Procter	1	1	0	1	1	1.00	-	-	1	-
R.W.Hanley	2	4	0	0	0	0.00	-	-	1	-

BOWLING AVERAGES

Name	Overs	Mdns	Runs	Wkts	Avge	Best	5wI	10wM
R.P.Snell	37.5	16	66	6	11.00	4-38	-	-
D.B.Rundle	6	2	14	1	14.00	1-9	-	-
A.A.Donald	90	26	224	12	18.66	4-29	-	-
A.P.Kuiper	104.5	17	307	16	19.18	5-50	1	-
C.J.P.G.van Zyl	35	7	99	5	19.80	4-83	-	-
V.A.P.van der Bijl	256	81	576	29	19.86	5-25	3	1
C.E.B.Rice	262.1	63	627	28	22.39	4-19	-	-
W.K.Watson	90.3	22	276	12	23.00	4-63	-	-
G.S.le Roux	493.2	98	1373	59	23.27	6-55	2	-
S.T.Jefferies	392	110	1167	39	29.92	4-58	-	-
R.W.Hanley	45	9	121	4	30.25	2-26	-	-
B.M.McMillan	113	26	312	10	31.20	3-44	-	-
P.N.Kirsten	164.1	36	422	13	32.46	3-61	-	-

A.J.Kourie	480	124	1277	38	33.60	6-55	3	-
H.A.Page	269.1	47	740	20	37.00	3-19	-	-
O.Henry	120.5	39	261	5	52.20	3-96	-	-
D.L.Hobson	156	29	478	7	68.28	3-87	-	-
S.J.Cook	2	1	1	0	-	-	-	-
M.J.Procter	6	3	6	0	-	-	-	-

ENGLAND XI (1981-82 and 1989-90)

BATTING AVERAGES - Including fielding

Name	M	Inns	NO	Runs	HS	Avge	100s	50s	Ct	St
D.L.Amiss	3	5	2	226	73*	75.33	-	3	1	-
G.A.Gooch	3	5	0	338	109	67.60	1	2	5	-
W.Larkins	3	5	0	185	95	37.00	-	1	-	-
R.A.Woolmer	3	5	1	138	100	34.50	1	-	-	-
B.C.Broad	1	2	0	48	48	24.00	-	-	-	-
R.T.Robinson	1	2	0	48	31	24.00	-	-	1	-
P.Willey	3	4	0	79	39	19.75	-	-	1	-
G.Boycott	3	5	0	89	36	17.80	-	-	-	-
N.A.Foster	1	2	0	32	21	16.00	-	-	-	-
J.K.Lever	3	4	2	31	10*	15.50	-	-	-	-
K.J.Barnett	1	2	0	24	24	12.00	-	-	-	-
M.W.Gatting	1	2	0	22	22	11.00	-	-	1	-
C.W.J.Athey	1	2	0	19	16	9.50	-	-	-	-
A.P.E.Knott	3	4	0	36	16	9.00	-	-	12	-
R.M.Ellison	1	2	0	18	12	9.00	-	-	-	-
A.P.Wells	1	2	0	15	11	7.50	-	-	-	-
C.M.Old	3	4	0	23	11	5.75	-	-	1	-
L.B.Taylor	3	3	1	10	10*	5.00	-	-	-	-
D.L.Underwood	2	3	0	14	8	4.66	-	-	-	-
J.E.Emburey	1	2	0	3	2	1.50	-	-	1	-
B.N.French	1	2	0	1	1	0.50	-	-	4	1
P.W.Jarvis	1	2	2	1	1*	-	-	-	-	-
M.Hendrick	1	0	0	0	0	-	-	-	1	-

BOWLING AVERAGES

Name	Overs	Mdns	Runs	Wkts	Avge	Best	5wI	10wM
M.W.Gatting	6	1	17	2	8.50	2-17	-	-
R.M.Ellison	22	7	54	5	10.80	4-41	-	-
L.B.Taylor	91.3	22	206	11	18.72	5-61	1	-
M.Hendrick	33	12	65	3	21.66	3-28	-	-
W.Larkins	5	0	24	1	24.00	1-24	-	-
J.E.Emburey	14	5	30	1	30.00	1-30	-	-
J.K.Lever	106.4	25	335	11	30.45	6-86	1	-
P.W.Jarvis	28.5	9	96	3	32.00	3-71	-	-
N.A.Foster	25	6	74	2	37.00	2-54	-	-
D.L.Underwood	45	10	128	2	64.00	1-36	-	-
C.M.Old	73	22	171	2	85.50	1-8	-	-
C.W.J.Athey	1.1	1	1	0	-	-	-	-
A.P.E.Knott	1	0	5	0	-	-	-	-
P.Willey	4	1	8	0	-	-	-	-
G.A.Gooch	2	0	15	0	-	-	-	-

SRI LANKA XI (1982-83)

BATTING AVERAGES - Including fielding

Name	M	Inns	NO	Runs	HS	Avge	100s	50s	Ct	St
H.H.Devapriya	1	2	0	82	53	41.00	-	1	-	-
B.de Silva	1	2	0	73	70	36.50	-	1	-	-
G.J.A.F.Aponso	2	4	0	144	81	36.00	-	1	-	-
A.N.Ranasinghe	1	2	0	63	54	31.50	-	1	-	-
J.B.N.Perera	2	4	0	117	102	29.25	1	-	1	-
J.F.Woutersz	2	4	0	114	51	28.50	-	1	1	-
P.L.J.Fernando	1	1	0	21	21	21.00	-	-	1	-
B.Warnapura	2	4	0	81	31	20.25	-	-	-	-
L.W.Kaluperuma	2	4	1	51	39	17.00	-	-	2	-
H.M.Goonatillake	2	4	1	46	19	15.33	-	-	2	1
A.R.Opatha	2	4	1	38	20	12.66	-	-	1	-
N.D.P.Hettiaratchi	2	4	0	16	10	4.00	-	-	-	-
G.R.A.de Silva	2	4	1	8	8*	2.66	-	-	-	-

BOWLING AVERAGES

Name	Overs	Mdns	Runs	Wkts	Avge	Best	5wI	10wM
L.W.Kaluperuma	61	7	233	5	46.60	5-123	1	-
J.B.N.Perera	61.2	5	202	4	50.50	2-48	-	-
A.R.Opatha	71	9	261	4	65.25	3-111	-	-
J.F.Woutersz	18	0	71	1	71.00	1-60	-	-
A.N.Ranasinghe	36	3	123	1	123.00	1-123	-	-
P.L.J.Fernando	7	1	24	0	-	-	-	-
G.R.A.de Silva	12	0	74	0	-	-	-	-

WEST INDIES XI (1982-83 and 1983-84)

BATTING AVERAGES - Including fielding

Name	M	Inns	NO	Runs	HS	Avge	100s	50s	Ct	St
S.F.A.F.Bacchus	2	3	1	161	76	80.50	-	2	-	-
B.D.Julien	1	2	1	51	33*	51.00	-	-	2	-
D.R.Parry	4	7	1	233	63*	38.83	-	2	4	-
A.I.Kallicharran	6	11	1	361	103	36.10	1	1	2	-
A.T.Greenidge	3	6	1	180	48	36.00	-	-	1	-
C.L.King	6	11	0	378	101	34.36	1	2	3	-
R.A.Austin	2	4	0	134	93	33.50	-	1	2	-
L.G.Rowe	5	9	1	249	157	31.12	1	-	3	-
F.D.Stephenson	6	10	2	212	56	26.50	-	2	5	-
E.N.Trotman	4	7	0	177	77	25.28	-	1	1	-
D.A.Murray	6	10	0	207	43	20.70	-	-	23	-
E.A.Moseley	4	6	1	84	33*	16.80	-	-	1	-
M.A.Lynch	3	5	0	67	26	13.40	-	-	-	-
S.T.Clarke	6	9	4	65	25	13.00	-	-	2	-
E.H.Mattis	5	10	0	123	32	12.30	-	-	3	-
R.A.Wynter	1	2	1	9	9	9.00	-	-	1	-
H.L.Alleyne	2	3	1	4	4	2.00	-	-	1	-

BOWLING AVERAGES

Name	Overs	Mdns	Runs	Wkts	Avge	Best	5wI	10wM
H.L.Alleyne	52	7	186	12	15.50	5-62	1	-
S.T.Clarke	248	72	598	37	16.16	7-34	6	2

E.A.Moseley	115.4	17	411	15	27.40	4-45	-	-
D.R.Parry	156	34	410	14	29.28	5-117	1	-
R.A.Wynter	20	3	59	2	29.50	2-26	-	-
F.D.Stephenson	161.4	21	564	12	47.00	3-47	-	-
B.D.Julien	26	5	82	1	82.00	1-71	-	-
C.L.King	30	7	110	1	110.00	1-3	-	-
R.A.Austin	10	1	36	0	-	-	-	-
A.I.Kallicharran	8.2	2	36	0	-	-	-	-

AUSTRALIA XI (1985-86 and 1986-87)

BATTING AVERAGES - Including fielding

Name	M	Inns	NO	Runs	HS	Avge	100s	50s	Ct	St
S.B.Smith	5	9	0	529	137	58.77	3	1	1	-
K.C.Wessels	4	7	1	327	135	54.50	2	-	2	-
M.D.Haysman	6	11	2	427	153	47.44	2	1	10	-
K.J.Hughes	7	13	3	461	97*	46.10	-	3	4	-
J.Dyson	7	13	1	518	198	43.16	2	1	6	-
T.G.Hogan	2	2	0	81	53	40.50	-	1	2	-
G.N.Yallop	3	6	1	163	51	32.60	-	1	2	-
G.Shipperd	4	8	0	190	59	23.75	-	2	-	-
M.D.Taylor	5	8	0	186	109	23.25	1	-	-	-
S.J.Rixon	7	10	1	169	61	18.77	-	1	36	1
T.V.Hohns	4	5	0	83	37	16.60	-	-	4	-
P.I.Faulkner	2	4	0	49	25	12.25	-	-	1	-
R.J.McCurdy	5	7	5	23	11*	11.50	-	-	-	-
J.N.Maguire	4	6	0	40	20	6.66	-	-	-	-
C.G.Rackemann	5	7	0	42	12	6.00	-	-	-	-
R.M.Hogg	5	7	1	27	12*	4.50	-	-	-	-
T.M.Alderman	2	2	1	4	3*	4.00	-	-	2	-

BOWLING AVERAGES

Name	Overs	Mdns	Runs	Wkts	Avge	Best	5wI	10wM
K.C.Wessels	12	6	18	1	18.00	1-18	-	-
R.M.Hogg	175	46	462	19	24.31	5-88	2	-
C.G.Rackemann	269	39	849	34	24.97	8-84	2	1
T.V.Hohns	195.5	46	472	14	33.71	6-98	1	-
R.J.McCurdy	217.5	33	765	20	38.25	6-67	1	-
J.N.Maguire	177.4	40	475	12	39.58	6-61	1	-
T.M.Alderman	102	15	326	6	54.33	4-116	-	-
P.I.Faulkner	55	6	171	2	85.50	1-58	-	-
T.G.Hogan	60.4	11	220	1	220.00	1-77	-	-
J.Dyson	1	1	0	0	-	-	-	-
S.B.Smith	2	0	9	0	-	-	-	-
M.D.Haysman	4	1	9	0	-	-	-	-

THE TEST MATCHES 1992-1994

Scorecards and averages for the Test matches played against India,West Indies, Sri Lanka and Australia

WEST INDIES vs. SOUTH AFRICA

at Bridgetown on 18th, 19th, 20th, 22nd, 23rd April 1992
Toss : West Indies. Umpires : D.M.Archer and S.A.Bucknor
West Indies won by 52 runs

WEST INDIES				
D.L.Haynes	c Wessels b Snell	58	c Richardson b Snell	23
P.V.Simmons	c Kirsten b Snell	35	c Kirsten b Bosch	3
B.C.Lara	c Richardson b Bosch	17	c Richardson b Donald	64
R.B.Richardson *	c Richardson b Snell	44	lbw b Snell	2
K.L.T.Arthurton	c Kuiper b Pringle	59	b Donald	22
J.C.Adams	b Donald	11	not out	79
D.Williams +	c Hudson b Donald	1	lbw b Snell	5
C.E.L.Ambrose	not out	6	c Richardson b Donald	6
K.C.G.Benjamin	b Snell	1	lbw b Donald	7
C.A.Walsh	b Pringle	6	c Kirsten b Snell	13
B.P.Patterson	run out	0	b Bosch	11
Extras	(lb 7,nb 17)	24	(b 17,lb 11,nb 20)	48
TOTAL		262		283

SOUTH AFRICA				
M.W.Rushmere	c Lara b Ambrose	3	b Ambrose	3
A.C.Hudson	b Benjamin	163	c Lara b Ambrose	0
K.C.Wessels *	c Adams b Ambrose	59	c Lara b Walsh	74
P.N.Kirsten	c Lara b Benjamin	11	b Walsh	52
W.J.Cronje	c Lara b Adams	5	c Williams b Ambrose	2
A.P.Kuiper	c Williams b Patterson	34	c Williams b Walsh	0
D.J.Richardson +	c Ambrose b Adams	8	c Williams b Ambrose	2
R.P.Snell	run out	6	c Adams b Walsh	0
M.W.Pringle	c Walsh b Adams	15	b Ambrose	4
A.A.Donald	st Williams b Adams	0	b Ambrose	0
T.Bosch	not out	5	not out	0
Extras	(b 4,lb 6,w 1,nb 25)	36	(b 4,lb 3,nb 4)	11
TOTAL		345		148

SOUTH AFRICA	O	M	R	W	O	M	R	W
Donald	20	1	67	2	25	3	77	4
Bosch	15	2	43	1	24.3	7	61	2
Snell	18	3	84	4	16	1	74	4
Pringle	18.4	2	61	2	16	0	43	0

WEST INDIES	O	M	R	W	O	M	R	W
Ambrose	36	19	47	2	24.4	7	34	6
Patterson	23	4	79	1	7	1	26	0
Walsh	27	7	71	0	22	10	31	4
Benjamin	25	3	87	2	9	2	21	0
Arthurton	3	0	8	0				
Adams	21.4	5	43	4	5	0	16	0
Simmons					5	1	13	0

FALL OF WICKETS	WI	SAF	WI	SAF
1st	99	14	10	0
2nd	106	139	66	27
3rd	137	168	68	123
4th	219	187	120	130
5th	240	279	139	131
6th	241	293	164	142
7th	250	312	174	142
8th	255	316	196	147
9th	262	336	221	148
10th	262	345	283	148

SOUTH AFRICA vs. INDIA

at Kingsmead, Durban on 13th, 14th, 15th, 16th, 17th November 1992
Toss : India. Umpires : S.A.Bucknor, K.E.Liebenberg and C.J.Mitchley
Match drawn

SOUTH AFRICA				
S.J.Cook	c Tendulkar b Kapil Dev	0	c & b Kumble	43
A.C.Hudson	b Kapil Dev	14	c More b Srinath	55
K.C.Wessels *	c Azharuddin b Kumble	118	c More b Srinath	32
P.N.Kirsten	c More b Srinath	13	not out	11
J.N.Rhodes	c Azharuddin b Kumble	41	not out	26
B.M.McMillan	c Prabhakar b Shastri	3		
D.J.Richardson +	lbw b Prabhakar	15		
O.Henry	c Tendulkar b Shastri	3		
M.W.Pringle	lbw b Kapil Dev	33		
A.A.Donald	lbw b Prabhakar	1		
B.N.Schultz	not out	0		
Extras	(lb 6,nb 7)	13	(b 1,lb 2,nb 6)	9
TOTAL		254	(for 3 wkts)	176

INDIA		
R.J.Shastri	lbw b Pringle	14
A.Jajeda	c McMillan b Schultz	3
S.V.Manjrekar	lbw b McMillan	0
S.R.Tendulkar	run out	11
M.Azharuddin *	run out	36
P.K.Amre	c Rhodes b McMillan	103
Kapil Dev	c Richardson b McMillan	2
M.Prabhakar	c McMillan b Donald	13
K.S.More +	lbw b Henry	55
A.R.Kumble	b Henry	8
J.Srinath	not out	1
Extras	(b 1,lb 7,w 4,nb 19)	31
TOTAL		277

INDIA	O	M	R	W	O	M	R	W
Kapil Dev	22	6	43	3	19	11	19	0
Prabhakar	24.4	7	47	2	14	3	47	0
Srinath	18	3	69	1	16	3	42	2
Kumble	28	8	51	2	16	4	36	1
Shastri	11	1	38	2	14	2	22	0
Tendulkar					2	1	3	0
Manjrekar					1	0	4	0

SOUTH AFRICA	O	M	R	W	O	M	R	W
Donald	29	6	69	1				
Schultz	14.5	7	25	1				
McMillan	37	18	52	3				
Pringle	34	10	67	1				
Henry	19.1	3	56	2				

FALL OF WICKETS	SAF	IND	SAF	IND
1st	0	18	68	
2nd	41	22	129	
3rd	101	38	138	
4th	183	38		
5th	194	125		
6th	206	127		
7th	215	146		
8th	251	247		
9th	253	274		
10th	254	277		

SOUTH AFRICA vs. INDIA

at Johannesburg on 26th, 27th, 28th, 29th, 30th November 1992
Toss : South Africa. Umpires : S.A.Bucknor, S.B.Lambson and C.J.Mitchley
Match drawn

SOUTH AFRICA				
S.J.Cook	c More b Prabhakar	2	c More b Srinath	31
A.C.Hudson	c Azharuddin b Prabhakar	8	b Kumble	53
K.C.Wessels *	c Azharuddin b Srinath	5	(4) run out	11
P.N.Kirsten	lbw b Prabhakar	0	(5) b Kumble	26
J.N.Rhodes	lbw b Kumble	91	(6) b Kumble	13
W.J.Cronje	c & b Kapil Dev	8	(7) b Kumble	15
B.M.McMillan	c Manjrekar b Srinath	98	(8) c Prabhakar b Kumble	5
D.J.Richardson +	lbw b Kumble	9	(3) b Kumble	50
C.R.Matthews	b Prabhakar	31	c Tendulkar b Prabhakar	18
M.W.Pringle	retired hurt/ill	3	absent hurt/ill	
A.A.Donald	not out	14	(10) not out	7
Extras	(lb 10,w 4,nb 9)	23	(b 1,lb 14,w 1,nb 7)	23
TOTAL		292		252

INDIA				
R.J.Shastri	c Wessels b Matthews	7	b Matthews	23
A.Jajeda	lbw b McMillan	14	c Wessels b Donald	43
S.V.Manjrekar	b McMillan	7	(5) not out	32
S.R.Tendulkar	c Hudson b Cronje	111	lbw b Donald	1
M.Azharuddin *	c Wessels b Matthews	9	(3) c Richardson b Matthews	1
P.K.Amre	lbw b McMillan	7	not out	35
M.Prabhakar	c Richardson b Donald	2		
Kapil Dev	c McMillan b Donald	25		
K.S.More +	c Richardson b McMillan	10		
A.R.Kumble	not out	21		
J.Srinath	c Richardson b Donald	5		
Extras	(lb 4,w 4,nb 1)	9	(b 2,lb 2,nb 2)	6
TOTAL		227	(for 4 wkts)	141

INDIA	O	M	R	W	O	M	R	W
Kapil Dev	25	4	62	1	24	6	50	0
Prabhakar	29	3	90	4	23.2	3	74	1
Srinath	26.5	6	60	2	26	2	58	1
Kumble	26	8	60	2	44	22	53	6
Shastri	4	0	10	0				
Tendulkar					1	0	2	0

SOUTH AFRICA	O	M	R	W	O	M	R	W
Donald	31	9	78	3	20	6	43	2
McMillan	29	11	74	4	21	6	34	0
Matthews	29	13	41	2	20	10	23	2
Cronje	17	10	22	1	18	7	32	0
Kirsten	2	0	8	0	3	1	5	0

FALL OF WICKETS	SAF	IND	SAF	IND
1st	10	27	73	68
2nd	11	27	108	70
3rd	11	44	138	71
4th	26	77	170	73
5th	73	124	194	
6th	158	127	199	
7th	186	155	209	
8th	251	174	239	
9th	292	212	252	
10th		227		

SOUTH AFRICA vs. INDIA

at Port Elizabeth on 26th, 27th, 28th, 29th December 1992
Toss : South Africa. Umpires : W.Diedricks, R.E.Kortzen and D.R.Shepherd
South Africa won by 9 wickets

INDIA				
R.J.Shastri	c Henry b McMillan	10	c Richardson b McMillan	5
W.V.Raman	c Richardson b Donald	21	b Donald	0
S.V.Manjrekar	c Henry b McMillan	23	lbw b Donald	6
S.R.Tendulkar	c Richardson b Donald	6	c Richardson b Schultz	0
M.Azharuddin *	c Richardson b Donald	60	c Wessels b Donald	7
P.K.Amre	c McMillan b Donald	11	c Richardson b Schultz	7
Kapil Dev	c Kirsten b McMillan	12	c McMillan b Donald	129
M.Prabhakar	c McMillan b Matthews	11	c Richardson b Donald	17
K.S.More +	c Richardson b Donald	20	b Donald	17
A.R.Kumble	c McMillan b Schultz	14	c Richardson b Donald	17
Venkatapathy Raju	not out	0	not out	2
Extras	(lb 13,w 4,nb 7)	24	(lb 4,w 1,nb 3)	8
TOTAL		212		215

SOUTH AFRICA				
A.C.Hudson	b Venkatapathy	52	(2) c Azharuddin b Tendulkar	33
K.C.Wessels *	b Prabhakar	0	(1) not out	95
W.J.Cronje	b Kumble	135	not out	16
P.N.Kirsten	c More b Venkatapathy	0		
B.M.McMillan	lbw b Venkatapathy	25		
J.N.Rhodes	c Prabhakar b Kumble	2		
D.J.Richardson +	run out	1		
O.Henry	lbw b Kapil Dev	16		
C.R.Matthews	c Azharuddin b Kapil Dev	17		
A.A.Donald	b Kumble	6		
B.N.Schultz	not out	0		
Extras	(b 2,lb 13,nb 6)	21	(b 8,lb 3)	11
TOTAL		275	(for 1 wkt)	155

SOUTH AFRICA	O	M	R	W	O	M	R	W
Donald	27	11	55	5	28	4	84	7
Schultz	20.5	4	39	1	16	5	37	2
McMillan	20	9	41	3	12	2	30	1
Matthews	17	7	34	1	9	1	43	0
Henry	11	2	30	0	8	2	17	0

INDIA	O	M	R	W	O	M	R	W
Kapil Dev	24	6	45	2	5	1	9	0
Prabhakar	15	3	57	1	5	2	7	0
Kumble	50.3	16	81	3	20	5	65	0
Venkatapathy	46	15	73	3	18	5	50	0
Tendulkar	1	1	0	0	3	0	9	1
Shastri	2	1	4	0				
Azharuddin					0.1	0	4	0

FALL OF WICKETS

	IND	SAF	IND	SAF
1st	43	0	1	98
2nd	49	117	10	
3rd	59	117	11	
4th	98	171	20	
5th	143	182	27	
6th	152	185	31	
7th	160	215	88	
8th	185	259	120	
9th	208	274	197	
10th	212	275	215	

SOUTH AFRICA vs. INDIA

at Cape Town on 2nd, 3rd, 4th, 5th, 6th January 1993
Toss : South Africa. Umpires : S.B.Lambson, K.E.Liebenberg and D.R.Shepherd
Match drawn

SOUTH AFRICA				
A.C.Hudson	c & b Srinath	19	(2) c More b Srinath	11
K.C.Wessels *	b Prabhakar	0	(1) c & b Srinath	34
W.J.Cronje	c Manjrekar b Kumble	33	c More b Srinath	0
P.N.Kirsten	c More b Kapil Dev	13	c Manjrekar b Kapil Dev	13
D.J.Cullinan	c Prabhakar b Venkatapathy	46	c More b Srinath	28
J.N.Rhodes	c More b Srinath	86	c Srinath b Kumble	16
B.M.McMillan	c sub b Kumble	52	not out	11
D.J.Richardson +	c Tendulkar b Kumble	21	not out	10
O.Henry	run out	34		
C.R.Matthews	not out	28		
A.A.Donald	not out	1		
Extras	(b 2,lb 22,w 2,nb 1)	27	(lb 4,nb 3)	7
TOTAL	(for 9 wkts dec)	360	(for 6 wkts dec)	130

INDIA				
A.Jajeda	c Kirsten b McMillan	19	not out	20
M.Prabhakar	c Wessels b Henry	62	c Richardson b Matthews	7
S.V.Manjrekar	c Hudson b Donald	46	not out	2
P.K.Amre	c McMillan b Donald	6		
S.R.Tendulkar	c Hudson b Cronje	73		
M.Azharuddin *	c Richardson b McMillan	7		
Venkatapathy Raju	c Cullinan b Matthews	18		
Kapil Dev	c Hudson b Cronje	34		
K.S.More +	lbw b Matthews	0		
A.R.Kumble	c Hudson b Matthews	0		
J.Srinath	not out	0		
Extras	(lb 7,w 3,nb 1)	11		0
TOTAL		276	(for 1 wkt)	29

INDIA	O	M	R	W	O	M	R	W
Kapil Dev	29	8	42	1	17	4	29	1
Prabhakar	23	6	48	1	10	4	19	0
Venkatapathy	47	15	94	1	20	8	25	0
Srinath	25	6	51	2	27	10	33	4
Kumble	47	13	101	3	23	11	20	1

SOUTH AFRICA	O	M	R	W	O	M	R	W
Donald	36	13	58	2	4	0	7	0
McMillan	36	9	76	2				
Matthews	28	12	32	3	6	1	17	1
Cronje	18.4	8	17	2	3	3	0	0
Henry	33	8	86	1				
Rhodes					1	0	5	0

FALL OF WICKETS	SAF	IND	SAF	IND
1st	0	44	20	21
2nd	28	129	28	
3rd	57	138	61	
4th	78	144	61	
5th	177	153	95	
6th	245	200	107	
7th	282	275		
8th	319	276		
9th	345	276		
10th		276		

SRI LANKA vs. SOUTH AFRICA

at Moratuwa on 25th, 26th, 28th, 29th, 30th August 1993
Toss : Sri Lanka. Umpires : B.L.Aldridge and K.T.Francis
Match drawn

SRI LANKA				
R.S.Mahanama	b Schultz	53	lbw b Symcox	17
U.C.Hathurusinghe	c Richardson b Donald	1	b Donald	9
A.P.Gurusinha	c Richardson b Donald	26	(4) b Schultz	27
P.A.de Silva	c Wessels b Schultz	27	(5) c Richardson b Symcox	68
A.Ranatunga *	c Richardson b Donald	44	(6) b Schultz	131
H.P.Tillekeratne	lbw b Schultz	92	(7) not out	33
R.S.Kalpage	c Richardson b Cronje	42	(8) not out	0
P.B.Dassanayake +	b Schultz	7		
P.Wijetunga	b Donald	10	(3) c Hudson b Symcox	0
G.P.Wickremasinghe	c Rhodes b Donald	11		
M.Muralitharan	not out	2		
Extras	(lb 11,w 1,nb 4)	16	(b 3,lb 6,nb 6)	15
TOTAL		331	(for 6 wkts dec)	300

SOUTH AFRICA				
K.C.Wessels *	c Tillekeratne b Muralitharan	47	(2) c Wickremasinghe b Muralitharan	16
A.C.Hudson	c Gurusinha b Wijetunga	90	(1) c Dassanayake b Hathurusinghe	4
W.J.Cronje	b Muralitharan	17	c sub b Wickremasinghe	1
D.J.Cullinan	lbw b Hathurusinghe	33	lbw b Wickremasinghe	46
S.J.Cook	b Wickremasinghe	7	c Tillekeratne b Wijetunga	24
J.N.Rhodes	c Tillekeratne b Muralitharan	8	not out	101
D.J.Richardson +	c & b Wickremasinghe	2	c Tillekeratne b de Silva	4
P.L.Symcox	c Mahanama b Muralitharan	48	c Hathurusinghe b de Silva	21
C.E.Eksteen	b Muralitharan	1	not out	4
A.A.Donald	not out	0		
B.N.Schultz	lbw b Kalpage	0		
Extras	(lb 4,w 1,nb 9)	14	(b 10,lb 4,w 3,nb 13)	30
TOTAL		267	(for 7 wkts)	251

SOUTH AFRICA	O	M	R	W	O	M	R	W
Donald	28	5	69	5	22	5	73	1
Schultz	31.2	12	75	4	20	2	82	2
Eksteen	14	4	44	0	9	2	34	0
Cronje	26	14	32	1	8	2	27	0
Symcox	28	3	100	0	21	2	75	3

SRI LANKA	O	M	R	W	O	M	R	W
Wickremasinghe	19	4	58	2	22	6	59	2
Gurusinha	3	0	3	0				
Kalpage	17.5	6	23	1	8	2	21	0
Wijetunga	29	2	58	1	23	2	60	1
Muralitharan	39	8	104	5	31	11	48	1
de Silva	1	0	3	0	17	3	35	2
Hathurusinghe	4	0	14	1	9	5	9	1
Tillekeratne					2	0	5	0

FALL OF WICKETS

	SRI	SAF	SRI	SAF
1st	5	104	26	13
2nd	77	152	26	15
3rd	100	179	34	48
4th	157	203	75	92
5th	168	203	196	126
6th	258	206	299	138
7th	273	240		199
8th	285	262		
9th	313	267		
10th	331	267		

SRI LANKA vs. SOUTH AFRICA

at Colombo on 6th, 7th, 8th, 10th September 1993
Toss : Sri Lanka. Umpires : B.L.Aldridge and T.M.Samarasinghe
South Africa won by an innings and 208 runs

SRI LANKA				
R.S.Mahanama	c Richardson b Schultz	7	b Schultz	0
U.C.Hathurusinghe	c McMillan b Donald	34	c Cronje b Donald	0
H.P.Tillekeratne	c Cronje b McMillan	9	c Richardson b Snell	9
P.A.de Silva	c Richardson b Schultz	34	c & b Donald	24
A.Ranatunga *	c Cullinan b Snell	11	(6) c Richardson b Schultz	14
S.T.Jayasuriya	b Schultz	44	(7) b Schultz	16
P.B.Dassanayake +	c Richardson b Donald	0	(8) c Richardson b Snell	10
H.D.P.K.Dharmasena	c Richardson b Schultz	5	(9) c Richardson b Schultz	2
C.P.H.Ramanayake	not out	3	(5) lbw b McMillan	0
G.P.Wickremasinghe	b Schultz	17	c Donald b Snell	21
M.Muralitharan	c Rhodes b Snell	0	not out	14
Extras	(lb 3,nb 1)	4	(lb 4,nb 5)	9
TOTAL		168		119

SOUTH AFRICA		
K.C.Wessels *	c Dassanayake b Muralitharan	92
A.C.Hudson	lbw b Wickremasinghe	58
W.J.Cronje	b de Silva	122
D.J.Cullinan	c & b Muralitharan	52
J.N.Rhodes	run out	10
B.M.McMillan	b Muralitharan	0
D.J.Richardson +	c Jayasuriya b Muralitharan	11
P.L.Symcox	st Dassanayake b de Silva	50
R.P.Snell	st Dassanayake b de Silva	48
A.A.Donald	not out	4
B.N.Schultz	st Dassanayake b Muralitharan	6
Extras	(b 5,lb 20,w 1,nb 16)	42
TOTAL		495

SOUTH AFRICA	O	M	R	W	O	M	R	W
Donald	12	4	22	2	10	7	6	2
Schultz	20	8	48	5	16	4	58	4
Snell	19	3	57	2	12	4	32	3
McMillan	9	1	38	1	4	0	11	1
Symcox	2	2	0	0	1	0	8	0

SRI LANKA	O	M	R	W	O	M	R	W
Ramanayake	20	5	63	0				
Wickremasinghe	31	6	111	1				
Hathurusinghe	7	4	12	0				
Dharmasena	45	12	91	0				
Muralitharan	54	17	101	5				
Jayasuriya	9	1	47	0				
de Silva	13	1	39	3				
Ranatunga	2	0	6	0				

FALL OF WICKETS	SRI	SAF	SRI	SAF
1st	7	137	1	
2nd	27	179	1	
3rd	72	284	30	
4th	85	306	31	
5th	117	307	49	
6th	119	333	54	
7th	145	401	69	
8th	147	480	76	
9th	167	487	101	
10th	168	495	119	

SRI LANKA vs. SOUTH AFRICA

at Colombo on 14th, 15th, 16th, 18th, 19th September 1993
Toss : South Africa. Umpires : B.L.Aldridge and B.C.Cooray
Match drawn

SOUTH AFRICA				
A.C.Hudson	c Tillekeratne b Dharmasena	22	(2) b Ramanayake	28
K.C.Wessels *	b Liyanage	26	(1) c Mahanama b Hathurusinghe	7
W.J.Cronje	b Ramanayake	24	not out	73
D.J.Cullinan	c Ramanayake b Jayasuriya	102	c sub b Dharmasena	4
J.N.Rhodes	st Dassanayake b Muralitharan	7	b Muralitharan	19
B.M.McMillan	c Jayasuriya b Muralitharan	2	not out	0
D.J.Richardson +	c de Silva b Muralitharan	62		
P.L.Symcox	c Tillekeratne b Ramanayake	30		
R.P.Snell	not out	13		
A.A.Donald	lbw b Ramanayake	1		
B.N.Schultz	c de Silva b Muralitharan	0		
Extras	(b 6,lb 10,nb 11)	27	(b 4,lb 17,nb 7)	28
TOTAL		316	(for 4 wkts)	159

SRI LANKA		
R.S.Mahanama	c McMillan b Schultz	25
U.C.Hathurusinghe	c Richardson b Donald	1
P.B.Dassanayake +	run out	8
P.A.de Silva	lbw b Symcox	82
A.Ranatunga *	c Richardson b Schultz	50
H.P.Tillekeratne	c Richardson b Schultz	37
S.T.Jayasuriya	c Cronje b Schultz	65
H.D.P.K.Dharmasena	c Richardson b Schultz	5
D.K.Liyanage	b Donald	0
C.P.H.Ramanayake	not out	0
M.Muralitharan		
Extras	(b 7,lb 9,nb 7)	23
TOTAL	(for 9 wkts dec)	296

SRI LANKA	O	M	R	W	O	M	R	W
Ramanayake	25	4	75	3	10	1	26	1
Liyanage	21	4	58	1	4	1	17	0
Hathurusinghe	6	4	6	0	8	4	7	1
Dharmasena	28	5	79	1	18	8	29	1
Muralitharan	35.1	8	64	4	15	3	39	1
de Silva	1	0	9	0	3	1	3	0
Jayasuriya	5	1	9	1	3	1	17	0

SOUTH AFRICA	O	M	R	W	O	M	R	W
Donald	30	12	62	2				
Schultz	36.5	9	63	5				
McMillan	30	8	64	0				
Snell	25	8	44	0				
Symcox	18	5	47	1				

FALL OF WICKETS

	SAF	SRI	SAF	SRI
1st	51	1	11	
2nd	53	27	58	
3rd	96	55	65	
4th	108	156	159	
5th	128	202		
6th	250	263		
7th	281	273		
8th	311	294		
9th	315	296		
10th	316			

AUSTRALIA vs. SOUTH AFRICA

at Melbourne on 26th, 27th, 28th, 29th, 30th December 1993
Toss : Australia. Umpires : D.B.Hair and T.A.Prue
Match drawn

AUSTRALIA		
M.A.Taylor	b Symcox	170
M.J.Slater	c Kirsten b Donald	32
S.K.Warne	lbw b de Villiers	0
D.C.Boon	b Matthews	25
M.E.Waugh	lbw b Matthews	84
A.R.Border *	c Richardson b Matthews	2
D.R.Martyn	b Symcox	8
I.A.Healy +	not out	7
P.R.Reiffel		
T.B.A.May		
C.J.McDermott		
Extras	(b 2,lb 7,nb 5)	14
TOTAL	(for 7 wkts dec)	342

SOUTH AFRICA		
A.C.Hudson	retired hur	64
G.Kirsten	c Taylor b Waugh	16
W.J.Cronje	c Boon b Warne	71
D.J.Cullinan	c Border b McDermott	0
J.N.Rhodes	not out	35
K.C.Wessels *	not out	63
D.J.Richardson +		
P.L.Symcox		
C.R.Matthews		
P.S.de Villiers		
A.A.Donald		
Extras	(lb 2,nb 7)	9
TOTAL	(for 3 wkts)	258

SOUTH AFRICA	O	M	R	W	O	M	R	W
Donald	30	4	108	1				
de Villiers	32	6	83	1				
Matthews	24	5	68	3				
Cronje	13	4	25	0				
Symcox	16.5	3	49	2				

AUSTRALIA	O	M	R	W	O	M	R	W
McDermott	23	5	60	1				
Reiffel	21	4	55	0				
Waugh	12	3	20	1				
May	28	7	58	0				
Warne	31	8	63	1				

FALL OF WICKETS	AUS	SAF	AUS	SAF
1st	57	49		
2nd	58	157		
3rd	127	157		
4th	296			
5th	300			
6th	327			
7th	342			
8th				
9th				
10th				

AUSTRALIA vs. SOUTH AFRICA

at Sydney on 2nd, 3rd, 4th, 5th, 6th January 1994
Toss : South Africa. Umpires : S.G.Randell and W.P.Sheahan
South Africa won by 5 runs

SOUTH AFRICA				
A.C.Hudson	lbw b McGrath	0	c Healy b McDermott	1
G.Kirsten	st Healy b Warne	67	b McDermott	41
W.J.Cronje	c Waugh b McDermott	41	b McDermott	38
D.J.Cullinan	b Warne	9	(5) lbw b Warne	2
J.N.Rhodes	lbw b Warne	4	(6) not out	76
K.C.Wessels *	c & b Warne	3	(4) b Warne	18
D.J.Richardson +	c Taylor b Warne	4	lbw b McGrath	24
P.L.Symcox	b Warne	7	c Healy b McDermott	4
C.R.Matthews	c Taylor b Warne	0	c Waugh b Warne	4
P.S.de Villiers	c Waugh b McDermott	18	lbw b Warne	2
A.A.Donald	not out	0	c Healy b Warne	10
Extras	(b 1,lb 4,nb 11)	16	(b 13,lb 1,nb 5)	19
TOTAL		169		239

AUSTRALIA				
M.J.Slater	b Donald	92	(2) b de Villiers	1
M.A.Taylor	c Richardson b Donald	7	(1) c Richardson b de Villiers	27
D.C.Boon	b de Villiers	19	c Kirsten b de Villiers	24
M.E.Waugh	lbw b Symcox	7	(5) lbw b Donald	11
A.R.Border *	c Richardson b de Villiers	49	(6) b Donald	7
D.R.Martyn	c Richardson b de Villiers	59	(7) c Hudson b Donald	6
I.A.Healy +	c Richardson b Donald	19	(8) b de Villiers	1
S.K.Warne	c Rhodes b Symcox	11	(9) run out	1
C.J.McDermott	c Cronje b de Villiers	6	(10) not out	29
T.B.A.May	not out	8	(4) lbw b de Villiers	0
G.D.McGrath	b Donald	9	c & b de Villiers	1
Extras	(b 1,lb 2,nb 3)	6	(lb 3)	3
TOTAL		292		111

AUSTRALIA	O	M	R	W	O	M	R	W
McDermott	18.1	2	42	2	28	9	62	4
McGrath	19	5	32	1	14	3	30	1
Warne	27	8	56	7	42	17	72	5
May	10	1	34	0	22	4	53	0
Border					3	1	8	0

SOUTH AFRICA	O	M	R	W	O	M	R	W
Donald	31.2	8	83	4	17	5	34	3
de Villiers	36	12	80	4	23.3	8	43	6
Matthews	28	11	44	0	6	5	9	0
Symcox	46	11	82	2	10	3	22	0

FALL OF WICKETS

	SAF	AUS	SAF	AUS
1st	1	10	2	4
2nd	91	58	75	51
3rd	110	75	101	51
4th	133	179	107	56
5th	134	179	110	63
6th	141	229	182	72
7th	142	250	188	73
8th	142	266	197	75
9th	152	281	203	110
10th	169	292	239	111

AUSTRALIA vs. SOUTH AFRICA

at Adelaide on 28th, 29th, 30th, 31st January, 1st February 1994
Toss : Australia. Umpires : D.B.Hair and T.A.Prue
Australia won by 191 runs

AUSTRALIA				
M.A.Taylor	b Kirsten G.	62	b Snell	38
M.J.Slater	c Rhodes b Donald	53	lbw b Donald	7
D.C.Boon	c de Villiers b Donald	50	c Hudson b McMillan	38
M.E.Waugh	c Snell b McMillan	2	c Richardson b Donald	12
A.R.Border *	c Richardson b McMillan	84	run out	4
S.R.Waugh	c Richardson b Donald	164	c Richardson b Snell	1
I.A.Healy +	c Rhodes b McMillan	0	not out	14
P.R.Reiffel	not out	32	not out	2
S.K.Warne	not out	4		
T.B.A.May				
C.J.McDermott				
Extras	(lb 9,nb 9)	18	(lb 7,nb 1)	8
TOTAL	(for 7 wkts dec)	469	(for 6 wkts dec)	124

SOUTH AFRICA				
A.C.Hudson	lbw b Waugh S.R.	90	c Waugh S.R. b McDermott	2
G.Kirsten	c May b McDermott	43	b Warne	7
W.J.Cronje *	c Healy b Reiffel	0	lbw b Warne	3
P.N.Kirsten	c Waugh M.E. b Warne	79	lbw b McDermott	42
J.N.Rhodes	b Waugh S.R.	5	(6) lbw b May	4
D.J.Cullinan	b Waugh S.R.	10	(7) c Healy b McDermott	5
B.M.McMillan	lbw b Waugh S.R.	2	(8) lbw b Warne	4
D.J.Richardson +	lbw b McDermott	6	(9) c Taylor b May	10
R.P.Snell	c Healy b McDermott	10	(10) c & b Warne	1
P.S.de Villiers	run out	4	(5) c Reiffel b McDermott	30
A.A.Donald	not out	1	not out	0
Extras	(b 3,lb 10,w 1,nb 9)	23	(b 9,lb 7,w 2,nb 3)	21
TOTAL		273		129

SOUTH AFRICA	O	M	R	W	O	M	R	W
Donald	38	7	122	3	11	2	26	2
de Villiers	41	11	105	0				
Snell	19	6	44	0	12	3	38	2
McMillan	30	3	89	3	11	0	33	1
Cronje	9	3	21	0	6	1	20	0
Kirsten G.	23	8	62	1				
Kirsten P.N.	4	0	17	0				

AUSTRALIA	O	M	R	W	O	M	R	W
McDermott	27	9	49	3	19	8	33	4
Reiffel	15	4	36	1	11	4	15	0
May	25	9	57	0	32	20	26	2
Warne	44.2	15	85	1	30.5	15	31	4
Waugh M.E.	3	1	7	0	3	2	3	0
Waugh S.R.	18	7	26	4	6	3	4	0
Border					4	3	1	0

FALL OF WICKETS

	AUS	SAF	AUS	SAF
1st	83	100	23	12
2nd	152	103	79	17
3rd	159	173	91	18
4th	183	179	99	100
5th	391	195	103	105
6th	391	203	109	113
7th	464	222		116
8th		243		128
9th		270		128
10th		273		129

SOUTH AFRICA vs. AUSTRALIA

at Johannesburg on 4th, 5th, 6th, 7th, 8th March 1994
Toss : South Africa. Umpires : S.B.Lambson and D.R.Shepherd
South Africa won by 197 runs

SOUTH AFRICA				
A.C.Hudson	c Healy b McDermott	17	b Warne	60
G.Kirsten	b Hughes	47	c Hughes b May	35
W.J.Cronje	c Border b Waugh S.R.	21	c Waugh S.R. b Hughes	122
K.C.Wessels *	c Hayden b Hughes	18	c Border b Warne	50
P.N.Kirsten	b May	12	c Boon b May	53
J.N.Rhodes	c Waugh M.E. b McDermott	69	c Healy b Waugh S.R.	14
B.M.McMillan	c Boon b May	0	(8) b Warne	24
D.J.Richardson +	lbw b Warne	31	(9) c Border b Warne	20
C.R.Matthews	c Boon b Hughes	6	(10) not out	31
P.S.de Villiers	b McDermott	16	(7) b McDermott	4
A.A.Donald	not out	0	not out	15
Extras	(b 1,lb 10,nb 3)	14	(b 13,lb 4,nb 5)	22
TOTAL		251	(for 9 wkts dec)	450

AUSTRALIA				
M.J.Slater	c Hudson b de Villiers	26	b de Villiers	41
M.L.Hayden	c Richardson b Donald	15	b de Villiers	5
D.C.Boon	c de Villiers b Donald	17	b Matthews	83
M.E.Waugh	run out	42	c Richardson b Donald	28
A.R.Border *	run out	34	c Kirsten G. b McMillan	14
S.R.Waugh	not out	45	c Richardson b Matthews	0
I.A.Healy +	b Matthews	11	c & b Donald	30
M.G.Hughes	c Kirsten G. b McMillan	7	not out	26
S.K.Warne	lbw b Matthews	15	lbw b McMillan	1
C.J.McDermott	lbw b Donald	31	b McMillan	10
T.B.A.May	lbw b de Villiers	2	c Kirsten G. b Cronje	11
Extras	(b 1,lb 1,nb 1)	3	(lb 5,nb 2)	7
TOTAL		248		256

AUSTRALIA	O	M	R	W	O	M	R	W
McDermott	15.2	3	63	3	35	3	112	1
Hughes	20	6	59	3	25	5	86	1
May	22	5	62	2	39	11	107	2
Waugh S.R.	9	2	14	1	10	3	28	1
Warne	14	4	42	1	44.5	14	86	4
Waugh M.E.					6	2	14	0

SOUTH AFRICA	O	M	R	W	O	M	R	W
Donald	19	0	86	3	23	3	71	2
de Villiers	19.3	1	74	2	30	11	70	2
McMillan	14	3	46	1	19	2	61	3
Matthews	15	4	40	2	20	6	42	2
Kirsten G.					4	0	7	0
Cronje					0.3	0	0	1

FALL OF WICKETS	SAF	AUS	SAF	AUS
1st	21	35	76	18
2nd	70	56	123	95
3rd	103	70	258	136
4th	116	136	289	164
5th	126	142	324	164
6th	126	169	343	191
7th	194	170	366	219
8th	203	201	403	225
9th	249	245	430	235
10th	251	248		256

SOUTH AFRICA vs. AUSTRALIA

at Cape Town on 17th, 18th, 19th, 20th, 21st March 1994
Toss : Not known. Umpires : K.E.Liebenberg and D.R.Shepherd
Australia won by 9 wickets

SOUTH AFRICA				
A.C.Hudson	run out	102	lbw b Waugh S.R.	49
G.Kirsten	run out	29	lbw b Warne	10
W.J.Cronje	b McGrath	2	c & b Waugh S.R.	19
K.C.Wessels *	c Waugh M.E. b McDermott	11	run out	9
P.N.Kirsten	lbw b Warne	70	c Taylor b Warne	3
J.N.Rhodes	lbw b McGrath	5	c Border b Waugh S.R.	27
B.M.McMillan	b Warne	74	(8) lbw b Waugh S.R.	3
D.J.Richardson +	lbw b McDermott	34	(9) c Healy b McGrath	31
C.R.Matthews	not out	7	(10) not out	0
P.S.de Villiers	c Taylor b Warne	7	(7) lbw b Warne	0
A.A.Donald	c Healy b McGrath	7	b Waugh S.R.	0
Extras	(lb 6,nb 7)	13	(b 4,lb 6,nb 3)	13
TOTAL		361		164

AUSTRALIA				
M.J.Slater	c Kirsten P.N. b de Villiers	26	(2) not out	43
M.A.Taylor	c Richardson b de Villiers	70	(1) b Donald	14
D.C.Boon	c Richardson b de Villiers	96	not out	32
M.E.Waugh	c Kirsten P.N. b McMillan	7		
A.R.Border *	c Richardson b Matthews	45		
S.R.Waugh	b Matthews	86		
I.A.Healy +	c de Villiers b Matthews	61		
M.G.Hughes	lbw b Matthews	0		
S.K.Warne	c McMillan b de Villiers	11		
C.J.McDermott	c Kirsten P.N. b Matthews	1		
G.D.McGrath	not out	1		
Extras	(b 6,lb 17,w 1,nb 7)	31	(b 1,nb 2)	3
TOTAL		435	(for 1 wkt)	92

AUSTRALIA	O	M	R	W	O	M	R	W
McDermott	27	6	80	2	13	3	39	0
Hughes	20	1	80	0	5	1	12	0
McGrath	26.1	4	65	3	16	6	26	1
Waugh S.R.	9	3	20	0	22.3	9	28	5
Warne	47	18	78	3	30	13	38	3
Waugh M.E.	10	3	23	0	3	1	11	0
Border	5	2	9	0	1	1	0	0

SOUTH AFRICA	O	M	R	W	O	M	R	W
Donald	35	10	111	0	5	0	20	1
de Villiers	44.4	11	117	4	6	0	20	0
Matthews	35	12	80	5	6	1	14	0
McMillan	29	9	82	1	5	0	23	0
Kirsten G.	4	0	13	0	1.1	0	10	0
Cronje	11	4	9	0	2	0	4	0

FALL OF WICKETS	SAF	AUS	SAF	AUS
1st	71	40	33	30
2nd	78	145	69	
3rd	100	153	94	
4th	189	244	97	
5th	198	310	97	
6th	260	418	97	
7th	335	418	103	
8th	339	430	164	
9th	348	434	164	
10th	361	435	164	

SOUTH AFRICA vs. AUSTRALIA

at Durban on 25th, 26th, 27th, 28th, 29th March 1994
Toss : Australia. Umpires : C.J.Mitchley and Mahboob Shah
Match drawn

AUSTRALIA				
M.J.Slater	c Rhodes b Matthews	20	lbw b Donald	95
M.A.Taylor	lbw b Donald	1	lbw b de Villiers	12
D.C.Boon	c Kirsten G. b Donald	37	c Kirsten P.N. b Donald	12
M.E.Waugh	c Richardson b Donald	43	(5) not out	113
A.R.Border *	c Rhodes b McMillan	17	(6) not out	42
S.R.Waugh	c Wessels b Matthews	64		
I.A.Healy +	b Matthews	55		
P.R.Reiffel	lbw b de Villiers	13		
S.K.Warne	c Wessels b Matthews	2	(4) c McMillan b Donald	12
C.J.McDermott	c Donald b de Villiers	6		
G.D.McGrath	not out	0		
Extras	(lb 1,w 1,nb 9)	11	(lb 6,w 1,nb 4)	11
TOTAL		269	(for 4 wkts)	297

SOUTH AFRICA		
A.C.Hudson	lbw b Reiffel	65
G.Kirsten	c Healy b Reiffel	41
W.J.Cronje	c Waugh S.R. b Warne	26
K.C.Wessels *	lbw b McDermott	1
P.N.Kirsten	lbw b Waugh S.R.	49
J.N.Rhodes	lbw b Warne	78
B.M.McMillan	c Slater b Waugh S.R.	84
D.J.Richardson +	c Reiffel b Warne	59
C.R.Matthews	lbw b Warne	1
P.S.de Villiers	lbw b Waugh S.R.	0
A.A.Donald	not out	0
Extras	(b 3,lb 10,nb 5)	18
TOTAL		422

SOUTH AFRICA	O	M	R	W	O	M	R	W
Donald	18	1	71	3	28	7	66	3
de Villiers	24.2	5	55	2	24	5	69	1
Matthews	29	9	65	4	28	12	56	0
McMillan	19	5	56	1	22	6	53	0
Cronje	5	1	8	0	18	5	40	0
Kirsten G.	6	1	13	0	3	1	7	0
Rhodes					1	1	0	0

AUSTRALIA	O	M	R	W	O	M	R	W
McDermott	38	11	76	1				
Reiffel	30	7	77	2				
McGrath	41	11	78	0				
Warne	55	20	92	4				
Waugh S.R.	27.2	12	40	3				
Waugh M.E.	11	3	38	0				
Border	3	0	8	0				

FALL OF WICKETS	AUS	SAF	AUS	SAF
1st	7	100	55	
2nd	45	117	81	
3rd	81	118	109	
4th	123	155	157	
5th	123	256		
6th	215	274		
7th	250	417		
8th	256	422		
9th	269	422		
10th	269	422		

AVERAGES

SOUTH AFRICA – TEST MATCHES (1992-1994)

BATTING AVERAGES - Including fielding

Name	M	Inns	NO	Runs	HS	Avge	100s	50s	Ct	St
T.Bosch	1	2	2	5	5*	-	-	-	-	-
S.J.Cook	3	6	0	107	43	17.83	-	-	-	-
W.J.Cronje	13	23	2	804	135	38.28	3	2	4	-
D.J.Cullinan	7	12	0	337	102	28.08	1	1	2	-
P.S.de Villiers	6	9	0	81	30	9.00	-	-	4	-
A.A.Donald	14	19	11	67	15*	8.37	-	-	4	-
C.E.Eksteen	1	2	1	5	4*	5.00	-	-	-	-
O.Henry	3	3	0	53	34	17.66	-	-	2	-
A.C.Hudson	14	25	1	1060	163	44.16	2	9	10	-
G.Kirsten	6	10	0	336	67	33.60	-	1	6	-
P.N.Kirsten	9	16	1	447	79	29.80	-	4	9	-
A.P.Kuiper	1	2	0	34	34	17.00	-	-	1	-
C.R.Matthews	8	11	4	143	31*	20.42	-	-	-	-
B.M.McMillan	10	16	2	387	98	27.64	-	4	12	-
M.W.Pringle	3	4	1	55	33	18.33	-	-	-	-
J.N.Rhodes	13	22	4	737	101*	40.94	1	5	8	-
D.J.Richardson	14	21	1	414	62	20.70	-	3	55	-
M.W.Rushmere	1	2	0	6	3	3.00	-	-	-	-
B.N.Schultz	5	5	2	6	6	2.00	-	-	-	-
R.P.Snell	4	6	1	78	48	15.60	-	-	1	-
P.L.Symcox	5	6	0	160	50	26.66	-	1	-	-
K.C.Wessels	13	23	2	789	118	37.57	1	6	9	-

BOWLING AVERAGES

Name	Overs	Mdns	Runs	Wkts	Avge	Best	5wI	10wM
T.Bosch	39.3	9	104	3	34.66	2-61	-	-
W.J.Cronje	155.1	62	257	5	51.40	2-17	-	-
.S.de Villiers	281	70	716	22	32.54	6-43	1	1
A.A.Donald	577.2	133	1568	63	24.88	7-84	3	1
C.E.Eksteen	23	6	78	0	-	-	-	-
O.Henry	71.1	15	189	3	63.00	2-56	-	-
G.Kirsten	41.1	10	112	1	112.00	1-62	-	-
P.N.Kirsten	9	1	30	0	-	-	-	-
C.R.Matthews	300	109	608	25	24.32	5-80	1	-
B.M.McMillan	347	92	863	25	34.52	4-74	-	-
M.W.Pringle	68.4	12	171	3	57.00	2-61	-	-
J.N.Rhodes	2	1	5	0	-	-	-	-
B.N.Schultz	175.5	51	427	24	17.79	5-48	2	-
R.P.Snell	121	28	373	15	24.86	4-74	-	-
P.L.Symcox	142.5	29	383	8	47.87	3-75	-	-

SOUTH AFRICA – ONE-DAY INTERNATIONALS (1991-1994)

BATTING AVERAGES - Including fielding

Name	M	Inns	NO	Runs	HS	Avge	100s	50s	Ct	St
T.Bosch	2	0	0	0	0	-	-	-	1	-
D.J.Callaghan	18	15	4	217	45*	19.72	-	-	2	-
S.J.Cook	4	4	0	67	35	16.75	-	-	1	-
W.J.Cronje	49	46	9	1260	112	34.05	1	5	17	-
D.J.Cullinan	20	19	2	351	70*	20.64	-	1	5	-
P.S.de Villiers	38	15	7	40	15	5.00	-	-	7	-
A.A.Donald	45	14	7	27	7*	3.85	-	-	5	-
C.E.Eksteen	1	1	1	6	6*	-	-	-	-	-
O.Henry	3	3	1	20	11	10.00	-	-	1	-
A.C.Hudson	43	42	0	1236	108	29.42	1	10	5	-
G.Kirsten	12	12	1	351	112*	31.90	1	2	4	-
P.N.Kirsten	39	39	6	1285	97	38.93	-	9	12	-
A.P.Kuiper	22	20	5	414	63*	27.60	-	1	3	-
C.R.Matthews	24	10	2	32	10*	4.00	-	-	3	-
B.M.McMillan	37	24	10	323	48*	23.07	-	-	21	-
M.W.Pringle	15	6	2	35	10	8.75	-	-	2	-
J.N.Rhodes	49	47	8	1166	66	29.89	-	3	22	-
C.E.B.Rice	3	2	0	26	14	13.00	-	-	-	-
D.J.Richardson	50	30	13	381	38*	22.41	-	-	65	8
D.B.Rundle	2	2	0	6	6	3.00	-	-	3	-
M.W.Rushmere	4	4	0	78	35	19.50	-	-	1	-
B.N.Schultz	1	0	0	0	0	-	-	-	-	-
T.G.Shaw	3	2	2	2	2*	-	-	-	-	-
E.O.Simons	7	5	2	58	23	19.33	-	-	2	-
R.P.Snell	35	22	6	213	51	13.31	-	1	4	-
E.L.R.Stewart	5	5	1	57	23*	14.25	-	-	3	-
P.L.Symcox	13	11	2	58	12	6.44	-	-	2	-
C.J.P.G.van Zyl	2	2	1	3	3*	3.00	-	-	-	-
K.C.Wessels	47	46	4	1456	90	34.66	-	11	27	-
M.Yachad	1	1	0	31	31	31.00	-	-	1	-

BOWLING AVERAGES

Name	Overs	Mdns	Runs	Wkts	Avge	Best	5wI
T.Bosch	8.3	0	66	0	-	-	-
D.J.Callaghan	52	2	221	6	36.83	2-15	-
W.J.Cronje	261.2	11	1109	28	39.60	5-32	1
P.S.de Villiers	334.3	44	1092	44	24.81	4-27	-
A.A.Donald	399	36	1567	60	26.11	5-29	1
C.E.Eksteen	2	0	18	0	-	-	-
O.Henry	24.5	0	125	2	62.50	1-31	-
P.N.Kirsten	30.3	1	153	6	25.50	3-31	-
A.P.Kuiper	98	0	518	18	28.77	3-33	-
C.R.Matthews	219.1	24	855	41	20.85	4-10	-
B.M.McMillan	302.5	16	1331	37	35.97	4-32	-
M.W.Pringle	128	11	520	21	24.76	4-11	-
C.E.B.Rice	23	0	114	2	57.00	1-46	-
D.B.Rundle	16	0	95	5	19.00	4-42	-
B.N.Schultz	9	1	35	1	35.00	1-35	-
T.G.Shaw	28	2	95	4	23.75	2-19	-
E.O.Simons	67.4	11	213	11	19.36	2-22	-
R.P.Snell	296.2	21	1317	35	37.62	5-40	1
P.L.Symcox	91	4	364	11	33.09	3-20	-
C.J.P.G.van Zyl	18	0	93	0	-	-	-
K.C.Wessels	2	0	11	0	-	-	-

FIRST-CLASS CAREER RECORDS OF LEADING SOUTH AFRICAN PLAYERS OF RECENT YEARS

(Figures include 1993-94 overseas tours but do not include the 1993-94 South African domestic season)

BATTING

Name	M	Inns	NO	Runs	HS	Avge	100s	50s
H.M.Ackerman	234	409	33	12219	208	32.49	20	60
A.Bacher	120	212	10	7894	235	39.07	18	45
E.J.Barlow	283	493	28	18212	217	39.16	43	86
D.J.Callaghan	70	110	12	3164	171	32.28	4	16
P.B.Clift	319	446	91	8383	106	23.61	2	31
S.J.Cook	255	449	53	19931	313*	50.33	59	82
W.J.Cronje	54	99	10	3158	161*	35.48	8	15
D.J.Cullinan	82	147	19	4681	140	36.57	10	27
B.F.Davison	467	766	79	27453	189	39.96	53	148
R.J.East	96	163	10	4817	191*	31.48	8	24
N.G.Featherstone	329	528	54	13922	147	29.37	12	88
A.M.Ferreira	245	386	70	9064	133	23.68	5	43
H.R.Fotheringham	147	247	27	8814	184	40.06	21	48
A.W.Greig	350	579	45	16660	226	31.19	26	97
I.A.Greig	253	339	50	8301	291	28.72	8	40
O.Henry	120	183	33	4322	125	28.81	5	19
A.C.Hudson	71	134	8	4445	184*	35.27	8	28
B.L.Irvine	157	271	26	9919	193	40.48	21	46
R.V.Jennings	159	220	46	4160	168	23.90	3	15
G.Kirsten	54	98	11	3655	189	42.01	8	17
P.N.Kirsten	281	491	52	19499	228	44.41	49	94
A.J.Kourie	127	175	45	4470	127*	34.38	5	21
A.P.Kuiper	130	210	25	5943	161*	32.12	6	37
A.J.Lamb	435	722	103	30223	294	48.82	84	153
D.T.Lindsay	124	214	15	7074	216	35.54	12	36
K.S.McEwan	428	705	67	26628	218	41.73	74	122
K.A.McKenzie	133	208	23	6756	188	36.51	13	34
B.M.McMillan	79	130	22	3862	136	35.75	5	22
R.C.Ontong	362	596	86	15071	204*	29.55	20	77
R.F.Pienaar	161	276	24	8984	153	35.65	17	51
R.G.Pollock	262	437	54	20940	274	54.67	64	99
M.J.Procter	401	667	58	21936	254	36.01	48	109
J.N.Rhodes	48	81	9	2617	135*	36.34	4	16
C.E.B.Rice	480	764	123	26262	246	40.97	48	136
B.A.Richards	339	576	58	28358	356	54.74	80	152
D.J.Richardson	141	225	33	4684	134	24.39	2	23
D.B.Rundle	67	104	24	1758	110	21.97	1	1
M.W.Rushmere	82	148	26	5224	177	42.81	15	22
L.Seeff	113	210	20	6558	188	34.51	11	36

C.L.Smith	269	466	60	18028	217	44.40	47	88
R.A.Smith	262	446	73	16550	209*	44.36	40	85
E.L.R.Stewart	27	51	3	1275	121	26.56	1	6
P.D.Swart	167	267	29	6093	122	25.60	6	33
K.C.Wessels	256	442	38	20336	254	50.33	54	105
B.F.Whitfield	83	150	15	5166	161	38.26	11	33
C.P.Wilkins	198	357	21	10966	156	32.63	18	61
M.Yachad	95	179	9	5957	200	35.04	13	30

BOWLING

Name	Runs	Wkts	Avge	Best	5wI	10wM
E.J.Barlow	13785	571	24.14	7-24	16	2
T.Bosch	3984	139	28.66	7-75	6	1
P.B.Clift	21610	876	24.66	8-17	26	2
P.S.de Villiers	5774	246	23.47	6-43	13	1
A.A.Donald	14955	632	23.66	8-37	35	5
C.E.Eksteen	4127	147	28.07	6-169	6	-
A.M.Ferreira	17708	583	30.37	8-38	18	2
A.W.Greig	24702	856	28.85	8-25	33	8
I.A.Greig	13023	419	31.08	7-43	10	2
R.W.Hanley	8491	408	20.81	7-31	23	3
O.Henry	10607	432	24.55	7-22	22	3
D.L.Hobson	10296	374	27.52	9-64	22	6
S.T.Jefferies	13028	469	27.77	10-59	19	4
A.J.Kourie	9869	421	23.44	8-113	24	3
A.P.Kuiper	4984	178	28.00	6-55	4	-
G.S.le Roux	17800	838	21.24	8-107	35	3
C.R.Matthews	3376	153	22.06	6-22	5	-
B.M.McMillan	5055	193	26.19	5-35	4	-
R.C.Ontong	25972	836	31.06	8-67	33	4
H.A.Page	6316	256	24.67	7-38	5	-
R.F.Pienaar	4910	148	33.17	5-24	3	-
P.M.Pollock	10620	485	21.89	7-19	27	2
M.W.Pringle	4753	194	24.50	7-60	9	1
M.J.Procter	27679	1417	19.53	9-71	70	15
N.V.Radford	24481	933	26.23	9-70	46	7
C.E.B.Rice	20873	929	22.46	7-62	23	1
D.B.Rundle	5142	165	31.16	6-37	7	2
B.N.Schultz	2791	114	24.48	6-72	4	-
T.G.Shaw	8108	300	27.02	7-79	12	2
E.O.Simons	6163	241	25.57	6-26	5	-
R.P.Snell	4435	167	26.55	6-33	6	1
P.D.Swart	9365	370	25.31	6-85	5	1
P.L.Symcox	3171	103	30.78	7-93	2	-
V.A.P.van der Bijl	12692	767	16.54	8-35	46	12
C.J.P.G.van Zyl	7642	331	23.08	8-84	12	2
W.K.Watson	11034	446	24.73	7-50	16	-

WICKET-KEEPING

Name	Ct	St
R.J.East	288	8
B.L.Irvine	240	7
R.V.Jennings	567	54
D.T.Lindsay	292	41
D.J.Richardson	399	31
E.L.R.Stewart	52	2

THE KEY BODIES IN SOUTH AFRICA'S CRICKET HISTORY

SACA: South African Cricket Association. Traditionally involved in whites-only cricket.

SAACB: South African African Cricket Board. Non-racial, formed in 1958. Claimed to be the only board to represent all colours in South Africa.

SACBOC: South African Cricket Board of Control, representing coloureds and Indians.

SACU: South African Cricket Union, formed in 1977 after amalgamation of SACA, SAACB and SACBOC. The first body that could claim to represent cricketers of all races.

SACB: South African Cricket Board. Breakaway group from SACU, whose president, Hassan Howa, adopted a militant stance towards SACU's policy of normalisation – 'no normal sport in an abnormal society'. In the 1980s, SACB represented the interests of black cricketers, organising its own leagues and refusing to co-operate with SACU until the government brought in political reforms.

UCBSA: United Cricket Board of South Africa, formed in 1990 after SACU and SACB agreed to join forces, under pressure from the African National Congress (ANC). The UCB now administers all cricket in South Africa.

LANDMARKS IN SOUTH AFRICAN CRICKET

1970 South Africa beat Australia 4-0 in its last Test series for 22 years.

The tour to England is called off by the British government.

1971 Leading South African cricketers walk off the field at Newlands, Cape Town in protest at their government's racial policies.

The tour to Australia is called off by the Australian Board of Control.

John Passmore stages a cricket week for the first time, in the township of Langa, near Cape Town.

1972 The South African Cricket Association vetoes a proposed tour by an England XI, including Basil D'Oliveira.

1973 The first Datsun Double Wicket Competition – the first time that blacks and whites compete together at international level.

Younis Ahmed and John Shepherd tour South Africa with the D.H.Robins side – the first non-whites to visit in a touring party.

1974 The Transvaal Cricket Union announces a plan to integrate its club leagues.

The International Cricket Conference (ICC) lays down four requirements for South Africa's return to Test cricket.

1976 Tours by an international Wanderers side, captained by Greg Chappell – the first tour involving games against representatives of all three rival cricketing bodies.

ICC vetoes South Africa's application for a return to international cricket.

Official mixed club cricket takes place in the Transvaal League for the first time.

'Normal cricket' is set up in most leagues.

1977 The Gleneagles Agreement is signed.

Kerry Packer signs up leading South African players for World Series Cricket.

The formation of the South African Cricket Union (SACU), the first official non-racial controlling body.

1979 ICC delegation to South Africa confirms its cricket is now non-racial.

1980 A full meeting of the ICC 'notes' last year's report by its fact-finding delegation.

1981 Sri Lanka becomes a full member country of the ICC and therefore eligible to play Test cricket.

1982 Graham Gooch leads an England rebel tour to South Africa.

SACU is refused a formal hearing at the ICC meeting.

A Sri Lankan rebel tour takes place.

1983 West Indian rebel tour – the first time a South African representative side has played one from the West Indies.

1984 Second West Indian rebel tour.

1985 Kim Hughes leads an Australian rebel tour.

1986 Ali Bacher starts his township programme.

Second Australian rebel tour.

Omar Henry, a Cape coloured, is selected to play for South Africa against the Australians.

1988 The ICC postpones a decision on South Africa's possible reinstatement.

1989 Mike Gatting confirms he will lead an England rebel tour to South Africa.

1990 President de Klerk lifts the ban on the ANC and releases Nelson Mandela from prison.
Gatting's tour is truncated because of civil unrest.
The United Cricket Board of South Africa is formed.

1991 The ICC readmits South Africa to international cricket.
The first international in Calcutta, November 10.

1992 South Africa reaches the semi-finals of the World Cup.
First Test on recall – against West Indies in Barbados, April 18.
Omar Henry becomes the first coloured player to represent South Africa in a Test.

1993 Test series in Sri Lanka. South Africa wins series.

1994 South Africa wins Sydney Test by 5 runs and draws series.
South Africa draws return series against Australia 1-1, winning the Johannesburg Test.

SOME SIGNIFICANT QUOTES

HASSAN HOWA

'When I started playing cricket I found a very sad set up, Moslems playing in one league, Christians in another, Indians in another. One had to be a Christian before one could play for Western Province, one had to be a certain lightness and one had to be able to run a pencil through one's hair. It was then that I learnt to fight the whole reactionary establishment.'

RASHID VARACHIA

On accepting the nomination of president of the newly-formed South African Cricket Union in 1977.

'For years many of us proclaimed loudly and clearly and persistently the need for better opportunities for our under-privileged cricketers and therefore even at this late hour my appeal is "Don't impede the progress of our cricketers or betray their trust". The politicians have their ideals, the sportsman his objective. There is no way anyone can stop this healthy and exhilarating wind of change that is blowing through the corridors of our world of cricket. We must forge ahead, ever mindful of the hungry and vicious outstretched hands that want to claw us. The collective responsibility of each player and administrator of every colour, is great. Succeed we must, and in our success lie the hopes and aspirations of hundreds of cricketers of all colours in this country.'

In a debate at the Cambridge Union in 1970, two opposing views on the intrusion of politics into sport.

TED DEXTER

'Something must be done actively to dissociate politics from sport. The people who play it, when they get on the field, by and large leave their other identities behind. Sport should be permitted by the politically committed to rediscover its former and traditional role.'

JOHN ARLOTT

'Political commitment is the only valid reason for breaking the sporting contacts... Any man's political commitment, if it's deep enough, is his personal philosophy and it governs his way of life, it governs his belief and it governs the people with whom he is prepared to mix.'

DR ALI BACHER

Guest speaker in London at the annual Wisden dinner in 1989.

'For years, cricket in South Africa shunned the black communities. It was shocked out of this by the introduction of the protest and isolationist policies of the anti-apartheid movement in the 1960s. It was a shock we fully deserved, and this was even more forcefully enforced for me when I received death threats from white South Africans for suggesting this publicly as the current Springbok captain in 1970. Death threats are still made against me, but as General Smuts once said: "The dogs may bark but the caravan moves on".'

February 26, 1992: South Africa beat Australia in its first match in the World Cup, at Sydney.

PRESIDENT F.W. DE KLERK

'Your victory is a victory for all of us over years of isolation and rejection.'

STEVE TSHWETE

'Damn it, man, we mustn't let apartheid get in the way of such a great team. Those guys struck a political blow with their bats today. They showed the world what a unified South Africa can do. I'm a proud man, a mighty proud man.'

INDEX

PICTURE ACKNOWLEDGEMENTS

The publishers are grateful to the following
for their permission to use copyright material
in the picture sections of this book:
(black & white section)
Argus Newspapers, South Africa
(colour section)
Allsport (Shaun Botterill, Mike Hewitt,
Ben Radford, Tertius Pickard, Thomas Turck)
(cover photographs)
(*front inset*) Allsport (Shaun Botterill)
(*front main*) Allsport (Adrian Murrell)
(*back*) Allsport (Shaun Botterill)